THE CONSTITUTION
THE REPUBLIC OF AUSTRIA

This book shows how the Austrian Constitution has been shaped and interpreted by the fundamental events in Austria's modern history. At the same time it emphasises the way in which the Constitution establishes a parliamentary system, with additional presidential features, limited, in turn, by Austria's federal structure and the parliaments of nine states. It charts the history and character of the Constitution; the political structure; the legislative and executive branches of the federal government; public bodies; jurisdiction and fundamental rights. This new edition explores the changing political landscape, particularly the development of a more competitive party system. It also looks at the response to COVID and the jurisprudence of the Austrian Constitutional Court in the face of the curtailment of rights in order to curb the pandemic. Offering the trademark combination of clarity of explanation and rigour of analysis that defines the series, this is an excellent guide to a fascinating constitutional structure.

Pictorial Narrative

At the centre of the composition is a metaphor of the constitutional court as the ultimate guardian of the constitution. This guardian[1] here assumes the form of a siren figure (half human, half eagle) perched on the diffused textual sources of the constitution,[2] performing the pivotal task of constitutional review. The legal tome that seems to slip away underfoot indicates that the court has lost some of its powers due to Austria's accession to the EU. At the same time, the double headed eagle reflects the decline of the monarchical and the increase of the republican influence. The guardian's right hand clutches two crosses (holy cross and cross potent, the latter alluding to the swastika) recognising the high profile of the Catholic Church and the nation's continuing struggle to grapple with its authoritarian and Nazi past. The left hand grasps the scales of justice to emphasise the recent strengthening of the judicial system. VSFGN in close formation alludes to a possible open political system.[3]

Austria's federal system is represented by red, white, yellow, blue and green which forms the background of the entire composition.[4]

The façade of the parliament building emerges from beneath the open volume, with a seated dog alluding to its reinforced watch dog function.

Bottom right there is a hand grabbing Euro notes referring to the fight against corruption while bottom left the unmistakeable yellow pointed stars on blue confirm the influence of the EU. Images of snow-covered mountain peaks symbolise Austria's neutrality status.

The *Blue Danube*'s musical score floating on water is a reminder of Austria's cultural heritage.

Putachad
Artist

---

[1] The figure is inspired in homage to Popova's 'Man Air Space'.

[2] Inspired by Juan Gris's still life paintings 'The Open Book' and 'Still Life with Guitar'.

[3] V (ÖVP), S (SPÖ), F (FPÖ), G (Green Party) and N (NEOS).

[4] Red and white for Vienna, Upper Austria, Salzburg, Tyrol, Vorarlberg; red-white-yellow for Carinthia; red and yellow for Burgenland; blue and yellow for Lower Austria; green and white for Styria.

Constitutional Systems of the World
General Editors: Benjamin L Berger, Rosalind Dixon,
Andrew Harding, Heinz Klug, and Peter Leyland

In the era of globalisation, issues of constitutional law and good governance are being seen increasingly as vital issues in all types of society. Since the end of the Cold War, there have been dramatic developments in democratic and legal reform, and post-conflict societies are also in the throes of reconstructing their governance systems. Even societies already firmly based on constitutional governance and the rule of law have undergone constitutional change and experimentation with new forms of governance; and their constitutional systems are increasingly subjected to comparative analysis and transplantation. Constitutional texts for practically every country in the world are now easily available on the internet. However, texts which enable one to understand the true context, purposes, interpretation and incidents of a constitutional system are much harder to locate, and are often extremely detailed and descriptive. This series seeks to provide scholars and students with accessible introductions to the constitutional systems of the world, supplying both a road map for the novice and, at the same time, a deeper understanding of the key historical, political and legal events which have shaped the constitutional landscape of each country. Each book in this series deals with a single country, or a group of countries with a common constitutional history, and each author is an expert in their field.

Published volumes

The Constitution of the United Kingdom; The Constitution of the United States; The Constitution of Vietnam; The Constitution of South Africa; The Constitution of Japan; The Constitution of Germany; The Constitution of Finland; The Constitution of Australia; The Constitution of the Republic of Austria; The Constitution of the Russian Federation; The Constitutional System of Thailand; The Constitution of Malaysia; The Constitution of China; The Constitution of Indonesia; The Constitution of France; The Constitution of Spain; The Constitution of Mexico; The Constitution of Israel; The Constitutional Systems of the Commonwealth Caribbean; The Constitution of Canada; The Constitution of Singapore; The Constitution of Belgium; The Constitution of Taiwan; The Constitution of Romania; The Constitutional Systems of the Independent Central Asian States; The Constitution of India; The Constitution of Pakistan; The Constitution of Ireland; The Constitution of Brazil; The Constitution of Myanmar; The Constitution of Czechia; The Constitution of New Zealand; The Constitution of Italy

Link to series website

www.bloomsbury.com/uk/series/constitutional-systems-of-the-world/

The Constitution of the Republic of Austria

A Contextual Analysis

Second Edition

Manfred Stelzer

•HART•

OXFORD • LONDON • NEW YORK • NEW DELHI • SYDNEY

HART PUBLISHING

Bloomsbury Publishing Plc

Kemp House, Chawley Park, Cumnor Hill, Oxford, OX2 9PH, UK

1385 Broadway, New York, NY 10018, USA

29 Earlsfort Terrace, Dublin 2, Ireland

HART PUBLISHING, the Hart/Stag logo, BLOOMSBURY and the Diana logo are
trademarks of Bloomsbury Publishing Plc

First published in Great Britain 2022

First published in hardback, 2022

Paperback edition, 2024

Copyright © Manfred Stelzer, 2022

A catalogue record for this book is available from the British Library.

A catalogue record for this book is available from the Library of Congress.

Library of Congress Control Number: 2022943187

ISBN: PB: 978-1-50995-673-9
        ePDF: 978-1-50995-671-5
        ePub: 978-1-50995-670-8

Typeset by Compuscript Ltd, Shannon

Acknowledgements

MORE THAN A decade has passed since the first edition appeared in 2011. That decade witnessed significant changes to Austria's constitution as well as its political system. I am grateful to the editors of this series for commissioning a second edition that allowed me to catch up with all these developments.

Helping me to collect relevant material, Tobias Fädler, Hanna Koppelent, Philip Wilfing and Clara Zimmermann did a magnificent job during the first phase of the pandemic, when libraries were closed more often than not.

Prablin Cheema, Sebastian Cody and Alexandra Kunesch made valuable comments on earlier drafts. So did Julia Bauer, Tobias Fädler and Teresa Radatz who additionally double-checked on the footnotes and supported me in drawing up all the requested lists and tables.

I am deeply indebted to Peter Leyland not only for the time he spent working through an entire draft version, offering useful feedback that gave me the chance to significantly improve the book, but also for countless hours of conversation during the last ten years, often accompanied by his and his wife's generous hospitality.

Putachad has graced the book with one of her inimitable cover paintings. I can only admire how she has caught the main ideas of my book in vibrant colours and powerful symbols and I hope that readers would not stop at studying the painting but still feel inclined to engage with the written part.

At Hart/Bloomsbury, Linda Goss and Ceri Warner edited the book with diligence and leniency for my shortcomings. Sasha Jawed and Jennifer Roberts further contributed to the production of the book as, surely, many others must have done, who were not brought to my attention.

Finally, as always, my family has been supportive throughout the process of writing.

None of the above mentioned contributions was to be taken for granted. I am entirely grateful for all of them.

Contents

List of Abbreviations

ABGB	Allgemeines bürgerliches Gesetzbuch (Civil Law Code)
BGBl	Bundesgesetzblatt[1] (Federal Law Gazette)
BVerfGE	Amtliche Sammlung der Entscheidungen des Bundesverfassungsgerichtes (Official Compilation of the German Federal Constitutional Court's rulings)
B-VG	Bundes-Verfassungsgesetz[2] (Federal Constitutional Law, the core document of the Austrian Constitution)
CJEU	Court of Justice of the European Union
ECHR	European Convention on Human Rights
ECtHR	European Court of Human Rights
EHRR	European Human Rights Reports
ESM	European Stability Mechanism
EU	European Union
F-VG	Finanz-Verfassungsgesetz (Constitutional Finance Law)
FFFA	Federal Finance Framework Act (Bundesfinanzrahmengesetz)
GDP	gross domestic product
GM	genetically modified
LGBl	Landesgesetzblatt (State Law Gazette)
OGH	Oberster Gerichtshof (Supreme Court)

---

[1] Laws that were published before 1997 are correctly referred to by numbers and the year of publication (eg BGBl 1013/1994, or, in reverse order: BGBl 1994/1013). From 1997 onward, the Federal Law Gazette has been divided into three parts. Part I largely contains Federal laws, part II mainly ordinances and part III state treaties.
   Correct citation therefore also requires indicating the part: BGBl I 2/1997 or BGBl I 1997/2.
[2] Available in English on the official website of the Austrian Federal Chancellery (www.ris.bka.gv.at).

RGBl	Reichsgesetzblatt (Imperial Law Gazette)
StGBl	Staatsgesetzblatt
TFEU	Treaty on the Functioning of the European Union
VfGH	Verfassungsgerichtshof (Constitutional Court)
VfSlg	Sammlung der Erkenntnisse und wichtigsten Beschlüsse des Verfassungsgerichtshofes (Official Compilation of the Constitutional Court's rulings)
VwSlg	Erkenntnisse und Beschlüsse des Verwaltungsgerichtshofes (Official Compilation of the Administrative High Court's rulings)
VwGH	Verwaltungsgerichtshof (Administrative High Court)

Table of Cases

Supreme Court

European Court of Human Rights (ECtHR)

European Court of Justice (ECJ)

Other National Courts

Germany

Netherlands

Table of Legislation

Constitutions

Other Federal Instruments

Other National Instruments

France

1

History and Character
of the Austrian Constitution

Introduction – Evolution of the Austrian Constitution – Characteristic Features of the Austrian Constitution – Basic Principles of the Constitution – Engineering Constitutional Changes – Conclusion

I. INTRODUCTION

THE REPUBLIC OF Austria, a small country situated in the heart of Europe, only emerged from the demise of the Habsburg monarchy in 1918. It united those German-speaking provinces of the former Empire which were not claimed by other nation states. From the very beginning, creating a new national identity proved to be rather difficult. Whether the *raison d'être* of a second, but considerably smaller German-speaking country bordering on the German Republic could be found was seriously doubted. Hopes of joining Germany were dashed at a very early stage. In 1920, after two years of intensive discussion, a new constitution was enacted. Although it introduced a democratic government, its core structure and elements, such as the courts system, the administrative system, the bill of rights and others, were adopted from the monarchical constitution and had therefore been originally designed in the nineteenth century. Significantly amended in 1929, the constitution was invalid between 1934 and 1945, but re-enacted after World War II. It is still in force today.

The period between 1934 and 1945 marked the darkest years in Austria's history, as the country was not only governed by an autocratic regime but, later, also annexed or occupied by Nazi Germany. After the war, the appetite for becoming a part of Germany was definitely gone. Establishing German 'otherness', contradicting the sense of belonging to the German-speaking world, seemed to be even more important than in the interwar period. In doing so, the republic drew on the great cultural heritage of the Habsburg Empire. Connecting post-war Austria with the pre-fascist period also helped the country to turn a blind eye to its own fascist and Nazi past. The post-war struggle for identity had an impact on the constitution and, moreover, the constitutional doctrine of that period.

However, this struggle was overlapped by a process of Europeanisation that had already started in the aftermath of Austria's 1958 adoption of the European Convention on Human Rights (ECHR) but became more apparent from the mid-1980s onwards. It ultimately led to Austria's accession to the European Union (EU). This process challenged the character of the constitution and the constitutional doctrine. It triggered significant constitutional changes, some of which were only effected during the second decade of the twenty-first century. Moreover, it went hand in hand with the demise of a stable party system that had supported the idea of a consociational democracy, one of the most characteristic features of post-war Austria. This demise not only led to a more competitive political system but also endorsed a eurosceptic, far-right populism that was further invigorated by the 2015 refugee crisis.

The first part of this chapter aims to provide the historical background as far as it might be necessary to understand Austria's constitutional law and the constitutional doctrine. The second part will discuss specific features of the 1920 Constitution and the methods developed to interpret it. Special attention will be given to the principles of the constitution – the democratic principle, the federal principle and the *Rechtsstaat* principle – which are regarded as core elements of the Austrian constitution and are deeper entrenched. The final section of the chapter will provide an overview on the different methods and ways to amend the constitution.

II. THE EVOLUTION OF THE AUSTRIAN CONSTITUTION

A. The Absolute Monarchy

At the time when the US Constitution was adopted in 1788 and the French Declaration on Human Rights was proclaimed in 1789, the Habsburgs[1]

---

[1] During the last decade the House of Habsburg has attracted fresh research interest – the most important books published in English arguably are: PM Judson, *The Habsburg Empire: A New History* (Cambridge, Mass, The Belknap Press of Harvard University Press, 2016, Kindle Edition), and M Rady, *The Habsburgs: The Rise and Fall of a World*

were busy transforming their hereditary lands into a modern, territorial state. Traditionally, the Habsburgs ruled over a more or less loose union of kingdoms, duchies and principalities. Two of them – the arch-duchies Austria upon and under the river Enns (today's provinces of Upper and Lower Austria) – became eponymous for a territory roughly covering today's Austria, South Tyrol and Slovenia. The term 'Austria' itself is alleged to be the Latin version of the old German '*austar*' meaning 'eastern'; that is to say, a country in the east.[2] Austrians could feel just how far in the east they were during several wars against the Ottoman Empire. In the course of these wars Vienna was besieged twice – in 1529 and in 1689. These wars, especially the second siege of Vienna, must have been traumatic events and the experience of being an eastern outpost of Christendom may be regarded as one of the reasons why this country became a stronghold of the counter-reformation and, consequently, the Roman Catholic Church.

In 1789, the reign of Joseph II, son of Maria Theresa, had almost come to an end. Not only did Joseph II rule over Habsburg's 'hereditary lands' like his mother, but also, like his father, Francis Stephen of Lorraine, he was the crowned Emperor of the 'Holy Roman Empire of the German Nation'. Vienna, the town of residence, was the political and cultural centre of large parts of Europe. Genuinely interested in the living conditions of his subjects, Joseph II travelled through his realm frequently and mostly undercover, hearing grievances and collecting (written) petitions which had to be worked through upon arrival in Vienna.[3] Taking him as far as Russia, Rome and Paris, where he visited his sister Maria Antonia who was married to the French king Louis XVI, he sensed the revolutionary mood in Europe, especially in France. Therefore, he speeded up reforming his territories. On top of the agenda was the abolishment of serfdom, in which he partly succeeded (entire abolishment was only achieved in 1848). Peasants were to be liberated from the feudal bonds to their noble masters, thus becoming equal citizens (and taxpayers). Additionally, necessary and ground-breaking reforms of the school system and the administration were brought on the way. The principles of reorganising the civil service were to survive centuries to come.

Power (UK, Penguin, 2020, Kindle Edition). These books and others shed a new light on the history of the Empire which will be reflected in this section.

[2] E Zöllner, *Der Österreichbegriff* (Wien, Böhlau, 1988) 18.

[3] See the illustrative book by M Czernin, *Der Kaiser reist inkognito. Joseph II und das Europa der Aufklärung*, 2nd edn (München, Penguin, 2021).

Joseph II reigned as an absolute monarch; however, he was described as 'enlightened'. Having studied Voltaire and other contemporary authors, he was determined to use his absolute powers in order to achieve the commonwealth of his subjects and his nations respectively. But it depended on his prudence and the prudence of his entourage to define the commonwealth of his nations. The idea that the common good could be defined in a parliamentary debate was completely alien to him, as he would have denied others the (intellectual) means to establish what was in the common interest. An 'enlightened absolute monarch' was seen as a loving and caring parent for all his subjects. The great German philosopher Immanuel Kant described and criticised such a relationship between a monarch (government) and the people as 'paternalistic'.[4] Nevertheless, the idea of a 'nanny state' became very powerful in Austria, certainly more powerful than the idea of a free market society, and this can be still felt today. Not only did it support the establishment of one of the world's most elaborate social welfare systems, but it is also present in everyday language when a Governor of a state is sometimes referred to as '*Landesvater*' or '*Landesmutter*' (the state's father or mother).

In 1792, Leopold II, who had succeeded his brother Joseph II only in 1790, died and his son Francis inherited the Habsburg throne. In 1804, he claimed the title Emperor of Austria to equal Napoleon I, who had crowned himself Emperor of France. Becoming the Emperor of Austria, he arguably took a decisive step in the nation-building process. In a further step, the 1811 Civil Law Code (*Allgemeines bürgerliches Gesetzbuch – ABGB*) was enacted. At least on a formal legal level, it introduced the concept of equal citizenship. After the end of the Napoleonic wars and the 1815 Congress of Vienna, there was no further appetite for reforms. At that time, the Austrian Monarchy, informed by the terror of the French Revolution, turned into one of the most reactionary countries in Europe. While constitutions had been introduced in several southern German principalities, Austria remained an absolute monarchy and relied upon an even more oppressive system based on censorship and spying.

In 1848, however, the revolutions that swept through Europe also reached the Austrian Monarchy and forced the Austrian Emperor to concede the formation of a '*Reichstag*' (a general assembly), which was entrusted with drafting a constitution. To avoid being impeded by insurgents, it was relocated from Vienna to Kremsier. Although it produced a draft constitution, the attempt eventually failed. The Emperor

---

[4] I Kant, *Über den Gemeinspruch: Das mag in der Theorie richtig sein, taugt aber nicht für die Praxis*, 5th edn (Hamburg, Meiner, 1992) 20ff.

Ferdinand I, son of Francis I, who had difficulties governing (possibly because he did not have sufficient mental ability), had to abdicate and his young nephew Francis Joseph ascended the throne. Francis Joseph dissolved the *Reichstag* and thus prolonged the absolute monarchy for more than another decade.[5] Nevertheless, as already mentioned, serfdom was finally abolished in 1848 and with that also the jurisdiction over peasants by their feudal lords. Consequently, a new judicial system had to be introduced in the fields of criminal and civil law. It featured a Supreme Court and several criminal and civil law courts – amongst others provincial courts and provincial courts of appeal. 1848 also saw the introduction of municipalities administering their affairs partially in an autonomous sphere.

B. The Constitutional Monarchy

After expensive wars were fought in the 1850s and, most notably, Lombardia was lost in the 1859 war against France and Piedmont, the debt-ridden monarch had to make concessions to citizens demanding a (liberal) constitution. In the 1860 October Diploma, Francis Joseph had promised the introduction of parliaments. In implementing this promise, an Imperial Council (*Reichsrat*) was established and also a diet (*Landtag*) was created in each of the provinces (kingdoms, duchies, etc). Although Francis Joseph initially had thought that these were only advisory bodies,[6] he quickly had to learn that they were meant to participate effectively in the law-making process. Future laws could therefore only be enacted if they passed the Imperial Council and – in a small field of legislative provincial powers – the respective diet. The monarch, of course, had to give his consent. With this step, the absolute monarchy was transformed into a constitutional monarchy.

Following the traumatic loss of the 1866 battle of Königgrätz (Sadowa),[7] the monarchy had to finally concede predominance in the

---

[5] Ferdinand, who lived until 1875, must have had a rather cynical view of his successor and the 1848 events. At each mishap of his successor and especially when Francis Joseph dramatically failed to win the 1866 war against Prussia, Ferdinand allegedly remarked: 'even I could have accomplished that'. See F Herre, *Kaiser Franz Joseph von Österreich – Sein Leben, seine Zeit* (Köln, Kiepenheuer & Witsch, 1992) 80; R Okey, *The Habsburg Monarchy c1765-1918. From Enlightenment to Eclipse* (Basingstoke-London, Macmillan Press, 2001) 189.

[6] Judson (n 1) 254.

[7] The defeat against the Prussian army had a devastating effect on the Empire and its population for various reasons. Consequently, in the carnival season 1866–67 many parties

German-speaking world to Prussia. As a consequence of this foreign policy disaster, Francis Joseph was forced to accept a settlement with Hungary (*Ausgleich*),[8] to form a dual monarchy (imperial and royal – *kaiserlich und königlich*, '*k.u.k.*') and to introduce further constitutional laws in the imperial part of the monarchy. Most notably, the power of parliament was increased by the introduction of ministerial responsibility. The Basic Law on the General Rights of Nationals (*Staatsgrundgesetz über die allgemeinen Rechte der Staatsbürger*, RGBl 142/1867) contained a bill of rights, and a 1867 Basic Law (*Staatsgrundgesetz über die Einsetzung eines Reichsgerichtes*, RGBl 143/1867) established the Imperial Law Court. This was attributed various powers, especially the power to pronounce on administrative rulings allegedly infringing on constitutionally guaranteed political rights after exhaustion of all other legal remedies offered by the administrative system. In 1875, the Administrative High Court (*Verwaltungsgerichtshof*)[9] was established. It was entitled to review administrative decisions for compliance with ordinary laws. The Administrative High Court developed an impressive jurisprudence especially with regard to administrative procedural law, which it derived from pre-legal principles rather than from codified statutes.[10]

Additionally, a 1868 law introduced a two-tier administrative system in the provinces, managed by a governor or a president. The provinces were divided into districts with a district administration authority in each (*Bezirkshauptmannschaft*) and managed by a district chief officer (*Bezirkshauptmann*).

---

and balls were cancelled. The '*Wiener Männergesangsverein*' (a men's choir) nevertheless gave a concert in which it performed a piece that offered a rather cynical and satirical view on the war. The tune had been written by Johann Strauß Jr. Initially not very popular, it became a great success in its instrumental version. Nowadays, it is known throughout the world as the 'Blue Danube Waltz'.

[8] Such a constitutional compromise was not reached with the Czechs: cf Z Kárník, 'Attempts to Achieve a German-Czech Ausgleich in Habsburg Austria and the Consequences of its Failure' in U Ra'anan et al (eds), *State and Nation in Multi-Ethnic Societies* (Manchester-New York, Manchester University Press, 1991) 81, 89.

[9] Until 2014, the English translation would have been 'Administrative Court'. This would still be correct as the German name has not been altered. However, with the introduction of administrative courts of first instance (in German: *Verwaltungsgerichte erster Instanz*) this traditional translation might lead to some confusion, as the linguistic difference between '*Verwaltungsgerichtshof*' and '*Verwaltungsgericht*' cannot be easily mirrored in English. But as the '*Verwaltungsgerichtshof*' has become a court of appeal, the English translation of Austria's constitution provided for by the Federal Chancellory suggests the term 'Administrative High Court'. This term will be used throughout the book.

[10] See, for instance, C Jabloner, 'Rechtskultur und Verwaltungsgerichtsbarkeit' (2001) 123 *Juristische Blätter* 137ff; T Olechowski, 'Entwicklung der Verwaltungsgerichtsbarkeit' in R Müller (ed), *Verfahren vor dem VfGH, dem VwGH und den VwG*, 7th edn (Wien, Manz, 2020) 129ff.

Having lost its influence in the German-speaking world and being excluded from the formation of the German Reich 1870/71, the strategic interest of the monarchy focused more and more on the Balkan peninsula. In 1878, Bosnia-Herzegovina, part of the Ottoman Empire, fell to Austria and was administered as a Crown colony; in 1908 it was annexed. In 1914 the *k.u.k* army started manoeuvres in Bosnia, threatening to invade Serbia, as a war on the Balkans had already been considered by the Austrian General Staff.[11] Archduke Francis Ferdinand, heir to the throne after the 1889 suicide of Crown Prince Rudolf, was asked to visit Sarajevo, capital of Bosnia, in open support of the imperial troops. There, he and his wife were assassinated by a Serbian nationalist on 28 June 1914.[12]

The monarchy reacted by issuing an ultimatum to Serbia demanding to fully co-operate in the investigation of the assassination and to allow *k.u.k.* police forces to operate within its territory. This would have been a clear breach of its sovereignty, which everybody understood was unacceptable. Nevertheless, having been assured the support of Emperor Wilhelm II of Germany, the *k.u.k.* army attacked Serbia when it refused to follow the demand set out in the ultimatum, as had been expected. With the mutual assistance pacts falling into place, the world tumbled into the Great War.[13]

C. The First Republic, Armed Conflicts and the Authoritarian Regime

At the end of World War I, the Empire, which had been led to war carelessly by its noble elite and its ruling House, collapsed. As it became increasingly unable to feed its population during the war, it had lost its *raison d'être*:[14] famine and chaos[15] ensued. With the consent of the Allied forces, the multinational Empire broke up, and nationalist groups empowered themselves, secured territories and finally declared their independence.[16] Ironically, all successor states – like the Czechoslovakian Republic, Hungary and Yugoslavia – were multinational.[17]

---

[11] Judson (n 1) 385.

[12] G King and S Woolmans, *The Assassination of the Archduke: Sarajevo 1914 and the Murder that Changed the World* (London, Macmillan, 2013) 167.

[13] M Hastings, *Catastrophe – Europe Goes to War 1914* (London, William Collins, 2013) 41ff.

[14] Rady (n 1) 320; Judson (n 1) 387; for more details on the lack of food supply, ibid, 400.

[15] Judson (n 1) 423.

[16] Rady (n 1) 322; Judson (n 1) 406ff.

[17] Judson (n 1) 446ff, 451.

In the remaining German-speaking part of Austria, a Provisional National Assembly (*Provisorische Nationalversammlung*) seized control of the government. The assembly consisted of (former) members of the Imperial Council, who represented different political parties, mainly German Nationalists, Conservatives and Social Democrats, with the Social Democrats probably having the most developed plan to found a republic.[18] The assembly elected a State Council (*Staatsrat*) and drew up a provisional constitution in which the 'Republic of German Austria' was declared part of the recently formed German Republic. Questions concerning the participation of German Austria in the legislation and administration of the German Republic were to be addressed in future legislation. The desire to join Germany was widespread because of the fear that the small country – the remnants of the former monarchy – stripped of 90 per cent of its former territories and 90 per cent of its former population, had neither an economic nor a political chance of surviving on its own. Not only the German Nationalists, but also in particular the Social Democrats supported this idea. The Conservatives became rather reluctant due to the initial success of left-wing parties in Germany. The Germans, on the other hand, did not show an overall enthusiasm either.[19]

Mainly on the initiative of the French delegation,[20] the 1919 State Treaty of St Germain[21] prohibited Austria from merging with Germany. German Austria was thus transformed into the Republic of Austria; nevertheless, the German language was proclaimed the official language. Subsequently, a Constituent National Assembly (*Konstituierende Nationalversammlung*) was elected. Its main task was to draft a new, Federal Constitution which was passed by parliament on 1 October 1920 and entered into force on 10 November 1920.

Although its leaders insisted that the republic should not be regarded as the successor state to the monarchy, there is remarkable continuity between the 1920 Constitution and the constitution of the nineteenth century. The administrative system and the judicial system, for example, both established under the monarchy, were adopted by the 1920

---

[18] R Saage, 'Die deutsche Frage – Die Erste Republik im Spannungsfeld zwischen öster-reichischer und deutscher Identität' in H Konrad and W Maderthaner (eds), *Das Werden der Ersten Republik … der Rest ist Österreich*, Vol 1 (Wien, Gerold, 2008) 65, 75.

[19] See Saage (ibid) 77.

[20] L Mikoletzky, 'Saint-Germain und Karl Renner – Eine Republik wird "diktiert"' in Konrad and Maderthaner (eds) (n 18) 179, 180.

[21] See also B Jelavich, *Modern Austria: Empire and Republic, 1815–1986* (Melbourne, Cambridge University Press, 1987) 155, 162.

Federal Constitution. The crucial difference between the monarchy and the republic lay in two fields.

First, the republic introduced a democratic government, based on the principle of popular sovereignty (Art 1 of the Federal Constitution). Parliament was no longer restricted to participation in the legislative process, but became – at least in theory – the central political institution. The (former monarchic) administration was completely subordinated to parliamentary legislation. Being a republic, the state was to be headed and represented internationally by a Federal President (*Bundespräsident*), who was initially elected by and accountable to the Federal Assembly (*Bundesversammlung*) and was equipped with the more ceremonial powers of the former monarch.

The second important structural change was enshrined in Art 2 of the Federal Constitution, according to which Austria became a federal state. The federal system had its roots in the monarchy as its provinces had the legal status of self-governing bodies and were attributed some legislative powers, as already mentioned. Members of the former diets had claimed power over the respective territories in the chaotic aftermath of the war but were ready to join the republic, after their points of interest were clarified in two conferences.

From the very beginning, the political parties were in charge of building the new state and drafting the constitution. Founded in the late nineteenth century, the Social Democrats (*Sozialdemokratische Arbeiterpartei – SDAP*), uniting social democrats and communists, and the Christian Socials (*Christlich-soziale Partei – CSP*), a conservative and predominantly catholic movement, formed the core of so-called 'camps' (*Lager*).[22] These 'camps' were based on fundamentally different moral concepts, ideologies and ideas about the state. German nationalist parties, often referred to as 'third camp', supported the Christian Socials in coalition governments. Amongst the parties constituting the 'third camp', a party could be found which, originating from Northern Bohemia and founded in the early 1900s, renamed itself the German National Socialist Labour Party in 1918 (*Deutsche Nationalsozialistische Arbeiter Partei – DNSAP*).[23] National Socialism, therefore, also had its roots in the Austro-Hungarian Monarchy.[24]

[22] See ch 2.
[23] G Jagschitz, 'Die Nationalsozialistische Partei' in E Tálos et al (eds), *Handbuch des Politischen Systems Österreichs – Erste Republik 1918–1933* (Wien, Manz, 1995) 231, 233f.
[24] G Stourzh, 'Problems of Conflict Resolution in a Multi-Ethnic State: Lessons from the Austrian Historical Experience, 1848–1918' in Ra'anan et al (eds) (n 8) 67, 80.

The atmosphere between these 'camps' can be described as highly fraught and mischievous, but there was one view all three camps had in common: democracy as proclaimed in Art 1 of the Constitution was seen merely as a transitional phase that should be replaced by an authoritarian regime. It is probably worth mentioning that there was no genuine liberal party, embracing, for instance, a free market society. Even today, liberal parties – as far as they exist – find it difficult to win a significant share of the electorate.

The parties' fundamental differences affected basic issues of the new constitution, such as federalism and fundamental rights. Whereas the idea of federal power sharing was alien to the Social Democrats, the Christian Social Party advocated a more powerful position for the states. The result was (and still is) a rather 'weak' federalism, at least on first sight. As it was not possible to pass the provisions containing the division of powers between the Federation and the states in 1920, they only entered into force on 1 October 1925.

In 1920, the main political groups could not agree on a new bill of fundamental rights, basically because the Social Democrats demanded the incorporation of social rights, which was emphatically rejected by the Conservatives. As a consequence, the 1867 Basic Law on the General Rights of Nationals remained in force. A possible reform of both the Austrian federalism and the fundamental rights charter, although deemed to be desirable, has never been facilitated because of the traditional partisan differences.[25] Nowadays, however, the historical bill of rights plays only a minor part as Austria has joined the ECHR as well as the European Union, which, in the meantime, has adopted its own bill of rights. Reforming the 1867 Basic Law no longer seems to be that urgent.

The conflict between the parties became increasingly fierce during the 1920s, as political programmes further drifted apart. While the Conservatives dominated on the federal level (mostly) in coalition governments with the German Nationalists, the Social Democrats were especially strong in Vienna where they implemented elements of a social welfare state, predominantly in the field of municipal housing.[26] Fortress-like council estates still leave their mark on Vienna's townscape. The Social Democrats may have prided themselves that they solved the

---

[25] See A Pelinka, *Austria: Out of the Shadow of the Past* (Oxford, Westview Press, 1998) 38, 39.

[26] H Konrad, 'Das rote Wien – Ein Konzept für eine moderne Großstadt?' in Konrad and Maderthaner (eds) (n 18) 223, 232f.

housing problem after World War I, but Conservatives may point to the fact that the private housing market collapsed under heavy taxation and may question whether membership to the Social Democratic Party was a prerequisite for obtaining a (fairly small) flat in one of the council estates. With more than 700,000 members, the Viennese Social Democratic Party was the largest political party of that time.[27] While the Social Democrats might have dreamed of establishing a Soviet system in Austria (in their '*Linzer Programm*' they even opted for violence to push it through), the Conservatives drifted more and more towards fascism.[28]

Unfortunately, violence did not remain merely a threat, as political parties were supported by armed militias. These militias had been formed in the chaotic aftermath of World War I, either to protect borders and guard rural assets (among others, the so-called '*Heimwehr*' siding with the Conservatives) or to protect factories and industries (the so-called '*Republikanischer Schutzbund*', supporting the Social Democrats).[29]

In a 1927 serious armed clash between those militias a Social Democrat was assassinated. As the perpetrator was acquitted, an uproar by Social Democrats saw files being burnt and thrown out of the Palace of Justice, home to the Supreme Court. Following that incident, a comprehensive amendment to the Constitution was discussed and set into force in 1929. To maintain law and order, the position of the Federal President was strengthened (direct election by the people; power to appoint the Federal Chancellor; power to dissolve parliament and to govern on emergency decrees). These changes resulted from a compromise between two totally opposed positions: whereas the Conservatives would have preferred to restore the monarchy, the Social Democrats wanted to maintain or even strengthen the position of parliament.[30]

However, attempts to stabilise Austria's domestic political situation by reforming the Federal Constitution did not succeed. The experiment of establishing a democracy without democrats was bound to fail. And there were not many democrats in the 1920s. One of the most prominent was Hans Kelsen, law professor and member of the Constitutional Court, who had already helped to design the Constitution. He advocated

---

[27] W Maderthaner, 'Die Sozialdemokratie' in Tálos et al (eds) (n 23) 177, 180.
[28] See T Kirk, 'Ideology and Politics in the State that Nobody Wanted: Austro-Marxism, Austrofascism, and the First Austrian Republic' in G Bischof et al (eds), *Global Austria* (New Orleans, University of New Orleans Press, 2011) 81ff.
[29] BM Buchmann, *Insel der Unseligen: Das Autoritäre Österreich 1933-1938* (Wien, Molden, 2019) 54ff.
[30] See Pelinka (n 25) 39.

the intrinsic value of democracy.[31] He emphasised that democracy was not just a means to autocratic ends (which was the common view of many Austrian politicians), but an end in itself. Introducing the compromise as the core element of a democratic government, his thoughts informed the script of the Second Republic after 1945, when everything had to be built around a compromise between the Conservatives and the Social Democrats – even if it were a shabby one.

But Hans Kelsen's ideas on democracy did not influence the course of history in the late 1920s and 1930s. Armed confrontations between the militias carried on. In 1934, the government took advantage of what was described as the self-elimination of parliament. In a fierce debate over the validity of votes cast in a roll call vote, all three presidents resigned from office. In the ensuing chaos, members of parliament left the premises without the session being officially closed. The government argued that with no president in office, parliament could not be reconvened.[32] Taking advantage of this situation, it introduced an authoritarian-corporate constitution, by means of a cabinet decree based on a 1917 law designed to manage the economic crises caused by the war (*Kriegswirtschaftliches Ermächtigungsgesetz*). Although this law was adopted by the republic and played a certain part still in 1919, it is fairly clear that its scope did not cover the enactment of a totalitarian constitution in 1934.

The cabinet even betrayed its view that parliament had eliminated itself and could not be reconvened by convening a rump-parliament (without the social democratic members) that had to rubber-stamp the previously introduced constitution. The powers of parliament were transferred to the cabinet and parliament was ultimately dissolved.

Even with contemporary witnesses emphasising that Mussolini exercised pressure on the Austrian government to establish an authoritarian regime in order to prevent Austria from occupation by Nazi Germany,[33] the introduction of the constitution was a '*coup d'etat*'. In its aftermath, all political parties were dissolved and the Fatherland Front (*Vaterländische Front*) was founded as a corporation under public law. Symbols similar to those of the German Nazis were introduced. Instead of the swastika, for instance, the cross potent was displayed.[34]

---

[31] H Kelsen, *The Essence and Value of Democracy*, ed by N Urbinati and CI Accetti, trans by B Graf (Lanham, Maryland, Rowman and Littlefield Publishers, 2013, Kindle Edition).

[32] Indeed, the Standing Orders of the National Council did not provide for such a case in 1934. Nowadays, however, this lacuna is filled and it would be the task of the eldest member of parliament to chair the session should all three presidents be unavailable.

[33] J Deutsch, *Ein weiter Weg* (Wien, Amalthea, 1960) 196.

[34] It is significant that there is still no consensus to be found how to characterise this regime. E Tálos and F Wenninger, *Das Austrofaschistische Österreich 1933-1938* (Wien,

The 1934 constitution was authoritarian as it did not provide for any elections. It attributed legislative powers to a Federal Diet (*Bundestag*) consisting of delegates, who were nominated by various 'councils' representing different institutions and professions. Members of these councils had to be appointed either by the Federal President or by various corporations (*Berufsstände*) and churches. These councils had to pre-discuss all laws that were to be passed by the Federal Diet, which had the power to pass laws or to reject them but was not entitled to make any amendments.[35] The constitution was 'corporate' as it was based on a programme rooted in the papal social encyclicals: '*Rerum Novarum*' and '*Quadragesimo Anno*' respectively. Those encyclicals envisaged overcoming the class struggle by replacing 'the people as a single electoral body ... by cultural communities and occupational sections'.[36] Ideally, these corporations had to represent employers and employees alike. The 'corporate' part of the constitution remained a political programme at best and served as a moral whitewash.

Many laws were enacted by cabinet decrees on the basis of a 1934 constitutional law providing for 'extraordinary measures', effectively leading to a chancellor's dictatorship.

However, the authoritarian government already envisaged a new Austrian patriotism that drew on the great cultural past of the monarchy: though it was impossible to restore Vienna's former political importance, it nevertheless could become the capital of music and culture.

The important takeaways of this constitution are the role of parliament, which was basically restricted to passing laws that were pre-discussed by other bodies; the idea that the class struggle could be overcome in specific 'corporate' institutions; and that an Austrian identity and legitimation as a 'second German state' had to be connected with the great cultural past of the monarchy. All these elements informed Austria's (efficient) constitution after World War II.

Even if the introduction of a genuine Austrian authoritarian regime was designed to save Austria from seizure by Germany, this attempt failed.

LIT-Verlag, 2017) 159ff, for instance, argue that from a typological point of view, the Austrian regimen was similar enough to German and Italian fascism to call it austro-fascist, a term coined by the Social Democrats in the 1930s. But as it was coined by the Social Democrats it is strongly rejected in conservative quarters, especially amongst those whose relatives were involved. See the discussion in Buchmann (n 29) 11f. Buchmann himself refers to the 1934 Austrian system as the 'Dollfuß/Schuschnigg-Regime' (named after the two chancellors who governed at that time), effectively giving up on any characterisation.

[35] A more detailed description can be found in H Wohnout, 'A Chancellorial Dictatorship with a "Corporative" Pretext: the Austrian Constitution Between 1934 and 1938' in G Bischof et al (eds), *The Dollfuss/Schuschnigg Era in Austria* (New Brunswick-London, Transaction Publishers, 2003) 143, 144ff.

[36] Wohnout (ibid) 146.

Already destabilised by Nazi terror conducted from German soil, it was occupied by Nazi Germany in March 1938, thus ending a period that was later called 'The First Republic'. Although the Austrian government tried to save Austria's independence, it abstained from deploying troops against the German army – shying away from what it believed would only have been an unnecessary bloodshed. Others, however, felt liberated from a rather unpopular government and the German troops were cheered on as they marched through the country in their approach to Vienna.

Obviously, the ideas of fascism and anti-Semitism[37] were not in general alien to the Austrian population. Fascist concepts had their roots in Austria and anti-Semitism was already quite common in the monarchy, fuelled by the then view of the Roman Catholic Church (under Maria Theresa, for instance, Jews were not allowed to settle in large parts of the German-speaking Habsburg hereditary lands with the exception of Vienna, where bankers, in particular, were welcome to finance the notoriously debt-ridden monarchy[38]). Unemployment rates in Austria were very high and there was a hope that joining Germany could improve the economic situation – a hope that had already been expressed in 1918. Many Austrians, therefore, identified themselves with the Nazi regime. Some even became high-profile party members and were deeply involved in the horrible concept of the 'Final Solution' (*Endlösung*): the systematic murder of the Jewish part of the population. Others, however, fell victim to the Nazis. Thousands died in concentration camps, were deported, emigrated or went underground. Austria lost vast parts of its intellectual elite in the 1930s and 1940s – a loss the country has not yet recovered from and probably never will.

In 1939, Europe went to war again and Austrians were serving in the army of the aggressor.

D. The Second Republic

After World War II, mainly under the influence of the Soviet occupying power, as the first step, political parties were re-established. The Socialist Party of Austria, renamed the Social Democratic Party of Austria (*SPÖ*)

---

[37] See RS Wistrich, 'Social Democracy, Antisemitism and the Jews of Vienna' in I Oxaal et al (eds), *Jews, Antisemitism and Culture in Vienna* (London-New York, Routledge and Kegan Paul Inc, 1987) 111, 120. Also cf B Marin, 'Antisemitism Before and After the Holocaust: the Austrian Case' in Oxaal et al (eds) (ibid) 216, 233.

[38] See Judson (n 1) 67.

after the fall of the Iron Curtain, a centre-left party, was founded by representatives of the former social democratic camp. The Austrian People's Party (*Österreichische Volkspartei* – *ÖVP*), a centre-right party, was founded by former Christian Socials. The Communist Party of Austria (*KPÖ*) completed what initially was designed to be a three-party system. The Communist Party met only a Soviet demand – it never gained large support. In the first election it won 5 per cent of the vote, only to become more and more insignificant.

The three parties issued a declaration (proclamation) of independence (*Unabhängigkeitserklärung*) in which they promised to rebuild the democratic republic of Austria in the spirit of the 1920/1929 constitution (Art 1). The proclamation already set the tone for Austria's post-war, identity-building narrative that one-sidedly focused on victimhood and German otherness.[39] The three parties had not just declared Austria's independence but also asserted that 'the helpless Austrians' were occupied and annexed by a military force, thus being the first victims of Nazi Germany. (According to the later official doctrine, the seizure of Austria was an occupation rather than an annexation.[40]) The proclamation insisted that 'the powerless and will-less people' were dragged into 'a senseless and unwinnable war of conquering' that 'no Austrian had ever wanted, foreseen or endorsed'.[41] Only the last two paragraphs of the proclamation halfheartedly dealt with its co-responsibility for the Nazi crimes, which Austria was frequently reminded of by the Soviets.

Indeed, Austria's grappling with its contribution to Nazi atrocities was hardly consistent. In 1945, nevertheless, procedures were introduced to denazify Austrian society. Former members of the Nazi party and some of its affiliate associations had to register. They could, consequently, be banned from exercising their professions or had to stand trial before specific People's Courts ('*Volksgerichte*', not to be confused with the Nazi '*Volksgerichtshof*'). Between 500,000 and 600,000 (numbers vary) were registered. They were not eligible to participate in the first general elections after the war. As many of those former members were civil servants, judges or academics, it soon became clear that banning them all from their professions would have led to vacancies the republic could not have filled. In a next step, a law therefore distinguished

---

[39] M Tschiggerl, 'Significant Otherness Nation-Building and Identity in Postwar Austria' (2021) 27 *Nations and Nationalism* 782.

[40] Offering a different view on the annexation of Austria by Germany see H Wright, 'The Legality of the Annexation of Austria by Germany' (1944) 38 *The American Journal of International Law* 621, 635.

[41] See the Proclamation StGBl 1/1945.

between those former members who were incriminated (*belastet*) and those who were less incriminated (*minderbelastet*). The latter – around 90 per cent – were immediately cleared and were integrated into Austria's post-war society. Many of the 'incriminated' were later acquitted after the 1955 State Treaty when the appetite to sue former Nazis vanished in general.[42]

Restoring the 1920 Constitution instead of drafting a new one met two demands. First, it avoided a discussion about a new constitution that might have triggered the danger of either dividing Austria into two parts – like Germany – or involving the Communist Party and the Soviets in the drafting of a new constitution.[43] Second, it further helped to eradicate the fascist period between 1933 and 1945 from the collective memory and to connect the present with the glorious cultural heritage of the monarchy, completely ignoring that its noble elite and the ruling House had toyed with a war on the Balkans, ultimately triggering the Great War. Tourists visiting rural and/or alpine villages will be surprised to find war memorials listing the names of those young villagers who fell in the two World Wars claiming that they died in defending their homeland (*Heimat*)[44] – although their homeland had never been attacked in the first place. Austrians forgot that they were not only victims but that many of them were also perpetrators.[45] This dishonesty in grappling with the Nazi past would come back to haunt them 40 years later.[46]

'The spirit of the 1920 Constitution' in which the Second Republic was restored, nevertheless allowed for a complete change in the attitude of the political parties. Although they had almost triggered a civil war in the First Republic, they vowed to co-operate in the Second. As it was they who re-built the state, according to the proclamation of independence, the Social Democrats and the People's Party (the Communist Party

---

[42] For a more detailed account see WR Garscha, 'Entnazifizierung und gerichtliche Ahndung von NS-Verbrechen' in E Tálos et al (eds), *NS-Herrschaft in Österreich. Ein Handbuch* (Wien, öbv & hip, 2000) 852ff.

[43] E Loebenstein, 'Verfassungspolitische Zielvorgaben des Jahres 1945 und ihre Verwirklichung aus der Sicht eines Zeitzeugen' in E Weinzierl et al (eds), *Justiz und Zeitgeschichte*, Vol 2 (Wien, Jugend & Volk, 1995) 808, 820ff.

[44] See H Uhl, 'Vom Opfermythos zur Mitverantwortungsthese: NS-Herrschaft, Krieg und Holocaust im "österreichischen Gedächtnis"' in C Gerbel et al (eds), *Transformation gesellschaftlicher Erinnerung. Studien zur 'Gedächtnisgeschichte' der Zweiten Republik* (Wien, Turia + Kant, 2005) 50, 60ff.

[45] A Pelinka, 'The Reception of the Anschluss after 1945' in WE Wright (ed), *Austria, 1938-1988. Anschluss and Fifty Years* (Riverside, CA, Ariadne Press, 1995) 223, 224.

[46] See ch 4, where the Waldheim affair will be discussed.

being insignificant) regarded the republic as their inheritance. They gained an unprecedented influence not only in genuine political matters, but also penetrated society and the economy. Not only were the political 'camps' restored, large parts of Austria's industry and of the banking sector were nationalised to avoid those assets being deemed 'German property' and acquired by the Soviets. This gave rise to an ubiquitous culture of patronage appointments. The two parties have been described by Austrian political scientists – quite frankly – as 'feudal lord(s)'.[47] The country was literally split into a 'red' and a 'black' half.[48] Although the mutual distrust between the two parties never really subsided, disputes were mainly resolved behind closed doors where compromises could be found. 'Grand coalition' governments were the logical consequence in a consociational democracy.[49] These governments were further supported by the system of the so-called 'social partnership'.[50] The ability to manage conflicts through open, transparent argument, something parliamentarianism might suggest and the constitution might have intended, remained underdeveloped for a long period[51] and it is still debatable if it has reached a level comparable to Western democracies.

The 1955 State Treaty ended the Allied occupation and restored Austria's sovereignty. But it came at a price that Austria was more than willing to pay: according to the Moscow Memorandum, Parliament enacted the Federal Constitutional Law of 26 October 1955 on Austrian Neutrality (*Bundesverfassungsgesetz über die Neutralität Österreichs*, BGBl 211/1955). All relevant political powers were strongly in favour of this status, which has co-shaped the character of the Second Republic. As a consequence, Austria had a very specific position during the Cold War, which largely became obsolete with the fall of the Iron Curtain.[52] Austria's membership of the European Union and the evolution of the Common Foreign and Security Policy have cast doubt on the concept of

---

[47] See A Pelinka, 'The Decline of the Party State. The Rise of Parliamentarianism: Change within the Austrian Party System' in A Pelinka and F Plasser (eds), *The Austrian Party System* (Boulder-London, Westview Press, 1989) 21, 25.

[48] A Pelinka, 'Austrian Political Culture: from Subject to Participant Orientation' in KR Luther and P Pulzer (eds), *Austria 1945–1995. Fifty Years of the Second Republic* (Aldershot, Ashgate Publishing, 1998) 109, 112.

[49] See also DM Wineroither, 'Das Demokratiemodell des B-VG und die politische Realität der Zweiten Republik' (2020) 75 *Zeitschrift für Öffentliches Recht* 139ff.

[50] See ch 2.

[51] A Pelinka, 'Eine "Verwestlichung" Österreichs? Zum Wandel des Politischen Systems durch den EU-Beitritt' (1995) 26 *Zeitschrift für Parlamentsfragen* (Sonderband) 278.

[52] See G Bischof et al (eds), *Neutrality in Austria* (New Brunswick, Transaction Publishers, 2001); see also O Rathkolb, 'Superpower Perceptions of Austrian Neutrality' in Luther and Pulzer (eds) (n 48) 67.

neutrality: many scholars question whether the concept has changed or whether neutrality *de facto* has already been given up.[53]

In 1958, Austria adopted the ECHR in the form of a constitutional law and made it directly applicable. After an initial period of reluctance, the Constitutional Court followed the continuously evolving jurisprudence of the European Court of Human Rights (ECtHR), which had substantial effects on the Austrian legal system, especially with regard to the concept of administrative jurisdiction and the enhancement of fundamental rights.

After numerous amendments in the following decades, a further and probably more decisive step towards Europeanisation followed in 1994, when Austrians voted in favour of joining the European Union, which came into effect on 1 January 1995. This was arguably the most significant constitutional change since the end of World War II. Not only did it further constrain parliament's powers by shifting legislative competencies to the government, but it also had an even more centralising effect on the separation of powers between the Federation and the states. Furthermore, it significantly curtailed the power of the Constitutional Court. This all happened as a mere consequence of adopting the EU Treaties without amending the wording of the 1920 Constitution. Provisions were introduced to counterbalance the shift of powers between parliament and government enacted in the aftermath of accession to the European Union.[54]

Roughly a month before the European Union closed its Convention on a European Constitutional Treaty, Austrian politicians established a Constitutional Convention for Austria, as a comprehensive reform of the Austrian constitution seemed to be desirable. Austrian federalism, a system of public administration that seemed far too costly, along with a new bill of fundamental rights and other issues were targeted.

The Convention finished its work in 2005 and presented a draft for a new constitution. The attempt to enact a new constitution failed because of probably the same ideological gaps between the political parties that had previously prevented compromises in the 1920s. However, following the general election of October 2006 a commission of experts was established at the Federal Chancellery to draft a comprehensive reform based on the work of the Constitutional Convention.

---

[53] See, for example, S Griller, 'Verfassungsfragen der österreichischen EU-Mitgliedschaft' (1995) 36 *Zeitschrift für Europarecht, Internationales Privatrecht und Rechtsvergleichung* 107, 110ff.

[54] See ch 3.

Shying away from enacting a new constitution which might have been subject to a mandatory referendum, parliament opted for a piecemeal reform, implementing only parts of the commission's work. The most important amendment was only passed and effected during the second decade of the twenty-first century: the introduction of a two-tier system of administrative jurisdiction. This amendment along with all other major changes will be dealt with in the following chapters of this book.

III. CHARACTERISTIC FEATURES OF THE AUSTRIAN CONSTITUTION

The 1920 Federal Constitutional Law (*Bundes-Verfassungsgesetz*, B-VG – the hyphen is essential when quoting this law) is the core document of the Austrian constitution.[55] As the historical section above has already shown, the institutional setup of the Austrian constitution stands in the tradition of modern, liberal Western constitutions which may be regarded as offsprings of the Renaissance period.[56] The Austrian constitution contains the following major design elements: it separates state powers horizontally – mainly between a bicameral parliament consisting of the National and the Federal Council, a responsible government and independent law courts – as well as vertically – dividing powers between a federal level and sub-federal levels (states and self-governing bodies). It provides for regular general elections that allow an unpopular government to be dismissed in a peaceful manner.[57]

A. The Style of the Constitution

A specific feature of Austria's constitution is its entirely formal, legal and sometimes extremely detailed character. Due to the fundamentally opposed ideologies of the two political 'camps' whose representatives framed the constitution, no compromise could be reached on the moral concepts that might underlie the constitution. Therefore, the text of

---

[55] It is available in its German version as well as in an English version on the website of the Federal Chancellery: www.ris.bka.gv.at. The English version may be regarded as a more or less official translation albeit the text is not authentic.

[56] DS Lutz, *Principles of Constitutional Design* (Cambridge, Cambridge University Press, 2006) 209.

[57] It therefore perfectly meets the requirements of a democratic government as is defined as the absence of tyranny by K Popper, *The Open Society and Its Enemies* (Abingdon, Routledge, 2011) 118f.

the Austrian constitution is rather sober compared with other constitutions. In contrast to the US, German, French or Swiss constitution, just to name a few, the Austrian constitution does not include a preamble and therefore no references to 'the people', 'the nation', a higher authority or any aims or values. In this respect, the republican constitution stands in the tradition of the constitutional laws of the monarchy – they were all completely lacking the solemn and elevated language typical of so many other constitutions. As sobriety is a characteristic element of the style of legal texts throughout Austria, this tradition clashed with the style of EU law. Not only the EU Treaties, but also regulations and directives carry sometimes even excessive preambles. The role these preambles have in interpreting the law was completely alien to the Austrian administration. This initially triggered some misunderstandings.[58]

Because of its 'sober' character and despite some more recent introductions of state objectives (like environmental protection or gender equality), the constitution has never played a part in the nation's identity-building process. As a consequence of its amending formula (see below), it has become one of the most flexible constitutions in the world after World War II. This was mainly due to Austria's specific concept of consociational democracy, where the Social Democratic Party and the People's Party, together enjoying a supermajority in parliament, more or less amended the constitution at will. According to the widespread formal understanding of the 'constitution', not only rules of genuine 'constitutional' character but also provisions relating to other matters – often covering the single interest of a party – were enacted as constitutional laws. This is the reason why Austrian constitutional law is 'overloaded' with provisions that in many other countries would not even be considered as constitutional laws.

As constitutional amendments do not have to be incorporated into the core document, the constitution has become highly fragmented. Numerous constitutional laws (*Bundesverfassungsgesetze*, BVG – in this case cited without a hyphen) and even constitutional provisions as part of otherwise ordinary laws were enacted without simultaneously amending the core document. Even constitutional lawyers were unable to oversee all the constitutional laws and provisions that literally went into the hundreds and thousands. A 2008 amendment has brought some relief in rescinding and downgrading quite a number of these provisions.

---

[58] See, for instance, the decision of the Administrative High Court, VwSlg 14592 A/ 1997. The decision is discussed in G Loibl and M Stelzer, *Nationale Souveränität im Gentechnikrecht* (Wien, Bundeskanzleramt, 1997) 62ff.

Nevertheless, Austrians never have been nor will be able to have 'their' constitution at hand in a small yet comprehensive book.

B. Interpreting the Constitution

As already mentioned, the domestic political situation after World War II decisively influenced the interpretation of the constitution in the Second Republic. There is a tendency for public law scholars to adhere strongly to structural theories and rather formalistic interpretations without taking into account teleological or value-oriented considerations, again to (more or less unknowingly) fit Austria's post-war narrative. In that respect, Austrian constitutionalists would emphasise that there is a typical Austrian reading of the constitution (*modus austriacus*)[59] that is pitted against the German reading of the Bonner Basic Law (the German post-war constitution). Although Austrian scholars usually study German legal literature and are influenced by it, there is obviously a need to uphold a specific Austrian 'otherness': a general need for Austria to define its role as a 'second' German state (and a way to dissociate itself from National Socialism, purported to be an entirely German matter).[60] In particular, Hans Kelsen's writings and his Theory of Pure Law became points of reference after the war, at least in some quarters (not necessarily amongst staunch Catholics). His international reputation allowed Austria's jurisprudence to be connected with its great cultural heritage. But, further, with regard to his Jewish origin, his democratic attitude and his emigration to escape Nazi terror, he was immune to any suspicion of being involved in Nazi and/or fascist atrocities and gave perfect cover for those who were not immune.

Hans Kelsen himself did not develop a doctrine of interpretation, nor did he adhere to formal methods when working as a judge on the bench of the Constitutional Court. Rather, he endorsed the political task of the court of empowering the new constitution, in particular enhancing its democratic elements and the principle of equality, not paying attention to any 'methodological' restraints.[61] Nevertheless, after World War II,

---

[59] E Wiederin, 'Denken vom Recht her: Über den modus austriacus in der Staatsrechtslehre' (2007) 40 *Die Verwaltung* 293.

[60] Tschiggerl (n 39) 782, 790ff.

[61] E Wiederin, 'Hans Kelsen als praktischer Verfassungsrechtler' in N Aliprantis and T Olechowski (eds), *Hans Kelsen: Die Aktualität eines großen Rechtswissenschafters und Soziologen des 20. Jahrhunderts* (Wien, Manz, 2014) 109.

Austrian public law scholars felt much more bound by the phrasing of the law.[62]

In the case of unresolved ambiguities, conventions of 'retrospective' interpretations were established, that either relied on explanatory material provided with draft government bills (*Gesetzesmaterialien*) in order to follow the purported 'will' of the historical legislator, or asserted the 'petrification' of constitutional terms (that is, that they are 'set in stone'). Originally designed to interpret the provisions pertaining to the division of powers between the Federation and the states, the petrification doctrine (*Versteinerungsdoktrin*) became more or less a general method of reading the constitution.[63] According to this doctrine, a constitutional term must be understood in the light of the ordinary laws pertaining to the constitutional term that were in force at the moment the constitutional law in question was enacted. Thus, the meaning of the constitutional term is 'petrified'. This doctrine works best with certain terms that define the responsibility of the Federation vis-à-vis the states and will therefore be discussed in depth in Chapter 5.

The petrification doctrine, as peculiar as it may be, is perfectly in line with the needs of Austria's post-war culture of compromise. According to that, it should have been the responsibility of the two traditional parties to find a compromise to develop the law in the light of changing living conditions, rather than the Constitutional Court. Unsurprisingly, this kind of judicial self-restraint was one of the sources of frequent constitutional amendments.

In a similar retrospective manner, a doctrine was widely accepted that emphasised the 'responsive character' of the constitution (*Antwortcharakter der Verfassung*). This doctrine draws on the fact that the constitution adopted various institutions from the monarchy. It suggests a continuity between the monarchy and the republic, from which the republican parliament could only deviate explicitly. The republican constitution therefore 'responded' to the given legal system. In cases where the constitution was silent, it was consequently assumed that it had adopted the traditional legal system.[64] Very often, Austrian constitutional scholars analysed the legal situation of the monarchy in order

---

[62] See M Potacs, 'Die Auslegung der Verfassung' in P Bußjäger et al (eds), *100 Jahre Bundes-Verfassungsgesetz, Verfassung und Verfassungswandel im nationalen und internationalen Kontext* (Wien, Verlag Österreich, 2020) 109ff.

[63] H Schäffer, *Verfassungsinterpretation in Österreich* (Wien-New York, Springer, 1971) 97ff.

[64] For some good examples how this method of reading the constitution works see R Thienel, *Österreichische Staatsbürgerschaft*, Vol 2 (Wien, Österreichische Staatsdruckerei, 1990).

to interpret the republican constitution. This 'method' tries to tie post-war Austria to its monarchical past, thereby following the more general cultural programme, but often defies questions regarding the significance of a democratic constitution.

The conventions of interpreting the constitution as developed after World War II not only met the narrative of post-war Austria and the demands of the political system based on compromises, as already emphasised. Moreover, they also ensured that the belief in an autonomous legal doctrine could have been upheld. Only such a doctrine could have exercised at least some authority within a legal system that lacked an underlying moral concept, and it helped bridging the still severe political differences between the conservative and the social-democratic 'camps' as well as integrating former Nazis. Any theory that would have suggested that the interpretation of a norm was based on pre-legal (and in this way also political) assumptions would have severely jeopardised the Austrian constitutional and political system to its very foundations and would have been, therefore, emphatically rejected or – more likely – simply ignored.

Although still common in some quarters, the traditional Austrian conventions of reading the constitution have been challenged by the European influence, both the jurisprudence of the ECtHR and the Court of Justice of the European Union (CJEU). The accession to the ECHR has already led to a different perception of freedom rights in the same way as the ECtHR has unfolded its jurisprudence case-by-case. As will be shown in Chapter 7, the jurisprudence of the ECtHR, as well as the intensive debate of German fundamental rights doctrine within large parts of the academic community, encouraged the Constitutional Court to recognise the principle of proportionality as a standard test for reviewing laws. This test, therefore, worked not only for freedom rights enshrined in the ECHR but also for those guaranteed by the domestic 1867 bill of fundamental rights, especially the right to free employment (*Erwerbsfreiheit*, Art 6 of the 1867 Basic Law on the General Rights of Nationals). Some tentative approaches in the earlier jurisprudence of the Constitutional Court apart, the full power of the proportionality principle was not unfolded in Austria until the late 1980s.

However, the application of this principle implies a different theoretical underpinning than the traditional retrospective conventions of reading the constitution[65] and refers to more substantial, even moral, concepts. The Austrian government, as well as the administration,

---

[65] See M Stelzer, *Das Wesensgehaltsargument und der Grundsatz der Verhältnismäßigkeit* (Wien-New York, Springer, 1991).

therefore, had profound difficulties in understanding the reasoning of the Constitutional Court's rulings and in reacting accordingly. In some cases, the government failed in its attempt to respond to the rescission of a law accordingly. It passed a law that was unconstitutional for the very same reasons as the previous law, and which, therefore, shared the fate of that previous law.[66] In other cases, however, constitutional provisions were passed by parliament in order to counter the court's case law, only to raise questions under the principle of *Rechtsstaat*.

The court's methodological turnaround, therefore, challenged not only the traditional approach of reading the constitution[67] but parts of the political system as well.[68] Although this turnaround was also modelled on the jurisprudence of the German Federal Constitutional Court, the Austrian court did not necessarily arrive at the same results as the German court when applying the proportionality principle in comparable cases. Especially with regard to pre-legal concepts that might inform the balancing exercise, it can be observed that the Austrian court deviates from the views of the German court. The latter, for instance, puts more trust into the regulating powers of a free market than the Austrian court has ever done.[69]

Nevertheless, it might be argued that the Constitutional Court helped to prepare Austria's legal system for the accession to the European Union as the principle of proportionality was already deeply woven into the fabric of European law in the 1990s. The accession to the European Union, however, further challenged traditional conventions of interpretation, as European law forces scholars to reason teleologically, which means duly considering the aims and purposes of a law.

C. Written Constitution and Efficient Constitution

Although the constitutional setup may suggest how powers are shared between the different institutions and provide for the instruments they are equipped with, it is not possible to draw the conclusion that power sharing is effective nor that the instruments are used in the way the constitution had obviously envisaged. In practice, the constitution may

---

[66] See, for instance, VfSlg 10179/1984.

[67] The harshest criticism was probably aired by H Mayer, *Das österreichische Bundes-Verfassungsrecht*, 3rd edn (Wien, Manz, 2002) V.

[68] See ch 7.

[69] See M Stelzer, 'Proportionalität oder Plausibilität?' in C Jabloner et al (eds), *Vom praktischen Wert der Methode* (Wien, Manz, 2011) 737ff.

play out differently. This is not an Austrian peculiarity, as this observation can probably be made in every legal system that relies on a written constitution. There is a gap between the written constitution and what might be called the 'efficient' constitution (*Verfassungswirklichkeit*). Whether or not or in which way the constitutional design becomes effective depends on circumstances and/or prerequisites that the constitution itself cannot guarantee or provide for. Austrian constitutional scholars, for instance, would enthusiastically agree that parliament is the central political body under the Austrian constitution. But this does not necessarily mean that it is – effectively – also the most powerful body. Under the efficient constitution it may turn out that there are reasons why another body, for instance the cabinet, effectively holds more political power than parliament.

In general, the reasons for this observed gap may be manifold and may also differ from constitutional system to system. In Austria, at least three reasons can be identified. One of them is religion. As Austria has been a deeply catholic country,[70] its population has been prone to accept hierarchical structures rather than insisting on the equality of all citizens. This had a bearing on the development of democracy and parliamentarianism,[71] for both of which equality is a necessary prerequisite.

Further, constitutional life after the war was informed by experiences of the First Republic: the violent clashes between political groups spoiled the appetite for fierce, open parliamentary discussions and paved the way for a consociational democracy.

A third reason, and probably the most important one, can be found in the party system. In general, constitutions have been very successful in curtailing the (absolute) monarchical power by dividing it and sharing it between different constitutionally established bodies, and the Austrian constitution also follows this pattern. What constitutions in general have not achieved is to limit the power of political parties. The political

---

[70] Although one may argue that the number of Catholics has significantly decreased to about 64% of the Austrian population (cf Die Presse, 5 August 2017, diepresse.com/5264108/religion-in-oesterreich-mehr-konfessionslose-mehr-muslime, accessed 5 January 2022) and many of them may be Catholic but in name only, the Catholic Church has not only informed the legal system and society over centuries but still enjoys a great influence on so-called morality policies: it may block liberal policies as long as the People's Party is in government. See C Knill, C Preidel and K Nebel, 'Die katholische Kirche und Moralpolitik in Österreich: Reformdynamiken in der Regulierung von Schwangerschaftsabbrüchen und der Anerkennung gleichgeschlechtlicher Partnerschaften' (2014) 43 *Österreichische Zeitschrift für Politikwissenschaft* 275ff. It may need powerful antagonists, such as the Constitutional Court, to overcome a stalemate. See ch 7 for examples.

[71] See ch 3.

system is therefore preceding the constitution (although it may also be informed by it). Consequently, the power-sharing concept of the written constitution may be overlapped by party hierarchies and party discipline. It is therefore necessary to understand the party system in order to establish the efficient constitution.

IV. BASIC PRINCIPLES OF THE CONSTITUTION

Art 44 para 3 of the Federal Constitution demands a referendum in the case of a 'total revision' (*Gesamtänderung*) of the Federal Constitution. As this provision was designed on the model of the Swiss constitution, one might have expected that it would have been understood in the same, more formal manner as revising the whole constitution or enacting a new one. Contrary to that, in the first textbooks and commentaries on the Austrian constitution, the term 'total revision' was already connected with Arts 1 and 2 of the Federal Constitution[72] and thus with the democratic principle and the federal principle. In the light of the experiences of World War II, the Constitutional Court accepted a third principle: the principle of *Rechtsstaat*. The court assumed that this principle was inherent in the Austrian constitution although not explicitly mentioned. Arguably, the 1920 Constitution only explicitly referred to those principles that defined the new republic, thus distinguishing it from the monarchy. As the court system, adopted by the 1920 Constitution, had been established during the monarchy, it was purported that the monarchy, therefore, had already been a *Rechtsstaat*. Consequently, the republic was a *Rechtsstaat*. This assumption dodged the question of whether the monarchical courts system effectively had met the requirements of a *Rechtsstaat* in the nineteenth century and, moreover, if these requirements would suffice in the twentieth century, given the experience of the Nazi atrocities.

However, these three principles of the constitution have been accepted by the Constitutional Court.[73] After World War II, Austrian scholars have postulated a number of further principles, such as the liberal principle, the separation of powers,[74] the separation of state and church[75]

---

[72] See, for example, H Kelsen, G Fröhlich and A Merkl, *Die Verfassungsgesetze der Republik Österreich*, Vol 5 (Wien-Leipzig, Franz Deuticke, 1922) 124.

[73] See, for instance, VfSlg 17340/2004, 16241/2001, 11669/1988.

[74] H Mayer, G Kucsko-Stadlmayer, K Stöger, *Bundesverfassungsrecht*, 11th edn (Wien, Manz, 2015) 89ff.

[75] I Gampl, *Österreichisches Staatskirchenrecht* (Wien-New York, Springer, 1971) 12ff.

and many more. Flooding Austria's constitution with principles in the sense of Art 44 para 3 was hardly convincing from a dogmatic perspective. Rather, it resulted from the political realities of post-war Austria. It reflects the desire of public law scholars to set limits to grand coalition governments commanding a two-thirds majority in parliament, thus threatening the function of the constitution as a legal framework for ordinary legislation. Whenever it was feared that a law might be deemed unconstitutional, the grand coalition government would amend the constitution. Only a principle in the sense of Art 44 para 3 would have had limiting effects as a referendum would have been required should an amendment have affected it. Suffice to say, none of these additional principles were ever considered by the Constitutional Court.

The assumption of principles which may only be amended by a constitutional law subject to an additional mandatory referendum has a severe impact on the structure of the constitution. In a hierarchical concept[76] these principles are superordinated to all other constitutional laws and provisions and, as such, deeper entrenched. Should a constitutional provision violate such a principle, it would be held unconstitutional and could, consequently, be rescinded by the Constitutional Court. Under the Austrian constitution, even a constitutional law may, therefore, be unconstitutional.

Assessing the violation of a principle not only requires the clarification of its substance but also an assessment of the degree of the impact. The latter would have to be severe enough to trigger the need for a referendum. Both seem to be rather difficult tasks. The Constitutional Court thus far has had only few opportunities to pronounce on these questions. However, the few decisions it has issued allow at least some basic considerations.

The democratic principle primarily protects certain constitutional institutions and their powers. At the core of this principle sits the Austrian parliament, mainly with regard to its legislative powers. Substantial changes to the position of the Austrian parliament, especially the National Council, and its legislative powers may be seen as a modification of the democratic principle that would require a referendum. Correspondingly, Austria's accession to the European Union was considered to be a total revision to the constitution, as a large set of legislative powers were transferred from the Austrian parliament to the

---

[76] See H Kelsen, *Pure Theory of Law*, trans by M Knight (Berkeley-Los Angeles, University of California Press, 1967, Kindle Edition) chapter V.35, for the hierarchical structure of the legal order.

legislative bodies of the EU. Further, the position of the Austrian parliament would also be affected by the introduction of a 'plebiscite', which would entitle the Austrian people to pass laws without the agreement or against the will of parliament. According to the opinion of many scholars[77] (and presumably of the Constitutional Court[78]), a plebiscite would have a severe impact on the position of the Austrian parliament and its legislative powers and for that reason its introduction would need a referendum.

It seems peculiar that the introduction of an instrument enhancing democracy should violate the democratic principle. Effectively, the assumption that the democratic principle primarily protects parliament and its powers serves the interest of those established political parties which have a presence in parliament.

Further, the court has assumed that the principle of equality is somehow part of the democratic principle. Although this assertion is theoretically convincing, it has not yet been assessed in which way the principle of equality would be immune against (ordinary) constitutional amendments.

With regard to the federal principle and the *Rechtsstaat* principle, the Constitutional Court has followed a doctrine designed by Austrian scholars according to which successive partial amendments could amount to a 'total revision'. A total revision would be achieved, for instance, if the division of powers between the Federation and the states, a core element of Austria's federal system, would be severely interfered with.[79] Selective transfers of powers from states to the Federation – as frequently happened as a consequence of the retrospective interpretation of the constitution – were clearly rated as partial revisions (*Teiländerungen*). Only transferring a large set of powers in a single act, could amount to a total revision. Austrian scholars argued that the consecutive and frequent transfer of individual powers amounted to a 'creeping total revision' (*schleichende Gesamtänderung*).[80] As it was impossible to determine the point at which the partial revision turned into a total revision, the court has never rescinded a constitutional law on the basis of this doctrine.

---

[77] See, for example, HP Rill, *Möglichkeiten und Grenzen des Ausbaus direktdemokratischer Elemente in der österreichischen Bundesverfassung* (Wien, Orac, 1987).

[78] VfSlg 16241/2001.

[79] VfSlg 11669/1988.

[80] HP Rill, 'Die österreichische Bundesstaatlichkeit und die Gesamtänderungsschwelle des Art 44 Abs 3 B-VG' in M Akyürek et al (eds), *Staat und Recht in Europäischer Perspektive* (Wien, Manz, 2006) 717; E Wiederin, 'Gesamtänderung, Totalrevision und Verfassunggebung' in Akyürek et al (eds) (ibid) 961.

The Constitutional Court considered a similar approach in determining the *Rechtsstaat* principle. In a formal sense, a *Rechtsstaat* must guarantee legal certainty (*Rechtssicherheit*) and, above all, legal protection (*Rechtsschutz*), for example by establishing courts tasked with the judicial review of administrative decisions and/or laws. The principle of *Rechtsstaat* in its formal sense is different from the 'rule of law', the former being more static and structural, the latter a broader, more dynamic concept.[81]

According to the Constitutional Court, the principle of legal protection was generally undermined when laws, other than genuine constitutional laws, were enacted on a constitutional level. This would have prevented the court from assessing them against the constitution. That happened, as already pointed out, primarily during the 1980s, when parliament responded to court rulings rescinding provisions as disproportionate by re-enacting similar provisions as constitutional laws. The Constitutional Court noted that such measures would undermine its powers if taken too frequently and therefore would violate the *Rechtsstaat* principle.[82] But, again, it was almost impossible to determine the point at which the accumulation of measures reached an extent that infringed this principle.

It was ultimately parliament which gave the Constitutional Court a reason for rescinding a constitutional law, based on the arguments outlined above. In the field of public procurement law, the Federal parliament had adopted a constitutional provision that immunised all public procurement laws of the states that were in force on a certain day against constitutional review. This constitutional provision had simply stated that the respective laws of the states were held to be constitutional. Although parliament only intended to address specific constitutional problems, the Constitutional Court understood the provision as an abrogation of its power to review statutes in the entire field of state public procurement law. The Constitutional Court declared this to be incompatible with the *Rechtsstaat* principle and rescinded the provision,[83] noting that a referendum had been required to introduce it. It is quite obvious that a referendum would never have been held on this kind of

---

[81] See AV Dicey, *Introduction to the Study of the Law of the Constitution*, 8th edn reprint (Indianapolis, Liberty Fund, 1982) 120f. Parts of Dicey's concept would be covered in Austria by the principle of equality rather than the *Rechtsstaat* principle. For further discussion on this matter see P Leyland, *The Constitution of the United Kingdom*, 4th edn (Oxford, Hart Publishing, 2021) 64ff.

[82] VfSlg 11756/1988.

[83] VfSlg 16327/2001.

constitutional law – not only for financial, but even more importantly for political reasons: who would dare asking the people to give their consent to undermine the *Rechtsstaat* in a specific case? Although addressing only a procedural aspect, by means of this decision the Constitutional Court set an effective limit for amending the constitution.

Austrian scholars have recently begun to consider whether the basic principles of the constitution may be abolished by means of a mandatory referendum at all.[84] The majority of Austrian scholars[85] would hold the view that they can, and some would even claim that it is a specific feature of Austrian democracy that the constitution can be legitimately abolished by means of a referendum. This assumption is still in line with the view of the political parties in the 1920s, which considered democracy only to mark a transitional period. Nevertheless, this view is not necessarily to be derived from the Austrian constitution. It is crucial to determine which amendments to the legal system may legitimately be based on a constitution. If the aim of a 'constitution' is to provide a general framework for a society of free and equal people, regulations that deny these qualities to any human beings cannot be based on a 'constitution'. Consequently, barbaric acts such as the introduction of slavery, other forms of denying human dignity or the abolishment of democracy still might occur, but never could be legitimised by a 'constitution'. To which view the Constitutional Court may tilt is an open question that hopefully will never have to be answered. The academic discussion, however, may serve as an example that constitutional lawyers in Austria are increasingly split over the conventions of interpreting the constitution.

V. ENGINEERING CONSTITUTIONAL CHANGES

Although Art 1 para 2 of the 1919 Law on the Representative Body of the People (*Gesetz über die Volksvertretung*, StGBl 179/1919) instructed the framers of the new constitution to provide for amendments requiring (additional) referenda, they did not abide by this mandate because of the purported transitional and provisional nature of the constitution. The 1920 amendment formulae therefore made changing the constitution a

---

[84] P Oberndorfer, 'Artikel 1' in K Korinek and M Holoubek (eds), *Österreichisches Bundesverfassungsrecht* (Wien-New York, Springer, 2000) 1, 9f; P Pernthaler, *Der Verfassungskern* (Wien, Manz, 1998).

[85] See H Mayer, 'Gibt es ein unabänderliches Verfassungsrecht?' in Akyürek et al (eds) (n 80) 473.

comparatively easy task. According to its original version, Art 44 para 1 of the Federal constitution stipulated that constitutional laws or constitutional provisions enshrined in ordinary laws only needed a two-thirds majority in the National Council with half of its members present and had to be explicitly indicated as a 'constitutional law' or 'constitutional provision'. On the demand of at least one third of the members of the National Council or the Federal Council, such a law or provision could be subject to a referendum – an opportunity that has never been seized. Only in the case of a total revision of the constitution would such a referendum be mandatory. As outlined above, a 'total revision' was defined as an amendment of one of the basic principles of the constitution.

This amendment formula, pertaining to constitutional law in a formal sense, has created the situation previously analysed: in the First Republic, when the political parties found very few compromises, constitutional amendments were rather rare, with the exception of two important changes. The 1925 amendment entrenched the distribution of responsibilities between the Federation and the states and the 1929 amendment introduced features of a presidential system, which perhaps amounted to a total revision. The amendment was passed without a referendum and this was finally widely accepted. However, it was arguably a design-changing amendment.[86]

In the Second Republic, after establishing a consociational democracy, the two major parties changed the constitution at will, thus being responsible for frequent amendments and a highly flexible constitution. As amendments do not have to be incorporated into the original body of the constitution, the extensive use of 'fugitive' constitutional laws and, especially, provisions led to a high fragmentation of the law that was only partly addressed later. In the case of Austria's accession to the European Union, however, all relevant actors agreed that this step fulfilled the requirements of a total revision. Consequently, a referendum was held.

The 1920 Constitution provides for a special protection of the Federal Council, thus modifying the amendment formula: the rules pertaining to the election of its members (Art 35 of the Federal Constitution) and, as of 1925, also its institution and composition (Art 34 of the Federal Constitution) can only be amended if the Federal Council agrees and the majority of the representatives of four states consent. A fundamental

---

[86] For the classification of amendments in the light of constitutional design see M Stelzer, 'Constitutional Design Through Amendment' in X Contiades and A Fotiadou (eds), *Routledge Handbook of Comparative Constitutional Change* (Abingdon-New York, Routledge, 2021) 137, 142ff.

reform of the Federal Council, albeit frequently discussed, would therefore face an additional hurdle.

Aiming at strengthening the powers of the states, a 1984 amendment to the constitution conferred on the Federal Council the task of agreeing to all constitutional laws and provisions that would curtail the state's legislative and/or executive powers. Such a decision has to be taken by a two-thirds majority with at least half of the members present. It took 35 years until this provision was effectively used to deny the consent of the Federal Council to constitutional provisions arguably affecting the powers of the states. In 2019, the Social Democrats blocked a decision to consent to a law that would merely have extended the time limit for a provision allocating a single legislative power to the Federation that had entitled it to enact a specific ordinary law,[87] thus only aiming at prolonging the *status quo*. The government circumvented this situation by successfully invoking a different constitutional provision that covered the law in question.[88] Later in the year, the Social Democrats and members of the Green Party blocked a decision to entrench the so-called 'debt-brake'.[89] In both cases, arguments pertaining to specific state interests were not exchanged; the dispute was part of the conflict between the conservative/right-wing government and the Social Democrats in opposition and/or the different macroeconomic policy approaches by conservative and left-leaning parties.

These two events are highly significant for the changes the political system has undergone since the mid-1980s. With the rise of the Freedom Party and the emergence of the Green Party, the People's Party and the Social Democrats have declined, gradually losing their combined two-thirds majority. At the time of writing (in 2022), these two parties together command less than 60 per cent of parliamentary votes, needing the consent of a third party to change the constitution. The Social Democrats, out of government, can no longer prevent a constitutional amendment in the National Council. The party therefore has used its minority in the Federal Council to block constitutional amendments in rare cases when the Federal Council had to give its consent based on a two-thirds majority.

Following Austria's 1995 accession to the European Union, the constitution cannot only be changed by traditional, domestic procedures invoking the amendment clauses of the constitution but also

---

[87] www.parlament.gv.at/PAKT/PR/JAHR_2019/PK0140, accessed 5 January 2022.
[88] www.parlament.gv.at/PAKT/PR/JAHR_2019/PK0507, accessed 5 January 2022.
[89] www.parlament.gv.at/PAKT/PR/JAHR_2019/PK0992, accessed 5 January 2022.

by overriding European law. Austrian scholars in general believe that European law – primary as well as secondary – would take precedence over Austrian constitutional law with the only exception being its core principles. However, changes to European primary law would have to be ratified in a specific procedure. They would need the approval of the National Council and the consent of the Federal Council. In both cases a two-thirds majority and the presence of half of the respective members would be required. Should the amendment affect a core principle of the Austrian constitution, a referendum would have to be held.

Scholars might expect that the high flexibility of the Austrian constitution, at least after World War II, might have prevented any informal changes. That was definitely not the case. Changes in state practice as well as in the jurisprudence of the Constitutional Court have also contributed to modifying the constitution.[90]

All of the above pertains to constitutional laws in a formal sense. Although the constitution is rather detailed, at least in some parts, there are ordinary laws that are a prerequisite to implement the constitution and/or contain provisions that are 'constitutional' in a substantive sense. For instance, the Standing Orders of the National Council regulate the procedures of passing a bill and, especially, voting on it. Should they be violated, the law might be unconstitutional. The laws on the Federal Gazette provide for publishing a law; laws that are not published accordingly are either unconstitutional or cannot enter into force. These laws (and others, like the laws providing for general elections) are called 'constitutional laws in a substantive sense'. They can be amended either in the same way as ordinary laws or specific supermajorities apply. The Standing Orders of the National Council, for instance, can only be amended with a two-thirds majority and half of the members of the National Council present.

VI. CONCLUSION

Although Austrian politicians emphatically denied that the small republic was the successor to the Austro-Hungarian Monarchy, its constitutional and legal system was built on the heritage of the former empire. From the very beginning, the constitutional debate was overshadowed by the

---

[90] For further details see M Stelzer, 'Constitutional Change in Austria' in X Contiades (ed), *Engineering Constitutional Change. A Comparative Perspective on Europe, Canada and the USA* (Abingdon-New York, Routledge, 2013) 7, 12ff.

deep conflict between dominant political camps, foremost the (catholic) Conservatives and the Social Democrats, based on fundamentally opposed ideologies. This explains the comparatively 'legal' or 'technical' character of the constitution, which lacks an underpinning moral concept. While the disputes between these camps led to armed conflicts in the First Republic and the introduction of a (catholic) authoritarian regime in 1934, Hans Kelsen's idea of democracy yearning for compromise became the script of the Second Republic, at least initially. This had a bearing on the constitution, as it could be amended frequently by two parties joined in coalition governments commanding a supermajority in parliament. Austria's post-war narrative not only claimed it to be the first victim of Nazi Germany, masking its co-responsibility for Nazi crimes and especially the mass-murder of its (predominantly) Jewish compatriots, but also tried to connect itself with the great cultural heritage of the monarchy, thus establishing German 'otherness'. This was reflected in a constitutional doctrine that favoured a formal reading of the constitution and the application of retrospective methods. From the mid-1980s onwards, shifts in the party system and the process of European integration have continuously jeopardised the monarchical heritage, the dominant role of the two traditional political parties and the conventions of formal and retrospective reading of the constitution. This process accelerated during the last decade, ultimately depriving the legal and political system in Austria of some of its typical post-war features.

FURTHER READING

Bußjäger, P and Johler, MM, 'Power-Sharing in Austria: Consociationalism, Corporatism and Federalism' in Keil, S and McCulloch, A (eds), *Power-sharing in Europe. Past Practice, Present Cases and Future Directions* (Cham, Palgrave Macmillan, 2021) 43.

Judson, PM, *The Habsburg Empire: A New History* (Cambridge, Mass, The Belknap Press of Harvard University Press, 2016, Kindle Edition).

Konrad, H and Maderthaner, W (eds), *Das Werden der Ersten Republik ... der Rest ist Österreich,* Vol 1 (Wien, Gerold, 2008).

Luther, KR and Pulzer, P (eds), *Austria 1945–1995* (Aldershot, Ashgate Publishing, 1998).

Pelinka, A, *Austria: Out of the Shadow of the Past* (Oxford, Westview Press, 1998).

Pelinka, A, 'Austrian Politics: 1918 to 2019' (2020) 4 *Antisemitism Studies* 82.

Rady M, *The Habsburgs. The Rise and Fall of a World Power* (UK, Penguin, 2020, Kindle Edition).

Reiter, I, *Texte zur österreichischen Verfassungsentwicklung 1848–1955* (Wien, WUV, 1997).

Roháč, D, 'Why did the Austrian Empire Collapse? A Public Choice Perspective' (2009) 20 *Constitutional Political Economy* 160, 176.

Tschiggerl, M, 'Significant Otherness Nation-building and Identity in Postwar Austria' (2021) 27 *Nations and Nationalism* 782.

Weinzierl, E et al (eds), *Justiz und Zeitgeschichte*, Vol 2 (Wien, Jugend und Volk, 1995).

Wohnout, H, 'A Chancellorial Dictatorship with a "Corporative" Pretext: the Austrian Constitution Between 1934 and 1938' in G Bischof et al (eds), *The Dollfuss/Schuschnigg Era in Austria* (New Brunswick–London, Transaction Publishers, 2003) 143.

2

Political Parties and Social Partnership

Introduction – Development of the Party System – Law on Political Parties – Social Partnership – Conclusion

I. INTRODUCTION

POLITICAL PARTIES ARE essential in modern, representative democracies as they mediate between the state and the individual. Their most important task is aggregating and articulating the political views or interests of their clientele as well as participating in elections. A genuine competition between parties is vital for a democratic system. In addition, political parties select a large number of officials to carry out public functions. It is not surprising that they penetrate constitutional institutions. Even though they are private associations, they perform 'public' duties that are indispensable for a representative democracy. Hans Kelsen would have gone even further and identified them as 'organs of government'.[1]

Traditionally, Austrian political parties were far more than that. The conservative People's Party and the Social Democratic Party formed the core of what were called 'political camps'. They constituted societies within society that followed different cultural and moral patterns. A characteristic feature of these camps was – and to an extent, albeit shrinking, still is – their penetration of many fields of everyday life and the economy. Affiliated associations, such as sports clubs, hiking associations, car driver clubs, just to name a few, covered many aspects of leisure activities. Nationalised industry, banks, public social insurance

---

[1] H Kelsen, *The Essence and Value of Democracy*, ed by N Urbinati and CI Accetti, trans by B Graf (Lanham, Maryland, Rowman and Littlefield Publishers, 2013, Kindle Edition) 38.

companies and the school system – they were all dominated by the two political parties. The republic was allegedly shared between those two parties. Party membership paved the way to a better job or accommodation. Needless to say, such a party system is prone to corruption. Austrian political scientists quite frankly characterised political parties as 'feudal lord(s)'.[2] It is impossible to understand Austria's efficient constitution without taking into account the degree of party penetration.

The first part of this chapter examines briefly the development of Austria's party system. It will be emphasised that until the 1980s all political parties of relevance after World War II carried a legacy that dated back to the Austro-Hungarian Monarchy. Austrian political scientists describe the party system after the war as a two-and-a-half party system that showed remarkable stability until the mid-1980s. With the rise of the Freedom Party and the emergence of the Green Party the traditional parties started to erode and gradually a moderate pluralistic party system evolved.[3]

The second part of the chapter will deal with the 2012 Political Parties Act which regulates the founding of political parties and provides for their public and private funding. Both issues will be discussed in depth.

The final part of the chapter introduces and critically analyses the so-called 'social partnership': an Austrian peculiarity which supported grand coalition governments and allegedly was (co-)responsible for Austria's peaceful development and prosperity after World War II.

II. THE DEVELOPMENT OF THE PARTY SYSTEM

A. Political Parties versus Electoral Parties

In 1920, political parties, arguably the founders of the First Republic as well as the Second Republic, were neither anchored nor even mentioned in the constitution, very much to Hans Kelsen's criticism.[4] The 1929 amendment made references to political parties, but only in an unfavourable way as party officials were banned from the bench of the

---

[2] See A Pelinka, 'The Decline of the Party State. The Rise of Parliamentarianism: Change within the Austrian Party System' in A Pelinka and F Plasser (eds), *The Austrian Party System* (Boulder-London, Westview Press, 1989) 21, 25.

[3] DM Wineroither and C Moser-Sollmann, 'Metamorphose des europäischen und österreichischen Parteiensystems' in A Kohl et al (eds), *Österreichisches Jahrbuch für Politik 2018* (Wien, Böhlau, 2019) 285, 286.

[4] Kelsen (n 1) 38.

Constitutional Court. The electoral laws, although based on the principle of proportional representation, did not and do not provide for political parties to compete in general elections but rather so-called 'electoral parties'. This is a heritage of the monarchy, whose electoral system was based on the majority principle; hence its territory was divided into many fairly small constituencies. Electoral candidates in these constituencies had to be backed by supporters. The supporters and candidates formed electoral parties which ceased to exist once the election was over.[5] Even today, from a legal point of view, electoral parties and not political parties compete at elections, although in most cases electoral parties are set up by political parties. This legal distinction is not generally apparent to the public as electoral parties usually use the same names as the political parties that establish them.

B. The Emergence of the Party System

Most of the contemporary political parties carry a legacy that dates back to the nineteenth century, the time of the Austro-Hungarian Monarchy. In fact, the core of the contemporary party system was developed in the late 1800s.

As in many other countries, the emergence of political parties was deeply linked with the development of parliamentarianism and the electoral system. In the 1848 *Reichstag*, which attempted to draft a constitution, but was dissolved in the same year, a distinction between the political 'right' and 'left' was already made according to the seating order: the German-speaking 'Liberals' sat on the left-hand side, while the German-speaking Conservatives and the Slavic delegates sat on the right-hand side.[6] This seating order was resumed in 1861, when the *Reichsrat* was established. The German-speaking Liberals, who again sat on the left side, advocated for a constitution, which was eventually created in 1867. Also called the Constitution Party or the Constitutionalist's Party, it had to redefine its political aims after this achievement. It carried on mainly as a representation of the German-speaking majority in a

---

[5] F Koja, 'Die Rechtsfähigkeit der Wahlparteien und der Politischen Parteien' (1958) 80 *Juristische Blätter* 487, 488; M Stelzer, 'Akzeptanz oder Inkorporation? Zur Einbindung der Politischen Parteien in die österreichische Rechtsordnung' (2007) *Österreichische Juristenzeitung* 807, 809.

[6] L Höbelt, *Kornblume und Kaiseradler. Die deutschfreiheitlichen Parteien Altösterreichs 1882–1918* (Wien-München, Oldenbourg, 1993) 18.

multi-ethnic parliament.[7] Thus, liberal and German-national elements were closely linked in Austrian party history. This might be the reason why a party that is largely seen as a right-wing party with a close affinity to German nationalism may bear the name 'Freedom Party' and still may pride itself on its liberal past and its merits in developing parliamentarianism and democracy.

The first period of parliamentarianism, lasting roughly until the 1870s, saw parties only as loose unions of delegates that formed parliamentarian groups.[8] They had no thorough political programme and no organisation outside parliament. As long as the members of the Imperial Council were elected by the Diets there was no need for political parties in the modern sense. This all changed with the introduction of direct elections in 1873.[9] New parties emerged, forming a party system that survived not only the monarchy but was re-established after World War II and remained stable until the mid-1980s. Although mass-party movements were not to be observed before the beginning of the twentieth century,[10] it consisted of three camps:[11] social democratic; Christian conservative; and German national.

i. The Social Democrats

For the social democratic camp, the fact that it was already unified at a party convention at Hainburg in 1888/89 and re-organised in 1892 proved to be decisive.[12] The Social Democrats were able to avoid splitting into two parties, which would have been a social democratic and a communist party. For that reason, communist parties have never played a part in Austrian domestic politics. The communist party that was established after World War II on the initiative of the former Soviet Union merely served as a vassal for the Soviets controlling or partly influencing

---

[7] WF Czerny, 'Parteien und Parlamentsfraktionen' in A Pelinka and F Plasser (eds), *Das österreichische Parteiensystem* (Wien-Köln-Graz, Böhlau, 1988) 579, 588.

[8] Czerny (ibid) 588.

[9] K Berchtold, 'Die Politischen Parteien und ihre parlamentarischen Klubs bis 1918' in H Schambeck (ed), *Österreichs Parlamentarismus – Werden und System* (Berlin, Duncker & Humblot, 1986) 137, 147; Czerny (ibid) 588.

[10] See for instance W Maderthaner, 'Das Werden der disziplinierten Massenpartei – Die Entwicklung der Organisationsstruktur der deutschen Sozialdemokratie in Österreich 1889–1913' (1989) 18 *Österreichische Zeitschrift für Politikwissenschaft* 347.

[11] Czerny (n 7) 579, 589.

[12] Maderthaner (n 10) 347; W Maderthaner, 'Die Sozialdemokratie' in E Tálos et al (eds), *Handbuch des Politischen Systems Österreichs – Erste Republik 1918-1933* (Wien, Manz, 1995) 177, 178.

Austria's re-emerging republic. The Communist Party lost all its seats in parliament shortly after the post-war occupation by Allied forces came to an end in 1955. Since 1959, it has never held a seat in the federal parliament.[13] On the other hand, the early unification of the social democratic camp may also explain why, traditionally, it comprises a left or even Marxist wing that has to be satisfied from time to time. Thus, socialist ideas play an effective part in Austrian domestic politics.

Initially politically prosecuted, the rise of the Social Democrats began only with the introduction of universal suffrage (at least for the male part of the population) in 1907.[14] Although they probably had the clearest idea of establishing a republic in 1918, after an initial grand coalition government, they were in opposition for the remainder of the First Republic as the Christian Socials coalesced with the German Nationalists instead. The Social Democratic Party was dissolved following the authoritarian revolution in 1933.

After the war the Social Democratic Party re-emerged but under the new name 'Socialist' Party of Austria, only to be renamed 'Social Democratic' after the fall of the iron curtain when the term 'Socialist' seemed to be outdated. However, no significant amendment of their programme ensued. Until the 1960s, the Social Democrats were the so-called 'junior partner' in grand coalition governments (meaning they held fewer seats in parliament than the Conservatives), albeit they were disadvantaged by the electoral system. In 1953 and 1959, for example, they won more votes than the Conservatives but still gained fewer seats in parliament. This all changed in the 1970s, when the Social Democrats took advantage of an amendment of the electoral system[15] and, with the sole exception of the 2002 elections, won more votes and seats than any other party until 2017.

ii. The Conservatives

The Christian Social Party, at the core of the conservative camp, was founded in 1890–91 in Vienna, merging several political associations and groups affiliated to Catholicism and the Catholic Church.[16] From the beginning, their policies were strongly influenced by the pontifical social

---

[13] In 2021, however, the Communist Party won the largest share of votes in the municipal elections in the capital of Styria, Graz, and its leader became mayor.

[14] Maderthaner (n 10) 347.

[15] See ch 3.

[16] A Staudinger, WC Müller and B Steininger, 'Die Christlichsoziale Partei' in Tálos et al (eds) (n 12) 160. See also KR Luther, 'Consociationalism, Parties and the Party System'

encyclical 'Rerum Novarum'.[17] With these catholic traditions in mind, the Conservatives have never been forceful embracers of a free market society. Merging with the Catholic Conservative Party, the Christian Socials proved to be one of the strongest pillars of the Habsburg Empire.[18] Therefore, some Christian Socials had a strong inclination to maintain the monarchy after World War I and/or restore it in the late 1920s. On the basis of this inclination, the Christian Socials developed a new Austrian patriotism and only reluctantly supported the idea of joining Germany. But they were also responsible for establishing the catholic-authoritarian government in 1933–34, even if this was meant to maintain Austria's independence.

After World War II, the Conservatives accepted their responsibility insofar as they renounced their old name 'Christian Socials' and adopted the name 'Austrian People's Party' (*Österreichische Volkspartei*),[19] although their programme was still based on Christian-catholic ideas. The Catholic Church and the People's Party have been strong allies on many issues up to the present day. Catholic students and/or academic associations play an important part in the academic world, administrative authorities, judiciary and nationalised industry, representing the conservative camp.

The People's Party, traditionally strong in the rural parts of Austria, was the 'senior partner' in grand coalition governments after World War II until the mid-1960s. From the 1970s up to 2017 its share of the vote in general elections gradually dropped, with the only exception of the 2002 elections.

iii. The German Nationalists

The German national camp, the 'third camp', is the smallest albeit the oldest camp, as its roots date back to liberal parties fighting for the 1867 Constitution. Traditionally, this camp was (and still is) highly affected by fragmentation; the 1860s Liberals were already split into various parliamentary groups.[20] During the First Republic, this camp was

---

in KR Luther and WC Müller (eds), *Politics in Austria: Still a Case of Consociationalism?* (London, Frank Cass Limited, 1992) 45.

[17] Staudinger et al (ibid) 160.

[18] Ibid.

[19] For political scientists, the German term '*Volkspartei*' also describes a certain type of political party, characterised by mass membership and attempting to attract various groups of people. In that case the term would rather translate to 'catch-all'-party. In this respect, the Social Democrats are also a '*Volkspartei*', albeit left-leaning.

[20] Berchtold (n 9) 137, 142.

mainly represented by the Grand German People's Party (*Großdeutsche Volkspartei – GDVP*). The supporters of the German Nationalists were probably most likely to sympathise with the German Nazis, although they were not the only ones. For many of them it might have been fairly easy to join the NSDAP (*Nationalsozialistische Deutsche Arbeiterpartei*) after the German occupation in 1938.

As the former members of the NSDAP and some of its affiliated organisations were excluded from the 1945 elections, the 'third camp' was only restored in 1949 when the less incriminated former members became eligible for general elections. The 'Union of Independents' (*Verband der Unabhängigen*) was formed and, competing in the 1949 elections, won more than 10 per cent of the vote. In 1956, the Freedom Party (*Freiheitliche Partei Österreichs*) was founded. It merged with the Union of Independents, thus becoming the sole representative of the third camp for more than three decades. It gained about 5–8 per cent of the vote in general elections until the mid-1980s. From 1959 to 1986 it was the only party apart from the Social Democrats and the People's Party with a presence in the National Council, and therefore the only 'opposition' to grand coalition governments. Despite some local success, it had only a marginal role in the states and in the Federal Council.

This started to change in the 1970s when the Social Democrats relied on the Freedom Party to back a minority government[21] after the 1970 elections. It was part of Social Democrats' strategy to raise the profile of the Freedom Party in order to weaken the People's Party, as in the 1970s both parties were considered to appeal to conservative voters. This was all done with the aim of ensuring at least a relative majority for the Social Democrats in the years to come. This strategy worked for about two decades, with the Freedom Party even supporting the Social Democrats in a coalition government from 1983 to 1986.[22]

C. From the mid-1980s Onwards

Political scientists have emphasised that this party system was 'very stable' until the mid-1980s.[23] The People's Party and the Social Democrats were

[21] See D Art, *The Politics of the Nazi Past in Germany and Austria* (New York, Cambridge University Press, 2006) 113, 115.

[22] S Puntscher-Riekmann, 'The Politics of Ausgrenzung, the Nazi-Past and the European Dimension of the New Radical Right in Austria' in G Bischof et al (eds), *The Vranitzky Era in Austria* (New Brunswick, Transaction Publishers, 1999) 78, 85.

[23] WC Müller, 'Austria: Tight Coalitions and Stable Government' in WC Müller and K Strom (eds), *Coalition Governments in Western Europe* (New York, Oxford University Press, 2000) 93.

both mass movements, counting up to 700,000 members each,[24] and in practice they shared the political power of the country. The Freedom Party, on the contrary, was a fairly small party, counting roughly 40,000 members. Because of the small size of the Freedom Party, the system was characterised as a two-and-a-half party system rather than a three-party system. Differences between the political programmes could be identified along various cleavages – between labour and property, between pro-cleric and anti-cleric tendencies and between centralistic and federal concepts. In this system, the Social Democrats sided with labour, anti-cleric and centralistic tendencies; the People's Party with property, clerical and federal tendencies; and the third camp traditionally with property, anti-cleric and centralistic tendencies.

The system started to change in the 1980s[25] with the emergence of the Green Party, and the beginning of the rise of the Freedom Party, rebranded into a far-right populist movement. Today, its politics follow the typical pattern of right-wing parties all over the world.

The reasons for this changes were manifold. One reason offered by Austrian political science is that the traditional divisions ('cleavages') lost their importance and new ones occurred: questions concerning environmental protection, the gender issue, immigration, the accession to the European Union and other issues.[26]

In the 1986 general elections, for the first time since 1959, a fourth party won a presence in the National Council. Different groups with some experience in organising mass demonstrations voicing concerns over the destruction of the environment had merged into a Green Party that successfully participated in these elections. It became an inventive opposition party, gaining between 4.8 per cent, initially, and 12.4 per cent of the vote in general elections.[27] In 2019, however, it managed to win 13.9 per cent of the votes and entered a coalition government with the People's Party. At the time of writing (in 2022) it is difficult to assess this government as it has been almost completely occupied in containing the Covid-19 pandemic.

The rise of the Freedom Party that also started with the 1986 general elections can only be described as dramatic: with 9.7 per cent in the 1986

---

[24] WC Müller, 'Die Österreichische Volkspartei' in E Tálos et al (eds), *Handbuch des politischen Systems Österreichs. Die Zweite Republik* (Wien, Manz, 1997) 265, 272; K Ucakar, 'Die Sozialdemokratische Partei Österreichs' in Tálos et al (eds) (ibid) 248, 259.

[25] MA Sully, 'Winds of Change in the Austrian Party System' in Pelinka and Plasser (eds) (n 7) 739.

[26] H Dachs, 'Grünalternative Parteien' in H Dachs et al (eds), *Politik in Österreich. Das Handbuch* (Wien, Manz, 2006) 389.

[27] These and all other election results can be found on the website of the Federal Ministry of the Interior: www.bmi.gv.at.

election, 16.6 per cent in 1990, 22.5 per cent in 1994, and 29.9 per cent at its peak in 1999. In the early years of the twenty-first century Austrian political scientists observed a fundamental change in the party system: there were no longer two large parties and two small parties, but three 'mid-sized' parties (next to the still small Green Party)[28] as the rise of the Freedom Party was combined with the demise of the People's Party and, from 1994 onwards, the decline of the Social Democrats. Since then, the success of the Freedom Party has proven to be more volatile: after another peak in 2017 gaining almost 26 per cent of the votes, it fell back to mere 16 per cent in the 2019 general election following the so-called 'Ibiza-scandal'.[29]

The tradition of fragmentation caught up with the third camp rising: as an obvious reaction to the right-wing policies of the Freedom Party, in 1993 five members of parliament, representing the more liberal wing of the party, broke away to found a new party, the Liberal Forum (*Liberales Forum – LIF*) that only survived two elections. In 2005, members of parliament supporting the coalition government with the People's Party broke away to found the Alliance (for the) Future of Austria (*Bündnis Zukunft Österreich – BZÖ*) which became especially strong as a regional party in Carinthia. In early 2010, a large group of the Carinthian part of the Alliance re-established itself as the Carinthian part of the Freedom Party (*Die Freiheitlichen in Kärnten – FPK*). On the federal level, the Alliance survived two elections (2006 and 2008). In 2012, the Austro-Canadian billionaire Frank Stronach decided to enter the political stage and to run for the 2013 election. He formed the 'Team Stronach' attracting members of parliament representing the Alliance (and taking financial advantage of forming a parliamentary group). The Team gained 5.7 per cent in the ensuing elections but with the party leader losing interest in Austrian politics the party was short lived and so was the Alliance.

In 2012, however, a new party was founded, partly as an offshoot of the People's Party. It was baptised 'NEOS' (from the Greek word for 'new') and merged with the remnants of the *LIF*. Ideologically, political scientists rank it between the People's Party and the Green Party and it

---

[28] See M Gehler, 'Die zweite Republik – zwischen Konsens und Konflikt. Historischer Überblick (1945–2005)' in Dachs et al (eds) (n 26) 47; A Pelinka, 'Wachsende Autonomie und Differenzierung: Parteien und Fraktionen im Parlamentarischen System Österreichs' in L Helms (ed), *Parteien und Fraktionen. Ein internationaler Vergleich* (Opladen, Leske & Budrich, 1999) 219, 222ff.

[29] See A Pelinka, 'Austrian Politics: 1918 to 2019' (2020) 4 *Antisemitism Studies* 82, 94ff; see ch 4 for further consequences of the Ibiza-scandal.

may be seen as a liberal party.[30] *NEOS* has been fairly successful so far, gaining between 5 and 8 per cent of the votes.

The emergence of new parties and the volatility of the voters also had a bearing on the two traditional parties: in 2008, for the first time in the history of democratic Austria, the Social Democrats' voter share dropped under 30 per cent, meaning that they could no longer block a constitutional amendment in the National Council. In 2017, the People's Party, on the brink of falling into oblivion, regrouped around its highly popular young chairman Sebastian Kurz and was rebranded into the 'New People's Party', changing its party colour from its traditional black into turquoise. It appeared to be more centralised, with more power assigned to its chairman, and adopted the anti-immigration attitude of the far right. It won a relative majority in the 2017 and the 2019 general elections, forming a government together with the Freedom Party and the Green Party respectively with Sebastian Kurz as chancellor presiding both cabinets. As he stepped down following corruption charges in 2021,[31] the future of the People's Party in particular and the party system in general seems to be rather unpredictable.

III. THE LAW ON POLITICAL PARTIES

It was only in 1975 that the recognition and regulation of political parties was incorporated as part of the constitution. Unsurprisingly, this was not done by amending the core document, but by passing a specific law, the Political Parties Act (*Parteiengesetz*, BGBl 404/1975). Its first article, a constitutional provision, proclaimed the plurality of the party system and regulated the founding of political parties. All other articles related to public funding of political parties, which was the real reason behind this act of legislation. As a result, the regulations regarding the organisation of political parties contained in the act were not comprehensive. The rules governing private party donations and party funding were insufficient to provide for transparency, thus giving ample opportunities for corrupt behaviour. Austria was therefore heavily and

---

[30] D Johann, M Jenny and S Kritzinger, 'Mehr Wettbewerb bei Österreichs Wahlen? Die neue Partei NEOS und ihre engsten Konkurrenten' (2016) 47 *Zeitschrift für Parlamentsfragen* 814. For the emergence of the multi-party system, see also K Stainer-Hämmerle, 'Kommen und Gehen. Neue Listendynamik im alten Parteiensystem' in A Kohl et al (eds), *Österreichisches Jahrbuch für Politik 2014* (Wien, Böhlau, 2015) 77ff.

[31] See ch 4.

repeatedly criticised by GRECO (Group of States against Corruption) reports.[32]

Changing the law accordingly failed mainly because of the resistance of the People's Party. Only in 2012 was this resistance broken, following a public outrage: a representative of the People's Party in the European Parliament and former minister of the interior had been caught on camera, offering to influence European legislation in exchange for money.[33] The Political Parties Act 1975 was thus replaced by the Political Parties Act 2012 (BGBl I 56/2012) which, although adopting the same structure, nevertheless eradicated some flaws of the 1975 Act; it established a system to facilitate and oversee the transparency of private donations but provided for even more generous public funding. A 2017 amendment limited private donations.

A. The Founding of Political Parties

According to Art 1 para 2 of the Political Parties Act, political parties are permanent associations whose statutes have been deposited with the Minister of the Interior and which, through common activities, aim to comprehensively influence the national decision-making process, predominantly by participating in elections. There are no restrictions on the founding of political parties unless a federal constitutional law states otherwise. Hence, the founding of political parties is 'free'. To form a political party, it is sufficient to adopt a statute that determines the party's bodies (a managing body, a general meeting and a supervisory body are compulsory), the rights and obligations of its members, its internal structure and its possible voluntary dissolution. The statute has to be deposited with the Minister of the Interior who in return has to publish the name of the political party and the date of the deposition of the statute in a public register.[34] The statute has to be published by the political party on the internet. With depositing the statute, the political party obtains legal personality. Around 1,130 organisations have been

---

[32] They are published on the website of the Federal Chancellery: www.bundeskanzleramt. gv.at/agenda/parteienfinanzierung/greco-berichte.html, accessed 4 January 2022.

[33] See for instance the report in the Wiener Zeitung, 14 January 2013, www.wienerzeitung. at/nachrichten/politik/oesterreich/515946-Der-tiefe-Fall-des-Ernst-Strasser.html, accessed 4 January 2022.

[34] The Political Parties Act 2012 is available on the website of the Federal Chancellery, www.ris.bka.gv.at, basically also in an English version. Unfortunately, the English version does not cover the sentence providing for this obligation.

registered as 'political parties'.[35] As a matter of course, the overwhelming majority do not play a part in Austria's domestic politics.

Under the 1975 Political Parties Act, the question had already arisen whether the Minister of Interior had any power to prohibit the founding of a political party, for instance, if its founding was unconstitutional or the statute did not meet the legal requirements. The Constitutional Court ruled that the Minister of the Interior does not have such a power nor would the Minister have the power to assess whether a political party has been founded or not.[36] The only legal consequence of an attempt at founding such a party is that the party does not obtain legal personality. In particular, this would be the case if a constitutional law restricts the formation of the party. The reasoning of the Constitutional Court is based on the parliamentary debate that led to the enactment of the 1975 Political Parties Act. Clearly, the representatives of the political parties wanted as much freedom as possible and no administrative authority or court to decide on the matter.

However, the outcome of the Constitutional Court's ruling was completely contrary to the reasoning of the court and to the aims of parliament. The court ruled that the Minister of Interior did not have the power to prohibit the founding of a party and/or to assess it. But by insisting that a group that aims to register as a political party without meeting the legal requirements would not obtain legal personality, it fell into the hands of all courts and all administrative authorities to – implicitly – decide on this matter once such a group started to operate in a legal context. Arguably, different courts and different administrative authorities might produce different decisions which would undermine the principle of legal certainty and thus the *Rechtsstaat* principle.

The jurisprudence of the Constitutional Court regarding the founding of political parties has one decisive consequence – the way the legal system deals with the formation or re-formation of national socialist or fascist organisations. According to a constitutional law, the 1945 National Socialism Prohibition Act (*Verbotsgesetz*),[37] any kind of national socialist activity is prohibited by law. This constitutional law would also inhibit the formation of a Nazi party.

If someone in Austria tried to found such a party, the attempt would be 'legally' unsuccessful. If the 'party' nevertheless appeared in a legal

---

[35] See www.parlament.gv.at/PERK/PK/PP/index.shtml, accessed 11 January 2022.
[36] VfSlg 9648/1983.
[37] StGBl 13/1945. Amended a couple of times, the law nowadays is correctly referred to as '*Verbotsgesetz 1947*' (in the applicable version).

context, the relevant courts and public authorities would have to deny it legal personality. To identify the party as a Nazi party, they would have to review its statutes and programmes against those of the *NSDAP* and its sub-organisations. Typical features that the courts and administrative authorities might look into are the use of Nazi terminology; the degradation of parliamentarianism and the call for a strong leader (*Führer*); the aim to abolish democracy; the glorification of the 1938 '*Anschluss*'; the attempt to legitimise the crimes committed by the Nazi regime; the denial of the Holocaust; as well as strong elements of xenophobia and racism, such as the call for expulsion of all migrant workers.[38] If there were enough or striking similarities to be found, the group would not obtain legal personality and, legally, would not exist as a party. It therefore could not be subject to rights and obligations and could not operate in a legal context. Cunningly, Austrian politicians can always argue that Austria has the strictest law on National Socialism: no Nazi party can ever be founded or exist – from a legal point of view. In practice, however, it hinges on what the courts might tolerate. The law may have a moderating effect, but at the end, it fails to draw a clear line under Austria's authoritarian past. Unfortunately, this fits the picture of Austria's postwar grappling with national socialism.

Art 1 of the Political Parties Act, which states that party-pluralism is essential to democracy, has provoked a discussion on whether there is a need for political parties to be organised democratically: a requirement the Germans have explicitly incorporated in their Political Parties Act.[39] Austrian lawyers are split over this issue. The traditional answer would be that there is no legal requirement for political parties to be organised democratically. This point of view is still backed by the idea that Austria's democracy is transient and may be abolished by means of a 'total revision'.[40] As it may be legally possible to abolish Austria's democracy – thus runs the argument – it must be allowable to form a political party to that end (which would be a Marxist or Stalinist party as fascist or even national socialist parties are banned by law). This argument is nevertheless astonishing, as Hans Kelsen's claim to anchor political parties in the constitution was accompanied by a demand to democratise their

---

[38] See VfSlg 11258/1987.

[39] See Art 21 of the Bonner Basic Law and especially Arts 6 and 9 of the German Law on Political Parties (*Parteiengesetz*, www.gesetze-im-internet.de/partg, accessed 11 January 2022).

[40] P Kostelka, 'Politische Parteien in der österreichischen Rechtsordnung' in O Martinek (ed), *Arbeitsrecht und Soziale Grundrechte* (Wien, Manz, 1983) 37, 49ff; H Schambeck, 'Politische Parteien und österreichische Staatsrechtsordnung' in H Mayer (ed), *Staatsrecht in Theorie und Praxis – Festschrift Walter* (Wien, Manz, 1991) 603, 612.

internal decision-making process. He rued the 'amorphous structure of the parties' as they allowed 'the political processes that occur within them to take on an explicitly aristocratic-autocratic character'.[41] Under the 1975 Political Parties Act some Austrian scholars[42] have already challenged the afore mentioned position. The 2012 Act may underpin this challenge as it forces party statutes to provide for a general meeting and, thus, a democratic assembly.

In reality, political parties in Austria are organised as oligarchies[43] rather than democracies, which follows not only from their statutes but also predominantly from the way these statutes play out in practice. Political scientists therefore question, for instance, the democratic value of an election of a chairperson when there is only one candidate. It therefore may be said that 'democracy' in Austria is restricted to the competition between parties rather than performed within the parties.[44] Party membership has not generally been seen as a way to participate in the political decision-making process but rather as a *quid-pro-quo* for a better career or an affordable apartment.

B. The Funding of Political Parties

As mentioned above, the main purpose of the Political Parties Act was to provide for a legal basis to fund political parties from tax revenues. The 2012 Act is also very clear about that as the full title reads: 'Federal Law on the Funding of Political Parties'. Public funding of political parties may arguably be reasonable since political parties have an essential role in a representative democracy as the system would not work without them. In Austria, public funding of political parties is granted not only on the federal level, but also on state and municipal levels and is extremely generous, only second to the public funding political parties receive in Japan.[45] Besides setting up a framework for public funding, the

---

[41] Kelsen (n 1) 41.

[42] M Stelzer, 'Innerparteiliche Demokratie' in M Akyürek et al (eds), *Staat und Recht in Europäischer Perspektive* (Wien, Manz, 2006) 779.

[43] WC Müller, W Phillip and B Steininger, 'Wie oligarchisch sind Österreichs Parteien? Eine empirische Analyse, 1945–1992' (1992) 21 *Österreichische Zeitschrift für Politikwissenschaft* 117.

[44] K von Beyme, *Parteien in Westlichen Demokratien*, 2nd edn (München-Zürich, Piper, 1984) 432; H Sickinger, *Politisches Geld. Parteienfinanzierung und öffentliche Kontrolle in Österreich* (Wien, Czernin, 2013).

[45] M Stelzer, 'Die Neuregelung der Parteienfinanzierung in Österreich' in S Bukow et al (eds), *Parteien in Staat und Gesellschaft. Zum Verhältnis von Parteienstaat und Parteiendemokratie* (Wiesbaden, Springer, 2016) 131, 132.

2012 Political Parties Act also regulates the admissibility of private donations and sponsorship.

i. Public Funding

A decisive characteristic of the Austrian party financing system has always been that funds are only supplied to parties which have won a presence in parliament (and other representative bodies such as local councils).[46] This system, in principle established by the 1975 Political Parties Act, has been entrenched by the 2012 Political Parties Act. Art 3, adopted as a constitutional provision, allows for annual subsidies that the Federation, the states or municipalities may grant to political parties with a presence in a representative body. They are compensated 'for their activities in participating in the formation of political will'.[47] The total amount of subsidies granted is calculated on the number of eligible voters. Per eligible voter the Federation shall spend not less than €3.10 but not more than €11, the exact sum to be determined by an ordinary law (currently, the Federal Act on Subsidising Political Parties provides for €4.6 per eligible voter[48]). The states are allowed to grant subsidies within double the lower and upper limits to also support political parties on the district and municipal levels. As municipalities are also entitled to party financing, the rationality of this provision might be questioned. Contrary to the 1975 Political Parties Act, specific subsidies for campaigning in general elections are prohibited by this constitutional provision. Further, limits to campaign expenses apply.

The distribution of the subsidies granted in total is regulated by the relevant (ordinary) laws. On the federal level, each party that has formed a parliamentary group[49] that commands at least five seats in the National Council, receives a basic amount of money. The rest is allotted to the political parties according to their vote share. Outside this system, a party that is not represented in the National Council may receive subsidies only in the year of a general election and only if it has gained more than one per cent of the votes.

---

[46] See WC Müller, 'Political Parties' in V Lauber (ed), *Contemporary Austrian Politics* (Oxford, Westview Press, 1996) 66, 68.

[47] Art 3 Political Parties Act 2012, quoted from the 'official' translation by the Federal Chancellery: www.ris.bka.gv.at.

[48] Art 1 para 2 of the Federal Act on Subsidising Political Parties (*Parteien-Förderungsgesetz 2012*, BGBl I 57/2012).

[49] See ch 3.

The formation of a parliamentary group is also decisive for receiving money under the Parliamentary Groups Funding Act 1985 (*Klubfinanzierungsgesetz 1985*, BGBl 1985/156 in the applicable version). Further, so-called academies of political parties are subsidised, arguably supporting political education, as long as the party is present in the National Council with at least five delegates. In 2021, political parties and parliamentary groups received a total of €212 million in public funding by both the Federation and the states.[50]

Restricting public funding to parties with a presence in the National Council leads to the creation of an exclusive club of political parties which receive abundant public subsidies,[51] or in other words: almost a party cartel.[52] New political parties face severe economic difficulties in gaining access to the political stage. Apart from the 1980s Green Party that managed to win a presence in the National Council as public funding was still less generous and election campaigns less costly, so far new political parties have exploited two avenues. The Liberal Forum, the Union (for the) Future of Austria and the Team Stronach – albeit the latter being backed by lavish amounts of private money – have emerged as parliamentary (breakaway) groups, immediately gaining access to funds allotted according to the Parliamentary Groups Funding Act. This road has been blocked after the (relative) success of the Team Stronach in 2013.[53] The *NEOS* were initially financed by a private donor. This road was blocked by the 2019 amendment to the 2012 Political Parties Act[54] (see below). Nowadays, it is difficult to imagine how a completely new party might run successfully in a general election on the Federal level. The system therefore is arguably incompatible with the constitutional commitment to a multiparty system (Art 1 para 1 Political Parties Act 2012).

The described system of publicly financing political parties had a decisive influence on the shape of the party system and especially on the development from the 1980s onwards.

Initially, the basic amount allotted to parties which had formed a parliamentary group was disproportionately high. Smaller parties therefore received more money than they would have if the distribution had

---

[50] Der Standard, 31 January 2021, www.derstandard.at/story/2000123756694/jeder-wahlberechtigte-zahlt-33-euro-jaehrlich-an-parteienfoerderung, accessed 4 January 2022.

[51] Sickinger (n 44) 226f.

[52] RS Katz and P Mair, 'Changing Models of Party Organization and Party Democracy. The Emergence of the Cartel Party' (1995) 1 *Party Politics* 5.

[53] See ch 3.

[54] BGBl I 55/2019.

only been based on vote share. For years, the Freedom Party gained subsidies that were completely out of proportion – both with regard to their membership and to their vote share. Benefitting disproportionately from the system prevented a small party challenging the system in a law court. According to the jurisprudence of the Administrative High Court and the Constitutional Court, a plaintiff who only benefits from a system has no standing when raising questions regarding the legality or constitutionality of such a system. While the People's Party and the Social Democrats needed most of the money to oil their party machinery, the Freedom Party with its small organisation had used it for public activities and election campaigns, giving the impression that the party was of the same size as the People's Party and the Social Democrats. But that never was the case. According to the latest numbers available, the People's Party claims to have around 500,000 members and the Social Democrats nowadays are down to 180,000; the Freedom Party still counts not more than 60,000. The Green Party counts around 7,300 members and the *NEOS* has around 2,500.[55]

Other than in Germany, the amount of public funding is not related to the social role of the relevant party. In one of its decisions regarding the public funding of political parties, the German Federal Constitutional Court has established a so-called 'relative upper limit', denying parties more public money than they have raised from private sources.[56] In Austria, however, – based on their statements of account – small parties have always been almost exclusively publicly funded. The yearly statements of all these parties show that only the Social Democrats and the People's Party obtain a significant amount of money from membership fees or private donations. With the restrictions following the 2019 amendment in place, it might be said that the whole system is publicly funded nowadays. Political scientists in Austria have pointed out correctly that the development of the Austrian political system was and is possible only because of the way in which political parties receive public funding.[57]

ii. Private Donations and Sponsorship

To tackle the lack of transparency of private party financing, the 2012 Political Parties Act provided for restrictions on private donations,

---

[55] See de.statista.com/statistik/daten/studie/288668/umfrage/mitgliederzahlen-der-politischen-parteien-in-oesterreich, accessed 10 January 2022.
[56] BVerfGE 85, 264 – Parteienfinanzierung II.
[57] Sickinger (n 44) 226ff.

detailed the structure of annual reports, obliged parties to disclose the identity of major donors and sponsors by having their names and the amount of money received published on the website of the Audit Court. It further set up a system of supervision and accountability in which the Audit Court had to review the annual statements and report any irregularity to the Independent Political Parties Transparency Panel, established by a constitutional provision, which could impose monetary penalties on political parties and fine individuals for committing an administrative offence. A 2019 amendment to the Political Parties Act, passed on a free vote in parliament after the demise of the coalition government between the People's Party and the Freedom Party, further limited the admissibility of private donations. According to this amendment, no individual nor legal person is entitled to donate more than €7,500 annually to a political party and, in general, a political party may accept donations only amounting to €750,000 annually. All money exceeding this limit has to be transferred to the Audit Court.

Although the amendment has met many demands of the GRECO reports, some issues still seem to be unresolved. The debate around the demise of the 2017 coalition between the People's Party and the Freedom Party which was due to the so-called 'Ibiza-scandal',[58] for instance, has demonstrated that there are still ways to circumvent the transparency rules when money is given to private associations affiliated with and working for political parties. Improvements of the Party Act are promised but have not yet been enacted.

The limits on party donations, however, raise different questions. Limiting the individual amount of donations, albeit infringing freedom of expression,[59] is probably proportionate as it prevents rich people from gaining more influence on politics than those who are poorer and may therefore be necessary in a democratic society. The same can hardly be said about the total limit on private donations, which makes even a small donation worthless once the total limit has been met, as it has to be transferred to the Audit Court. Such an infringement of the right to freedom of expression is arguably not necessary in a democratic society and, consequently, unconstitutional.

However, the limits on private donations have further contributed to political parties being overwhelmingly financed out of tax revenues. Financially, they are organs of government, betraying their role as intermediaries between state and society.

[58] See ch 4.
[59] Art 10 ECHR; see, for instance, *Bowman v UK* (App no 24839/94) ECtHR 19 February 1998.

IV. THE SOCIAL PARTNERSHIP

'Social Partnership' describes a neo-corporatist conflict resolution model, established after World War II, primarily in the fields of macroeconomic and welfare policies. It is deeply related to and/or intertwined with the two dominant political parties – the People's Party and the Social Democrats – and it served as a pillar of Austria's very own model of consociational democracy. Participating in the social partnership are the Austrian Chamber of Commerce (*Wirtschaftskammer Österreich*) formerly known as the Federal Chamber of Commerce (*Bundeswirtschaftskammer*); the Federal Chamber of Labour (*Bundesarbeiterkammer*); and the Conference of the Presidents of the Chambers of Agriculture (*Landwirtschaftskammer*), together with the Austrian Trade Union Federation (*Österreichischer Gewerkschaftsbund*).[60]

Under the Austrian constitution, chambers are self-governing or autonomous bodies under public law, based on compulsory membership and compulsory financial contributions. The organs of the chamber are elected by its members. In general, they are tasked with the representation of their members' interests and offering support in various ways. Almost all people working in Austria are members of chambers, regardless of whether they are employed or self-employed, with the only exception being civil servants. Further, there are some chambers representing different professions even outside the system of social partnership such as a chamber for pharmacists, for medical doctors or for solicitors and barristers. These chambers not only promote the professional interests of their members but also exercise disciplinary power over them.

The regional Chambers of Labour incorporate all other employees with the exception of civil servants and agricultural workers. Self-employed people are members of the (regional) Chambers of Commerce, while farmers are members of the (regional) Chambers of Agriculture. The Austrian Trade Union Federation is a private association, which means that membership is not compulsory. Nevertheless, in some fields, for instance among railway workers, membership has been seen as a moral or social obligation and the Austrian Trade Union Federation is by far Austria's largest association. Its distinctive feature is the high degree of centralisation: trade unions for specific industrial sectors operate under the roof of the Trade Union Federation which also oversees the finances. While the Chambers of Commerce and the Chambers of Agriculture are traditionally dominated by the conservatives, the Chamber of Labour

---

[60] See also E Tálos, 'Corporatism – The Austrian Model' in Lauber (ed) (n 46) 123.

and the Austrian Trade Union Federation are social democratic strongholds. The Chamber of Commerce and the Chamber of Labour employ many experts in various fields, so they are seen as the 'brain trust' of the People's Party and the Social Democrats respectively.

The idea of social partnership was to balance the interests of employers and employees in a more or less peaceful way by negotiations between their representatives. The instruments available were, on the one hand, collective agreements, in which, for instance, pay rises or working conditions for a whole industrial sector would be negotiated between the Trade Union and the Chamber of Commerce; on the other hand, the social partners could influence the prices of consumer goods. The Law on the Regulation of Market Prices (*Preisgesetz*, BGBl 1992/145, originally stemming from the 1950s, in the applicable version) allows government to fix prices for consumer goods if that would be justified from a macroeconomic point of view. It establishes a joint-commission to advise the responsible ministers. In this commission, representatives of the Austrian Chamber of Commerce, the Conference of the Presidents of the Chambers of Agriculture and the Chamber of Labour co-operate. These two instruments – fixing wages and fixing prices – were seen as 'communicating vessels': for macroeconomic reasons the Trade Union could limit its demands for pay rises and, instead, ask for the fixing of prices of specific consumer goods.[61]

Further, social partners were invited to assess every draft bill – or even pre-discuss it – filed by the Federal Cabinet. In that way, they could also influence other fields of policy. If they agreed on a specific phrasing of the law and/or reached a compromise, parliament seldom made changes. The main reason why this system could produce such 'cast iron' compromises was that the social partners and the two main political parties were also intertwined on a personal basis. Until the 1980s, it was very common that officials of the Chamber of Labour and leading representatives of the Trade Union Federation would sit in parliament on a social democratic ticket while officials of the Chambers of Commerce and the Chamber of Agriculture did the same on a conservative ticket. And they were also part of the Federal Cabinet, especially in grand coalition governments. Conventionally, the officials of the Trade Union Federation claimed the Ministry for Social Affairs while officials of the Chamber of Commerce and the Chamber of Agriculture claimed the Ministry of Economy and the Ministry of Agriculture respectively. Interestingly, the

---

[61] See E Tálos and T Hinterseer, *Sozialpartnerschaft. Ein zentraler politischer Gestaltungsfaktor der Zweiten Republik am Ende?* (Innsbruck, Studienverlag, 2019) 54ff.

law that forbids a minister's pursuit of any other job during the minister's tenure makes one exception: it allows combining the job of a minister with a job in a social partner institution.[62] In this way, representatives of the social partners who were at the same time influential members of the Federal Cabinet and/or parliament could guarantee that their compromises were never challenged there.

The social partnership embraced consensus and compromise oriented strategies to solve social conflicts.[63] It was the main reason why no serious labour disputes and industrial actions were observed in Austria in the post-war period and it contributed to Austria's image as an 'Island of the Blessed', as it was once called by Pope Paul VI.[64] The price to pay was a lack of transparency as all compromises were reached behind closed doors and the needs of those who were not integrated in this system were often disregarded. Further, parliament was circumvented as its role was diminished to rubber-stamp compromises which had been found outside parliament – reminiscent of the role parliament was attributed under the 1934 authoritarian constitution. The system was also intrinsically paternalistic and elitist: compromises reached were handed down to the members of the chambers and the unions. However, the social partnership was very popular. A 1981 survey still found that around 60 per cent preferred or even strongly preferred the social partnership over parliament.[65]

Arguably, the system worked best during the times of rapid economic growth, when there was increasing wealth to share, and as long as the two main parties represented about 90 per cent of the population.[66] It even survived the single government of the People's Party (1966–1970) and the single government of the Social Democrats (1971–1983). Around the mid-1980s, however, the environment of the social partnership started to gradually deteriorate. The globalisation of the economy gradually diminished the political leeway for national governments, and the accession to the European Union a decade later transferred legislative powers to Brussels and thus removed them from the influence of the social partners, who then had to engage in European organisations to lobby for

---

[62] Art 2 para 4 Incompatibility Act 1983 (*Unvereinbarkeits- und Transparenz-Gesetz*, BGBl 330/1983 in the applicable version).

[63] See A Pelinka, *Austria: Out of the Shadow of the Past* (Oxford, Westview Press, 1998) 91.

[64] *Arbeiterzeitung* 19 November 1971, 16; cf Pelinka (ibid) 29.

[65] Tálos and Hinterseer (n 61) 44.

[66] See also P Gerlich, 'A Farewell to Corporatism' in Luther and Müller (eds) (n 16) 132, 146.

their interests. A-typical careers as a result of economic changes and different working conditions and retirement schemes for younger employees, as a result of abolishing privileges older employees still enjoyed, led to questions over whose interests the unions effectively represented. With the emergence of the Green Party and the rise of the Freedom Party, new actors entered the political stage who were not part of the social partnership and therefore had no genuine interest in maintaining it.

The Freedom Party in particular challenged the system, and questioned the compulsory membership of the chambers. Consequently, during the coalition government formed by the People's Party and the Freedom Party (2000–06) techniques were implemented to minimise the influence of the social partners, especially those affiliated with the Social Democrats.[67] The subsequent coalition government between the Social Democrats and the People's Party revalued the social partnership and fulfilled a long-cherished wish of the social partner institutions by incorporating them into the constitution. According to that 2008 amendment, the republic now appreciates the role of the social partners, respects their autonomy and supports their dialogue by establishing self-governing bodies. As these self-governing bodies are all established, the provision serves as a constitutional guarantee to leave the institutions untouched but does not guarantee their specific influence. Consequently, the 2017 coalition between the People's Party and the Freedom Party further eroded the social partnership and the question of compulsory membership to the chambers was raised again. Abolishing it, however, would nowadays need a constitutional law as the 2008 constitutional guarantee most certainly comprises the relevant features of a self-governing body under public law. The majority needed was blocked by the People's Party – the Social Democrats would not have had the power to do that.

Although it was partly rekindled during the Covid-19 pandemic as a furlough scheme was negotiated between the social partners and the conservative/green coalition government,[68] the future of the social partnership is still in limbo. It may hinge on the Social Democrats participating in a future government as the conservatives seem to have largely lost their interest in it. Should it survive, it will most certainly be different to what was seen during the first four decades after World War II.[69]

---

[67] See ch 3.

[68] E Tálos and H Obinger, *Sozialstaat Österreich (1945-2020). Entwicklung – Maßnahmen – internationale Verortung* (Innsbruck, Studienverlag, 2020) 68.

[69] For the development of the Social Partnership and its possible demise, see the detailed analysis from Tálos and Hinterseer (n 61) 73ff.

V. CONCLUSION

In Austria, political parties have not only competed for influencing public decision making but also dominated everyday life. Three contemporary political parties emerged from political camps that date back to the nineteenth century: the Social Democratic Party; the People's Party, a conservative party which emerged from the Christian social camp; and the Freedom Party, despite some recent split-ups, successor to the so-called 'third camp', the German Nationalists. Until 1986, they formed a stable party system, which was rated as a two-and-a-half party system by political scientists, due to the small size of the Freedom Party. From the mid-1980s onwards the system became far more volatile with the rise of the Freedom Party, rebranded into a far-right populist party, and the emergence of the Green Party. Various other parties followed, albeit most of them were short lived.

Despite their relevance for the functioning of a democratic constitution, political parties were not anchored in the constitution until 1975. According to the 1975 Political Parties Act, followed by the 2012 Political Parties Act, the formation of a political party is fairly easy and quite unbureaucratic and only restricted by the prohibition of national socialist activity. In theory, no national socialist party may exist in Austria. In reality, of course, it is up to the discretion of courts and authorities to assess whether a party can be called national socialist.

The lavish public funding is almost exclusively reserved for parties represented in the National Council (and other representative bodies). By favouring smaller parties, this system was also responsible for the rise of the Freedom Party. Today, all parties are heavily subsidised with taxpayer's money – the smaller ones almost exclusively.

Underpinning the post-war grand coalition governments was the neo-corporatist system of social partnership. Notwithstanding their diminishing influence from the mid-1980s onwards, the social partners were incorporated into the Austrian constitution by a 2008 amendment. As this has not stopped the further decline of social partnership, its future is more than uncertain.

In general, given its high volatility, predictions in which direction the Austrian party system might move are impossible to make. How volatile it can be was especially felt by the Green Party, which dropped out of the National Council in the 2017 general elections only to return on a share of almost 14 per cent of votes in 2019 leading to participation in a coalition government. However, it might be observed that the party system as a whole tries to stabilise itself by making it increasingly more difficult for new parties to successfully compete in general elections. Thus, it is on the brink of becoming a party cartel.

FURTHER READING

Bischof, G and Plasser, F (eds), *The Changing Austrian Voter* (New Brunswick-London, Transaction Publishers, 2008) 12, 53.

Bischof, G et al (eds), *The Vranitzky Era in Austria* (New Brunswick, Transaction Publishers, 1999).

Dachs, H et al (eds), *Politik in Österreich. Das Handbuch* (Wien, Manz, 2006).

Luther, KR and Müller, WC (eds), *Politics in Austria: Still a Case of Consociationalism?* (London, Frank Cass Limited, 1992).

Müller, WC, 'Austria: Tight Coalitions and Stable Government' in Müller, WC and Strom, K (eds), *Coalition Governments in Western Europe* (New York, Oxford University Press, 2000).

Pelinka, A, *Austria: Out of the Shadow of the Past* (Oxford, Westview Press, 1998).

Pelinka, A, 'Austrian Politics: 1918 to 2019' (2020) 4 *Antisemitism Studies* 82.

Pelinka, A and Plasser, F (eds), *The Austrian Party System* (Boulder-San Francisco-London, Westview Press, 1989).

Sickinger, H, *Politisches Geld. Parteienfinanzierung und öffentliche Kontrolle in Österreich* (Wien, Czernin, 2013).

Stainer-Hämmerle, K, 'Kommen und Gehen. Neue Listendynamik im alten Parteiensystem' in A Kohl et al (eds), *Österreichisches Jahrbuch für Politik 2014* (Wien, Böhlau, 2015), 77.

Tálos, E and Hinterseer, T, *Sozialpartnerschaft. Ein zentraler politischer Gestaltungsfaktor der Zweiten Republik am Ende?* (Innsbruck, Studienverlag, 2019).

3

The Legislative Branch of the Federal Government

Introduction – Electoral System and the Composition of the National Council – Assembly and Legal Status of the Federal Council – Parliamentary Functions I: Legislation – Parliamentary Functions II: Overseeing the Executive Branch – Conclusion

I. INTRODUCTION

ACCORDING TO ITS original design, the 1920 Constitution introduced a parliamentary system, thus establishing parliament as the central state body. It consists of two chambers: the National Council (*Nationalrat*) and the Federal Council (*Bundesrat*), both chaired by presidents. Together they form the Federal Assembly (*Bundesversammlung*), whose responsibilities mainly relate to the Federal President. Originally, the Federal President, as well as the Federal Cabinet, were elected by and answerable to parliament. The 1929 amendment strengthened the position of the Federal President at the expense of parliament, which lost the power to elect the Federal Cabinet and the Federal President. Thus, elements of a presidential system were introduced.

While the National Council is elected by the Austrian people, the members of the Federal Council are delegated by the state parliaments. Both systems of election and delegation ensure the dominant influence of political parties. They also shape the role of these two chambers. This will be discussed in the first part of this chapter.

The other sections will deal with parliament's responsibilities. A pivotal function is to enact laws. It will be demonstrated how the executive branch of government and parliament effectively have to work together to pass laws and it will be argued that under the efficient constitution, the executive branch of government – despite the more competitive party system – still has a stronger influence on the substance of legislation than parliament. More recently, parliament's legislative competence has been considerably curtailed as a result of Austria's accession to the European Union, further strengthening the executive branch of government.

As the entire public administration has to be based on parliamentary statutes, all laws enacted by parliament must be sufficiently clear and detailed. The effects of this proposition, recently challenged by the Covid-19 pandemic, will be analysed in this chapter.

The other main function of the federal parliament is overseeing the executive branch of (the federal) government. The heads of the federal administration, the Federal Ministers, are legally and politically accountable to parliament. It will be argued that, in reality, the system of ministerial responsibility mostly hinges on party hierarchies. However, substantial reforms of the regulations regarding committees of inquiry and increasing competition between political parties have strengthened parliament's position as a watchdog.

In its task to oversee the executive branch of government, parliament is supported by the Audit Court and the Ombudsman Board. The chapter will conclude by analysing these two bodies.

II. THE ELECTORAL SYSTEM AND THE COMPOSITION
OF THE NATIONAL COUNCIL

A. The Electoral System

The 183 seats of the National Council are allocated on the basis of a general election conducted nationwide. The constitution entrenches the main principles of the electoral system in its Art 26. The Regulations on National Council Elections 1992 (*Nationalrats-Wahlordnung 1992*, BGBl 471/1992) provide for detailed procedures. Elections are based on the principles of proportional representation and the free, general, equal, direct, secret and personal vote.

All citizens, men and women, who are at least 16 years of age on the election day are entitled to vote. Citizens who are at least 18 years of age on this day may stand as candidates. In Austria, universal suffrage was introduced in 1907 for males and was extended to females in 1918. Austria was the first EU Member State to lower the voting age in national elections to 16.[1] Restrictions on the right to vote only apply for people imprisoned for certain crimes, provided that a court has pronounced on

---

[1] A 2017 survey shows that, with regard to their knowledge of the political system, 16 and 17 year olds seem to be mature enough to vote: D Johann and SJ Mayer, 'Stand und

these restrictions.[2] In 2007, postal voting, already available for expatriates, was introduced on a more general basis. It required a constitutional amendment[3] as the Constitutional Court had struck down earlier attempts to introduce absentee voting as it arguably violated the principles of secret and personal voting.[4] Postal voting is still disputed, especially by far-right politicians[5] – nourished mainly by conspiracy theories.

Although the electoral system of the republic was based on the principle of proportional representation in the 1920 Constitution, some elements of the former majority-system survived. So did the idea that representatives should primarily be elected in constituencies.[6] These elements initially favoured the two large parties – the People's Party and the Social Democrats – over smaller parties. In the 1950s and 1960s, smaller parties needed about three times as many votes to win a seat in parliament as the two major parties. The conservatives benefited most from this system, because seats were allocated to constituencies according to the number of inhabitants rather than the number of eligible voters. In constituencies which were inhabited by families with comparatively more children, it needed fewer votes to gain a seat. As these (mostly rural) constituencies were traditional strongholds for the conservatives, they were systematically favoured by the electoral system. This explains why in 1953, as well as in 1959, the People's Party gained fewer votes than the Social Democrats, but nevertheless won the majority of the seats in parliament.

The 1970 electoral reform, which the Social Democrats had promised in exchange for the Freedom Party supporting their minority government, turned this system around to significantly benefit minor parties. It needed a further electoral reform in 1992 to re-balance the allocation of seats according to the principle of proportional representation. This was effected by introducing a final round at the federal level that,

---

Struktur des politischen Wissens in Österreich: Ein Vergleich der 16- und 17-jährigen mit anderen Altersgruppen' (2017) 46 *Österreichische Zeitschrift für Politikwissenschaft* 1ff; nevertheless, a better political education focusing on the ideological position of political parties still seems to be desirable.

[2] The law had to be adapted according to the findings of the ECtHR (First Chamber) in the case of *Frodl v Austria* (App no 20201/04) ECtHR 8 April 2010. Austria's initial provision had arguably violated Art 3 Protocol No 1 ECHR as it had – according to the findings of the court – disproportionately disenfranchised prisoners.

[3] BGBl I 27/2007.

[4] VfSlg 10412/1985.

[5] See the case of the 2016 Presidential elections, analysed in ch 4.

[6] G Strejcek, *Das Wahlrecht der Ersten Republik* (Wien, Manz, 2009) 17f.

mathematically speaking, redistributes all 183 seats according to the d'Hondt method. Today, a party needs about 25,000 to 26,000 votes to win a seat. These figures may be of some importance for understanding Austrian domestic politics. Measures affecting a group of people that exceeds this number are probably considered extremely carefully before being taken.

Eradicating almost all majority-forming elements from the electoral system further contributed to the fragmentation of the political system, as described in Chapter 2, making it harder to establish (coalition) governments. Consequently, demands were made to abolish the principle of proportional representation and introduce a majority system instead;[7] however, nothing ensued from the subsequent debate. At the time of writing (2022), any fundamental changes to the electoral system seem highly unlikely as they would require amending the constitution. That would need the support of at least one smaller party, which would supply it only to its own peril.

It is a decisive feature of Austria's electoral system that the electorate has very little influence on the selection of the candidates. Generally, voters can only choose between party slates. Additionally, they may cast a so-called 'priority vote' (*Vorzugsstimme*) for one of the candidates. Candidates who receive a certain number of priority votes are given priority when seats are assigned. This would slightly upset the order of the candidates on the list. In practice, this system only occasionally shows any effect as it would need the combined effort of many voters to successfully prioritise a candidate. The composition of the party lists is otherwise a matter for the parties and party secretariats. Some party statutes define the criteria according to which the lists should be composed.

Traditionally, the People's Party and the Social Democrats had to respect the demands of their subdivisions, influential state governors[8] and, most notably, the social partners. It was a decisive cornerstone of the social partnership that representatives of their organisations were placed on promising positions of the party slates. Only then could they assure that their compromises would not be overturned in parliament. Nevertheless, in recent years, both parties tried to introduce more democratic procedures when composing the party list by carrying out so-called 'pre-elections' amongst party members. The People's Party,

---

[7] See, for instance, K Poier, *Demokratie im Umbruch – Perspektiven einer Wahlrechtsreform* (Wien, Böhlau, 2009).

[8] This is an important aspect of Austria's Federalism that explains why it may not be so 'weak' regarding the efficient constitution. See ch 5.

however, recently returned to more authoritarian methods by handing some selection powers to their chairman. Consequently, more personal loyalty between the chairman and delegates could be established.[9] After the 2021 government crisis[10] and the retirement of the chairman, it is difficult to predict whether these amendments to the statute will survive.

The Green Party, dedicated to grassroots democracy, has implemented a system of gender equality, according to which female candidates must make up at least 50 per cent of the party list.[11] The *NEOS* has established a rather complex procedure based on the votes of party members.[12] In the Freedom Party it is the federal executive committee (partly together with the executive committees in the states) which draws up the party list for general elections.[13]

The fact that it is basically the political party that decides on the composition of the slate triggers a strong bond between the party and the elected candidate. A candidate who hopes to be re-elected would therefore be more loyal to the party or the relevant group within the party that is responsible for the nomination than to a constituency. The electoral system therefore strengthens party hierarchies.

B. The Legal Status of Members of the National Council

Members of the National Council enjoy a number of privileges. This status becomes effective when the newly elected National Council meets for the first time and generally ends with the assembly of the succeeding National Council, unless the member is re-elected.[14] The Constitutional Court may pronounce on the loss of the seat on application by the National Council if the member has been absent from parliamentary sessions during a period of at least 30 days without good reason and/or if

---

[9] H Sickinger, 'Parlamentarismus' in E Tálos (ed), *Die schwarz-blaue Wende in Österreich* (Wien, LIT-Verlag, 2019) 90, 97f.

[10] See ch 4.

[11] Art 8.9.e of the Statute of the Green Party. See gruene.at/organisation/partei, accessed 10 January 2022.

[12] Art 16 of the *NEOS*' Statute. See www.neos.eu/_Resources/Persistent/972e636ffe31339 39c1d104788d9a12bfe9fa4d3/NEOS Satzung_18_06_21.pdf, accessed 10 January 2022.

[13] Art 14 para 6 of the Statute of the Freedom Party, www.fpoe.at/fileadmin/user_upload/ www.fpoe.at/dokumente/statuten/Satzungen_aktuell_2019.pdf, accessed 10 January 2022.

[14] See Art 55 para 2 and Art 141 para 1 of the Federal Constitution and Art 2 para 8 of the Federal Law on the Rules of Procedure of the National Council (*Geschäftsordnungsgesetz*, BGBl 410/1975) for other grounds on which the legal status as a member of parliament may be terminated.

the member pursues a profession incompatible with membership of the National Council. Remarkably, in its 1998 decision, the Constitutional Court held that being imprisoned (abroad) may generally justify absence from the sessions of the National Council, but as the delegate had refused to return to Austria once that became possible, his absence was no longer justified.[15]

Decades ago, a constitutional amendment introduced a further reason for a National Council member to lose her or his seat, which has remained highly controversial. In a parliamentary system, cabinet members normally hold seats in parliament but in Austria, Art 56 of the Federal Constitution allows them to relinquish their seats temporarily, which has become a standard procedure from the 1970s onwards. If they do so, their seats are taken by subsequent candidates on the respective party lists. If the ministers leave office, they have the right to return to their seats, thereby ending the mandates of the National Council members who have held them temporarily. In the Austrian constitutional doctrine, those members who are temporarily assigned to parliament are rated 'second class members'.[16] It might happen that a party is not happy to lose the stand-in member once the minister is set to return. In this case, it has the option to 'persuade' another member to resign instead.

But in general, members of the National Council cannot be forced out of their position, as the right to be elected entails the right to remain in parliament.[17] In particular, there is no procedure to deal with the situation where a National Council member becomes unpopular in her or his own party, which therefore wants the member to resign.

National Council members are not bound by any mandate in the exercise of their function (Art 56 para 1 of the Federal Constitution). With its historical meaning[18] irrelevant today, the purpose of the 'free mandate' can be seen in limiting the extent of control a party may exercise over its own delegates[19] – especially whether and to what extent National Council members may be forced to vote with their own party or parliamentary group. Parliamentary groups are set up by representatives of the same political party.

---

[15] VfSlg 15266/1998.

[16] B Wieser, 'Artikel 56' in K Korinek and M Holoubek (eds), *Österreichisches Bundesverfassungsrecht* (Wien-New York, Springer, 1999) 4.

[17] VfSlg 3426/1958, 3560/1959.

[18] See for instance UFH Rühl, 'Das "Freie Mandat": Elemente einer Interpretations- und Problemgeschichte' (2000) 39 *Der Staat* 23.

[19] H Fischer, 'Das Liberale Forum als parlamentarische Fraktion – eine Rechtliche und Rechtspolitische Betrachtung' (1993) 1 *Journal für Rechtspolitik* 3.

In fact, a comparatively high degree of party discipline can be observed in Austria.[20] Thus, the outcome of a vote is generally clear from the beginning and genuine discussions during plenary sessions are rare. Parliamentary groups – having discussed a matter internally – demand that all their members vote unanimously, irrespective of whether the internal discussions had produced consensus. Although a National Council member may be forced to vote against her or his will, it might be argued that this was the price for the advantages of being a member of a parliamentary group: groups are teams that can reach their goals only when co-operating and sharing the workload.

Questions can be raised on how open and 'democratic' internal discussions may be. As they are held behind closed doors, a definite answer is hard to give. Remarkably, a conservative member of parliament described the discussion within the group of the People's Party during the period of the coalition government with the Freedom Party (at the beginning of the twenty-first century) as receiving instructions by the party leaders rather than openly discussing a matter. The general mood he felt was that the representatives were asked to keep their mouths shut and fold their hands in prayer.[21]

In the 1950s and 1960s, parliamentary groups had adopted rather strict methods to guarantee unanimous voting, that in the end were considered to violate the constitution. Members had to sign undated letters of resignation in advance, which could be submitted to the electoral board whenever convenient. Thus, the majority of a group or even only its leaders could decide at any stage on termination of the mandate and thus the loss of the member's parliamentary seat. This approach was considered to be unconstitutional in the light of Art 56 para 1 of the Federal Constitution.[22] Nowadays, National Council members can be excluded from a group (as well as from their political party), but not forced out of parliament. A member, however, is free to leave a group or party and join another group or party. As these things happen every now and then, it therefore can be said that the principle of the 'free mandate' protects the individual member from being totally dependent on the political party that has provided the member with a ticket.

---

[20] C Konrath, 'Regierung und Parlament. Organisation und Praxis' in R Heinisch (ed), *Kritisches Handbuch der österreichischen Demokratie* (Wien, Böhlau, 2020) 203, 221ff.

[21] This statement was held against the People's Party in various parliamentary discussions, obviously criticising its attitude. This is documented in the protocols recording parliamentary sessions, see 14. Sitzung des Nationalrates vom 7. März 2007, 23 GP, Stenographisches Protokoll, 175.

[22] W Berka, *Verfassungsrecht*, 8th edn (Wien, Verlag Österreich, 2021) 173.

Until a 2013 amendment to the Standing Orders of the National Council, it was also admissible for five members to leave their party or parties and establish a new parliamentary group, thus participating in the public funding of parliamentary groups. This can be decisive for the formation and the success of a new party as it might – at least – to a certain extent help to diminish the competitive advantage established parties have due to the lavish public funds they receive. Various parties have exploited that avenue, the most recent one being the Team Stronach. In a fierce reaction to this development, the 2013 amendment[23] limited the ability to found parliamentary groups to the first month following the convening of a newly elected parliament. Arguably, this limitation infringes the 'free mandate' and might be unconstitutional, but this has not yet been tested in court.

Members of the National Council can never be held to account for votes cast in the exercise of their function. They are also not subject to prosecution or other legal proceedings in respect of their oral or written contributions to parliamentary debates, with two notable exceptions. They might be sued for defamation and/or leaking classified information.[24] Otherwise, their actions are subject only to disciplinary measures taken by the National Council itself. The obvious reason for this provision is to ensure freedom of speech and an uninhibited debate. Furthermore, members of the National Council are also accorded protection from prosecution, especially from arrest and house searches. These privileges date back to the monarchy and were nourished by the representatives' fear that the (monarchical) administration could interfere with their deliberations and influence law-making procedures by simply holding some of them under arrest.[25] The privileges still may be of some importance, especially for members of the opposition, but have been nonetheless curtailed during the past decades. They now amount to the right of parliament to consent to prosecution or to interfere with it depending on how closely the allegation is related to the delegate's parliamentary tasks.

Publishing the account of proceedings in public sessions of the National Council can never be subject to accountability. Nevertheless, civil law courts have surprisingly ruled that members of parliament are

---

[23] BGBl I 131/2013.

[24] According to the Information Rules Act (*Informationsordnungsgesetz*, BGBl I 102/2014), information submitted to these chambers may be classified. Depending on the degree of classification, leaking the information might constitute a criminal offence.

[25] C Kopetzki, 'Artikel 57' in Korinek and Holoubek (eds) (n 16) 4.

not free to repeat outside parliament what they had already said in a parliamentary debate, not even in the form of a mere report. They might still be liable for offences.[26]

The function of a National Council member is incompatible with some other public positions, such as a member of the Federal Council or of the European Parliament, the Federal President or a member of the Supreme Court, the Constitutional Court or the Administrative High Court. There may also be incompatibility with respect to certain positions in the private sector. Members of the National Council receive a public monthly emolument.[27] This sum is the reference amount of the so-called 'Income Pyramid' (*Einkommenspyramide*), which was introduced for holders of public offices (*Öffentliche Funktionäre*) in the 1990s. Holders of public offices, such as members of the Federal or State Government, the Federal President, the Chancellor, the Vice-Chancellor, members of the Federal Council and many others, receive emoluments which are expressed in percentages of the monthly salary of a National Council member.[28] Federal Ministers, for instance, are entitled to 200 per cent of the reference amount, the Federal Chancellor to 250 per cent, etc. This suggests a hierarchical order between these offices, which partly reflects the degree of political power that is effectively assigned to the office holder.

Holders of public offices are very well paid in Austria. However, one of the main reasons for the amounts granted is corruption. Political parties expect and demand holders of public offices to pay what is called a 'party tax' (*Parteisteuer*). This means that political parties receive a certain percentage of the income of holders of public offices as a reward for putting them on the party slate and/or supporting their appointment. This not only represents a part of a truly feudal system, but also means that political parties are (also) funded indirectly from tax revenue.[29]

---

[26] OGH 29.3.2000, 6 Ob 79/00m.

[27] At the time of writing in 2022, this is €9,228 paid 14 times a year (12 regular monthly payments plus an additional payment before the summer and before Christmas; preferably taxed, the two additional payments are a benefit all Austrian employees receive). See www.finanz.at/gehalt/politiker, accessed 28 September 2021.

[28] Federal Constitutional Act on the Limitation of Emoluments of Holders of Public Offices (*Bezügebegrenzungsgesetz*, BGBl I 64/1997); Emoluments Act (*Bezügegesetz*, BGBl 273/1972).

[29] Rather than abolishing this feudal system, the Political Parties Act 2012 has legalised it by introducing Art 5 para 4 no 4 according to which such 'contributions' have to be explicitly declared in the parties' annual statements.

III. ASSEMBLY AND LEGAL STATUS OF THE FEDERAL COUNCIL

The members of the Federal Council are elected by the state parliaments. These elections are based on the principle of proportional representation and mirror the partisan composition of the respective state parliament. The number of members a state parliament elects depends on the results of the latest census and is defined by the Federal President by means of an ordinance. The state with the largest population delegates 12 members, the one with the smallest at least three. At present, Lower Austria delegates 12 members, Vienna 11, Upper Austria 10, Styria nine, Tyrol five, Carinthia and Salzburg four and Vorarlberg and Burgenland three members each. The members are elected after every general election of the respective state parliament. As a result, the Federal Council is never dissolved, but it is partially renewed. The states succeed one another in alphabetical order (based on the German spelling) in chairing the Federal Council.

Members of the Federal Council enjoy a legal status comparable to that of members of the National Council. They are also supposed to exercise their function without being bound by a mandate and they enjoy immunity to the same extent as members of the respective state parliaments would. They also draw public salaries, though they receive only half of the amount a National Council member is entitled to.

The constitution provides for the Federal Council as a second chamber of parliament which is, by design, supposed to represent the states when participating in the legislation and administration of the Federation. As such, it is held to be a core element in Austria's concept of federalism.[30] However, reality is different. The way the members of the Federal Council are recruited already shows that party affiliations are more important than state interests. Remarkably, the seating order of the Federal Council is drawn along party lines and the members of the Federal Council join the parliamentary groups of the National Council according to party membership. It is fair to say that party hierarchies have effectively overridden the design of the constitution in this case. It should come as no surprise that this has a bearing on the way the Federal Council performs its tasks and that genuine interests of the states do not play a part.

Different concepts have been drawn up to reform the Federal Council and discussions emerge from time to time but it is rather unlikely that the

---

[30] VfSlg 2455/1952.

constitution will be amended as design changes would imbalance politi-cal powers.[31] State interests are therefore represented by their governors. The Conference of the State Governors (*Landeshauptleutekonferenz*), which in Austria works only on an informal basis, traditionally provides a much more effective forum for expressing the interests and needs of the states.

Further, the states created a new body to represent their interests relat-ing to European integration. Within the framework of the constitutional amendments designed to meet the requirements of Austria's participa-tion in the legislative procedures of the European Union, they established an 'Integration Conference of the States' (*Integrationskonferenz der Länder*)[32] in which the state governors and presidents of the state parlia-ments co-operate. The Presidency (*Präsidium*) of the Federal Council is merely entitled to participate in its meeting.

IV. PARLIAMENTARY FUNCTIONS I: LEGISLATION

According to the constitution, parliament has two main functions. First, it enacts laws. This is seen as parliament's most important task, as the law is – in theory at least – the pivotal instrument for governing a democratic society. Second, parliament oversees the executive branch of government. With Austria's accession to the European Union, the exer-cise of parliament's functions had to be partly reshaped and adapted to the demand of Austria's participation in EU legislation. In reality, it remains true that parliament has to pass every (domestic) law, otherwise it would not be valid. But this does not mean that parliament neces-sarily has a strong influence on its substance. On the contrary, it is primarily the Federal Cabinet in accordance with the administration, political parties, social partners and other institutions that decide on the substance of a law, as will be demonstrated. Parliament may be seen merely as the bottleneck through which laws have to pass.[33] Despite the shifts from a consociational democracy to a more competitive system, it seems that parliament has not gained decisively more influence on the

---

[31] See F Fallend, 'A Redundant Second Chamber? The Austrian *Bundesrat* in Comparative Perspective' in G Bischof and F Karlhofer (eds), *Austrian Federalism in Comparative Perspective* (Innsbruck-New Orleans, University of New Orleans Press, 2015) 34, 50ff.

[32] See, for instance, LGBl für Wien 29/1992.

[33] H Neisser, 'Planung der Gesetzgebung aus der Sicht des Parlaments' in T Öhlinger (ed), *Methodik der Gesetzgebung: Legistische Richtlinien in Theorie und Praxis* (Wien-New York, Springer, 1982) 108.

substance of the laws. Under the conservative/far-right government, the Federal Cabinet arguably exercised an even more effective control over the legislative process.[34]

A. Legislative Procedures

Formally, it takes several stages to pass a law. Only some steps have to be carried out by parliament. Others may have to be taken by the executive branch of government and the electorate respectively. The process starts with a legislative proposal. It must be considered and passed by the National Council and subsequently – at least in most cases – by the Federal Council. After a law has been passed by both chambers, it may be subject to a referendum, although this has only been the case twice. Usually, after being passed by the Federal Council, a law is submitted to the Federal President for authentication and is then counter-signed by the Federal Chancellor. Finally, the law must be published: publication is the basic condition for a law's validity under the *Rechtsstaat* principle. Authentication and publication are thus performed by the executive branch of government, both of which can be seen as a heritage of Austria's monarchical past. Although scholars have always vividly emphasised the dominant role of parliament as the central body of the republic, by design this role was already limited in the original 1920 Constitution.

i. Legislative Initiative

The initiative for legislation can stem from several sources. A proposal can be made by the National Council itself or by at least five of its members. The Federal Council, or at least a third of its members, the Federal Cabinet (*Regierungsvorlage*) and a certain part of the electorate are also entitled to submit proposals.

In practice, it is mainly the Federal Cabinet that submits a draft bill. In some legislative sessions almost 90 per cent of the laws enacted by parliament were based on cabinet bills. This is due to several factors.

First, to a certain extent, all parliamentary systems tend to shift powers from parliament to the government or the cabinet.[35] This is also

---

[34] See Sickinger (n 9) 90, 112.
[35] Sickinger (ibid) 90.

a consequence of party hierarchies.[36] The chairperson of the governing party will (quite regularly) hold the position of the Federal Chancellor (or Vice-Chancellor for the chairperson of the smaller partner in a coalition government). Ministers will be chosen either from the party's upper echelon or for their loyalty to the chairperson. Voting against the will of the Federal Cabinet would therefore trigger a party revolt. Nevertheless, the parliamentary groups of the governing parties will have to be kept informed and involved accordingly, which primarily is the task of the group's chairperson, who participates in preliminary talks with the cabinet members of the respective party.[37]

Second, there are some Austrian peculiarities that intensify these effects. The skills and information needed for drafting a bill lie with the ministerial bureaucracy and are therefore at the disposal of the Federal Ministers rather than parliament. Parliament, for instance, does not have its own legislative service, so that even in the case of members of the parliament drafting a bill they would rely on the support of the ministerial bureaucracy.

Traditionally, government bills, and only government bills, were subject to an assessment procedure, during which a number of institutions, most notably the social partners, were given the opportunity to comment on the draft. Coordinated statements by social partner organisations were in general not overruled by parliament. That was ensured by placing members of social partner institutions on the party slates of the People's Party and the Social Democrats.

While this assessment procedure gained significant importance for peace and prosperity in the post-war period under successive grand coalition governments, it purportedly delayed or jeopardised comprehensive reforms in various fields of legislation in the late 1980s/1990s. Notably, both the 2000/2002 and the 2017 conservative/far-right coalition governments developed strategies to outmanoeuvre the social partner institutions, predominantly those affiliated with the Social Democrats.[38]

Two different strategies were applied to achieve this. One aimed at shortening the time limits set for the assessment procedure, as these were not defined by law. This strategy worked extremely well with rather complex and comprehensive bills as the social partner institutions had

[36] A Pelinka, 'Wachsende Autonomie und Differenzierung: Parteien und Fraktionen im Parlamentarischen System Österreichs' in L Helms (ed), *Parteien und Fraktionen – Ein internationaler Vergleich* (Opladen, Leske & Budrich, 1999) 219ff.

[37] See Sickinger (n 9) 90, 94.

[38] Sickinger (ibid) 106.

no chance to analyse them properly and file a substantial statement. Alternatively, a minimum of five members of the governing parties was asked to submit the draft bill – in such cases no assessment procedure was required.[39] These motions, however, were prepared by the ministerial bureaucracy.

In 2021, the assessment procedure was completely reorganised by an amendment to the National Council's Standing Orders.[40] As of 1 August 2021, all draft bills submitted to parliament have to be published on its website. Everyone – associations, organisations and private individuals alike – is entitled to submit statements and comments which also have to be published on parliament's website (those of private individuals only with their explicit consent).

In addition, parliament occasionally carries out online consultations and crowdsourcing projects inviting every citizen to participate.

ii. Popular Petitions

Fifty-seven times in the Second Republic so far,[41] the electorate has exercised its right to submit a motion by means of a petition (Art 41 para 2 of the Federal Constitution, further detailed in the Petitions Act).[42] For voters to initiate a motion, the support of one per million of the electorate (currently about 8,400 voters) is required. In a subsequent procedure, members of the electorate supporting the legislative proposal have to register. It is truly remarkable that most of the petitions were launched by opposition parties rather than by other members or groups of the electorate. This was originally encouraged, as the initial support of one per million of the electorate required to start a registration procedure could be subsidised by the support of eight members of the National Council or a certain number of members of at least three different state parliaments.[43] Opposition parties have used this instrument instead of

[39] Apart from the Austrian assessment procedure, which is only required in the case of a government bill, there is a notification procedure, established according to European Law, particularly for norms on technical standards. This means that the Commission has to be informed before a relevant law may be passed. The Austrian implementation of the European directive envisages notification only in the case of government bills. This may fail to meet the requirements of European law, especially in cases described above.

[40] BGBl I 63/2021.

[41] According to the website of the Ministry of the Interior, see www.bmi.gv.at/411/Alle_Volksbegehren_der_zweiten_Republik.aspx, accessed 10 January 2022.

[42] *Volksbegehrengesetz*, BGBl I 106/2016 in the applicable version.

[43] See M Stelzer, 'Direkt-demokratische Elemente in der österreichischen Verfassung: ein rechtsvergleichender Blick' in M Geis and D Lorenz (eds), *Staat-Kirche-Verwaltung – FS für Hartmut Maurer* (München, CH Beck, 2001) 1019, 1026.

submitting a motion to parliament by (five of) its members to gain more publicity and to exercise pressure on the government to deal with the relevant issue.

Every motion signed by at least 100,000 voters or by one-sixth of the voters of three separate states must be submitted to the National Council, which has to discuss them according to its Standing Orders. It does not necessarily mean that the motion has to become law. Most petitions have not ended in laws, not even those that attained a particularly high degree of public support. From a sociological point of view, it can be observed that after petitions were signed by about a million voters but were not transferred into law, subsequent elections have resulted in a change of government. Petitions may therefore act as an indicator of the people's disagreement with the incumbent government.[44]

In recent years there have been political moves to make popular petitions more effective and attractive. It has been suggested that if a motion is supported by a certain percentage of the electorate but parliament does not see fit to legislate, a referendum should enable the people to enact a law without parliamentary consent.[45] As the Constitutional Court, as well as most constitutional lawyers, considers the introduction of such an instrument to be a total revision of the Federal Constitution,[46] such a change would have to be submitted to a referendum.

iii. Deliberation and Voting

Any legislative proposal that has been successfully launched, has to be considered by the National Council. There are basically two types of discussion. One is led during plenary meetings when the government is given the chance to substantiate its proposal and the opposition parties will be able to explain their views on it. This discussion is open to the public. Parties will therefore primarily try to address their clientele. These discussions are rather strictly regulated by the National Council's Standing Orders and time limits for contributions apply.

Although officially aimed at allowing for a more lively and focused discussion, setting strict limits to speaking times has at least partly to be seen as a reaction to the almost nine-hour speech of a member of the Green Party in the late 1980s. What might have been an attempt at

---

[44] Stelzer (ibid) 1027.
[45] Bundesregierung, *Zukunft im Herzen Europas: Österreich neu regieren* (Wien, Bundespressedienst, 2000).
[46] VfSlg 16241/2001.

filibustering, led neither to a decisive delay nor the prevention of the enactment of a law but gained much public attention. As a consequence, opposition parties were deprived of that instrument. In Austria, the main task of parliament is seen to be passing laws rather than debating public issues. The question may be permitted if that view is still informed by the 1934 constitution.

In contrast to the plenary sessions of the National Council, consultations in the committees normally take place *in camera*. The idea of opening all committee meetings to the public has been discussed, but political scientists insist that the purpose of meetings *in camera* is to enable committees to work efficiently without always having to pay attention to the likely perception of remarks and comments by the media and the wider public.[47] Discussions led in committee meetings are therefore said to be more informal and to focus more on substantive matters.

The legislative procedure in parliament ends with the voting on the bill. The majorities required for the approval of a law differ depending on the formal character of the law. The Standing Orders provide for rather strict and clear rules on voting procedures. Sometimes it so happens that parliament (the Presidency) does not meet all the requirements. Such a law would be held unconstitutional and may be subject to rescission by the Constitutional Court.[48]

iv. The Role of the Federal Council

The decision of the National Council is then passed to the Federal Council, if the latter has a veto power or, in some specific and rather rare cases, must approve the decision. Approval is required, for example, if the draft adopted by the National Council curtails the powers of the states or changes the legal framework of the Federal Council. There are also cases in which the Federal Council is not tasked with participating in the legislative process: the most important example being the Law on the Federal Budget.

If the Federal Council vetoes a bill, it may only delay the legislative process but cannot prevent the enactment of a law. 'A reasoned objection' to give the National Council the chance of a second thought has to be raised within eight weeks, but may be overridden by the National Council

---

[47] H Sickinger, 'Die Funktion der Nationalratsausschüsse im Prozess der Bundesgesetzgebung' (2000) 29 *Österreichische Zeitschrift für Politikwissenschaft* 157, 170.
[48] VfSlg 16151/2001.

in a so-called persistence decision (*Beharrungsbeschluss*) that requires the presence of at least half the members of the National Council. It is up to the Federal Council to allow eight weeks to pass without taking any action or to explicitly decide not to veto a law in order to speed up the law-making process.

In reality, however, contributions of the Federal Council to the legislation of the Federation have been of only marginal importance; this follows from the design of the constitution, which asymmetrically attributes legislative powers to the National Council and the Federal Council respectively. Vetoes are not submitted to pursue specific interests of the states but only result from party politics. Vetoes in significant numbers can therefore only be expected in periods when the opposition in the National Council commands a majority in the Federal Council. Then they are used as a tool to at least delay the law-making process in order to demonstrate disagreement with the law. Until 2008, laws were vetoed about 110 times;[49] since then, a further seven vetoes were submitted.[50] Amendments of the bill rarely ensued. Whenever the Federal Council was asked to approve a shift in power from the states to the Federation, it generally concurred. The only exception was in 2019,[51] when the Social Democrats used their power to block a two-thirds majority, thus denying the consent of the Federal Council.

The Federal Council is obviously betraying its constitutional mission, which explains the ongoing debate to reform the institution, with some scholars even demanding its dissolution.[52] But as reforms would imbalance political powers and therefore are unlikely to happen, a pragmatic solution has been found: in some cases, defined by the constitution, laws can only be passed if the states agree. In such a case, it would be the task of each state governor to agree or disagree within eight weeks; should a single governor disagree, the law could not be passed.

v. Referenda

After the conclusion of proceedings at the Federal Council, it would be at this stage that the law might be subject to a referendum. Such a referendum would be mandatory if a total revision of the constitution was

---

[49] The figures are taken from H Schäffer, 'Reformperspektiven für den Bundesrat' (2007) 15 *Journal für Rechtspolitik* 11.

[50] The vetoes of the Federal Council are documented on the website of the Austrian Parliament: www.parlament.gv.at.

[51] See ch 1.

[52] For this debate see Schäffer (n 49) 11, 13ff.

envisaged (Art 44 para 3 of the Federal Constitution), which would be the case if principles of the constitution were to be amended.[53]

If the National Council so decides, any other law may be submitted to a referendum.[54] In either case, the referendum must formally be ordered by the Federal President.[55] In exercising this power, the Federal President may only act on the recommendation of the Federal Cabinet. The Federal President therefore does not have power to order a referendum even in a case of an undisputed total revision. The Federal President can only indirectly force the Federal Cabinet to submit such a recommendation if she or he successfully denies signing the constitutional amendment. It is another but so far only academic question whether a Federal President might deny the order of a referendum that has been recommended by the Federal Cabinet and on which grounds the Federal President might be entitled to do so.[56]

Referenda play a marginal, albeit not uninteresting part in the history of Austrian legislation. Although Austrian scholars have argued on numerous occasions that constitutional provisions had violated constitutional principles and therefore would have required a referendum for the reasons outlined above,[57] there was only a single case in which the government was willing to accept such arguments and to submit a constitutional law to a referendum: Austria's accession to the European Union. In 1994, more than 66 per cent of the electorate voted in favour of the accession which was subsequently accomplished.

The 1970s saw the first and so far only case in which parliament decided to submit an ordinary law to a referendum. It did so for a highly strategic reason. When the first (and only) nuclear power station had been erected and was ready to start operating, a huge public debate emerged on the safety of nuclear power stations in general and of the Austrian one in particular. The then government led by Federal Chancellor Bruno Kreisky, who was strongly in favour of exploiting nuclear power, drew on the experience of the Swedish government, which had lost an election over safety concerns regarding nuclear power stations. Therefore, he decided to submit this question to a referendum. A law was passed in parliament explicitly providing for the peaceful

---

[53] See ch 1.

[54] See Arts 43 and 44 of the Federal Constitution.

[55] For further details see the Referendum Act (*Volksabstimmungsgesetz*, BGBl 79/1973 in the applicable version).

[56] R Thienel, 'Verfassungsfragen nach Art 49b B-VG – dargestellt am Beispiel der geplanten EU-Volksbefragung' (2000) 8 *Journal für Rechtspolitik* 327, 337.

[57] See ch 1.

exploitation of nuclear power.[58] Such a law was completely superfluous as at that time erecting and operating the power station was perfectly legal. The law was only passed for the sole purpose of giving the people the chance to cast their votes in a referendum. Although the government and the Federal Chancellor personally strongly supported this law in public, the referendum was lost by a small margin. The nuclear power station never came into operation and quite a lot of money was wasted. Nevertheless, the Social Democrats won the following 1979 elections, obtaining their best result ever.

After the referendum, parliament passed a new law which prevented the 'peaceful exploitation of nuclear power' (*Atomsperrgesetz*, BGBl 1978/676). In 1999 (BGBl 1999/149), this law was transferred into the rank of a constitutional law. Consequently, there are no nuclear power stations in Austria. Moreover, fighting nuclear power stations became a big issue in Austria's foreign and European policy.

The referenda discussed here are not to be confounded with the advisory referenda or 'consultation of the people' (*Volksbefragung*) provided for in Art 49b of the Federal Constitution. Accordingly, the National Council may decide to consult the people on a matter of fundamental and national importance which lies within the power of the federal lawmaker. The result is not binding on parliament. To date, only one such consultation has been held – this was a consultation in 2013 on maintaining general conscription which the electorate answered in the affirmative.

When the procedures in parliament are terminated (and/or in the rare case of a referendum, the electorate has concurred), the bill must be authenticated by the Federal President and published by the Federal Chancellor. Both duties fall in the responsibility of the executive branch of government and will be discussed in Chapter 4. These powers of the Federal President and the Federal Chancellor and thus the participation of the executive branch of government in the legislative process, which is no Austrian peculiarity, is a heritage of the constitutional monarchy. They diminish the powers of parliament by design: a really powerful parliament would be in control of publishing the laws it passes.

B. Delegation of Legislative Powers

Eventually, parliamentary systems face the question if and to what extent parliament may defer an issue to the administration. This is

---

[58] See 97. Sitzung des Nationalrates vom 28. Juni 1978, 14 GP, Stenographisches Protokoll.

because no law can be drafted to foresee every single situation it may be applied to, nor can it always be as clear and precise as may be intended. In cases of emergency, it might even be necessary for the government to react immediately rather than initiate a long lasting law-making procedure in parliament. The latest example being the outbreak of the Covid-19 pandemic, when measures had to be taken fairly quickly to be effective.

The basic question was raised by the Constitutional Court in the 1920s.[59] Over the decades, the court has developed a comparatively strict view, rescinding various laws that seemed too generous in conferring regulative powers on the executive branch of government. Thereby – at least formally – the court strengthened the position of parliament vis-à-vis the cabinet. The reasoning is derived from a specific reading of Art 18 of the Federal Constitution which provides for the entire public administration to be based on law, or, to put it more precisely: on statutes enacted by parliament.

This 'principle of legality' (*Legalitätsprinzip*), as it is called in the Austrian constitutional doctrine, is seen as a cornerstone of the Austrian democratic system as it subordinates the entire public administration to parliament. Thus it is part of the constitutional design that establishes a parliamentary system in Austria. The constitution only allows for some mild exceptions when it entitles the administration in some cases to take direct actions, for example to release ordinances directly based on the constitution (*verfassungsunmittelbare Verordnungen*).

The principle of legality binds (sovereign) administration in two ways. First, it establishes the supremacy of law. This means that all administrative acts must comply with the law. Second, it implies that the entire public administration may only act on the basis of legal authorisation. Without any such authorisation, it would be illegal for the administration to act at all.

By contrast, the administration of the monarchy was only selectively bound by law. The principle of monarchical legitimation enshrined in the 1867 Constitution empowered the administration to act without specific legal authorisation, provided it neither interfered with civil rights nor infringed on existing laws. The administration of the monarchy was thus

---

[59] VfSlg 176/1923; the court's ruling is based on a vote drafted by Hans Kelsen, who was a member of the Constitutional Court in those days. The decision may serve as an example that Kelsen's aim was to strengthen parliamentary democracy rather than to follow strict methods in interpreting the law. For a more detailed analysis of this ruling and Kelsen's influence see M Vašek, *Von den Genfer Protokollen zum COVID-19 Maßnahmengesetz* (Wien, Sramek-Verlag, 2021) 17ff.

restricted only by the condition that it had to act within the framework of the law.

The principle of legality is also seen to be relevant within the context of the principle of *Rechtsstaat*.[60] Binding the administration to law should make administrative actions predictable. Furthermore, it gives citizens the possibility of challenging administrative acts in administrative courts if they believe that those acts are unlawful and violate their substantive rights.

The principle of legality may only satisfy these two functions if laws do substantively determine administrative actions. A law stating that administration may act as it chooses would formally provide a legal basis for administrative actions and therefore meet the wording of the constitution, but would obviously not comply with the intention of the principle of legality to bind the administration to the will of parliament and to make administrative actions predictable. Such a provision, deferring all parliamentary powers to the administration (*formalgesetzliche Delegation*), would be unconstitutional, according to the Austrian constitutional doctrine. However, it is rather unrealistic to believe that the law will always clearly and precisely determine each and every administrative action. This is neither possible with regard to the ambiguity of language, nor is it always desirable.

The question to what extent a law must substantively determine the exercise of executive power has caused much controversy amongst Austrian legal scholars.[61] The Constitutional Court has established that legal provisions have to be '*sufficiently* clear and detailed' (*hinreichend bestimmt*). There are numerous cases in which the court has ruled whether particular legal provisions met this requirement. In general, the court holds that this is the case as long as the administrative courts and the Constitutional Court are able to test administrative actions for compliance with the contested legal provision.[62] However, this definition turns tautologic, as it is only possible to test administrative actions for compliance with a legal provision if the latter is sufficiently clear and detailed.

As a result, it is hard to predict how the Constitutional Court will rule on a particular legal provision and standards may even vary from time to time. Nevertheless, some common ground may be observed. Very often, the court has to deal with legal provisions that have been phrased

---

[60] See ch 1.
[61] HP Rill, 'Artikel 18 B-VG' in HP Rill and H Schäffer (eds), *Kommentar zum Bundesverfassungsrecht* (Wien, Verlag Österreich, 2001) 5ff.
[62] See VfSlg 11499/1987.

rather ambiguously (*unbestimmter Gesetzesbegriff*): the meaning of such a provision is always highly debatable and particularly open to different interpretations. Examples may be found in laws referring to technical standards, which they often do by using clauses like 'state of the art', or to economic issues by using terms like 'economic reasons'. Such terms and others like 'equity' or 'professional ethics' are in particular need of assessment. The court has established that all available conventions of interpretation must be applied before assuming that a legal provision is not sufficiently clear and detailed.[63] Therefore, legal provisions that are vaguely phrased do not automatically violate the principle of legality as enshrined in Art 18 of the Federal Constitution.

However, if the meaning of a provision remains unclear after all avenues of interpretation have been exhausted, the provision violates the principle of legality. This is, for instance, the case if the assessment of a provision demands a certain diligence in archive research[64] or a delight in solving brainteasers.[65]

Scholars have emphasised that the degree to which the administration is bound by law may vary according to the subject matter (*differenziertes Legalitätsprinzip*).[66] In fields that require particularly fast reactions to an ever changing environment (for instance in the fields of economy or technology), laws may not be as detailed as in other areas. On the other hand, provisions that entitle the administration to encroach upon fundamental rights should be binding to a very high degree.[67] However, in practice it does not appear that the court has systematically ruled that all provisions potentially affecting fundamental rights must meet this requirement.

Further, scholars of Austrian constitutional law have debated whether provisions that bind the administration only by providing for objectives comply with the principle of legality.[68] In contradiction with some scholarly opinion, the Constitutional Court has declared such laws to be compatible with Art 18 of the Federal Constitution.[69] However, in these cases, the court focuses particularly on procedural requirements.

---

[63] See VfSlg 8395/1978 and others.

[64] VfSlg 13740/1994.

[65] VfSlg 12420/1990.

[66] R Novak, 'Das differenzierte Legalitätsprinzip in der verfassungsgerichtlichen Rechtsprechung' in B-C Funk (ed), *Staatsrecht und Staatswissenschaften in Zeiten des Wandels* (Wien-New York, Springer, 1992) 491; G Winkler, *Gesetzgebung und Verwaltung im Wirtschaftsrecht* (Wien, Jupiter, 1970) 78.

[67] See VfSlg 10737/1985 and 11455/1987.

[68] B Raschauer, 'Finale Programmierung und Raumordnung' (1980) 5 *Zeitschrift für Verwaltung* 93, 94.

[69] VfSlg 8280/1978 and others.

In the field of planning law, the administrative authorities, for instance, have to rely on expert opinion and to submit their draft acts to hearings provided for by law. The results must be taken into consideration in settling conflicts between different objectives.

In a similar way, the court has upheld laws rather vaguely defining measures to be taken to contain the Covid-19 pandemic. In all these cases, however, ordinances that implemented such measures had to be based on a risk assessment as well as reasonable considerations why these measures were necessary and proportionate. This had to be demonstrated in the files, otherwise the ordinance was unlawful.[70]

The question to what extent the administration must be bound by law is further complicated by Art 130 para 3 and Art 133 para 3 of the Federal Constitution. These provisions relate to the judicial review of the administration by administrative courts. They state that administrative acts (or decisions by administrative courts of first instance) are not illegal if by law the matter was left to the authority's or court's discretion, and discretion was exercised in the spirit of the law. The Federal Constitution thus allows for exceptions from the concept of strict legal binding.

Even in the light of these possible exceptions, in Austria it is generally held that parliamentary statutes have to determine administrative actions in a more detailed way than might be the case in other countries. This may be illustrated by comparison of road traffic law in Austria and Germany. In Germany, ordinances contain many provisions regulating road traffic whereas in Austria similar provisions would have to be part of the Road Traffic Act according to the Austrian understanding of the principle of legality. Needless to say, anything amounting to 'Henry VIII clauses'[71] which would offer ample discretion in passing ordinances would be unconstitutional. But with regard to the Covid-19 legislation, it might be discussed whether the court has already started to deviate from its traditional standards.

The discussion around the principle of legality provides a good example for Austria's doctrine fitting its post-war narrative. A rather formal formula obscures the core element of the question: the division of powers between the legislative and the executive branch of government. Treating this question accordingly would have to be based on a more profound theory of a representative democracy. Such a theory would have political

---

[70] VfGH 1.10.2020, G 272/2020; 8.6.2021, V 587/2020; see further ch 7 for a more detailed analysis of the case law of the Constitutional Court concerning measures taken to curb the spread of the coronavirus.

[71] P Leyland, *The Constitution of the United Kingdom*, 4th edn (Oxford, Hart, 2021) 78.

implications and might also require a moral concept. It would also have to ask if the 1929 amendment that introduced the direct election of the Federal President who has to appoint the government, has provided a democratic legitimation for the executive branch of government that no longer only derives from parliament and thus might affect the balance of power between the legislative and the executive branch of government.

However, there has always been one major exception to the strict reading of the principle of legality: if the law had provided for the administration to achieve its ends by means of (private law) contracts, it was not bound by the principle of legality. This view was derived from the fact that the Constitution had established the Federation, the states and even the municipalities as full subjects under private law ignoring any division of responsibilities that would otherwise have curtailed these competencies. Public procurement, public subsidies, the administration of the nationalised industries – all of this could be performed without any legal determination and authorities could invoke the freedom of contract like any other private person although at the expense of the taxpayer. A major academic debate arose in the 1950–60s, with public law scholars claiming that the principle of legality should have its full effect also in the field of 'private law administration' (*Privatrechtsverwaltung* or *Privatwirtschaftsverwaltung*).[72] But this had no immediate consequences. Obviously, within this field the governing political parties could exercise their power almost at will: contracts could be handed out to party affiliates or in return for party membership or party loyalty, amounting to corruption. Gradually, parts of the so-called 'private law administration' were regulated by law; remedies in the field of public procurement law were only introduced after the accession to the European Union implementing the relevant directives. Nationalised industries were subject to an ongoing process of privatisation, thus reducing the field of 'private law administration'.

C. Participation in EU Legislation

Although the executive branch holds most of the power in the legislative process according to the efficient constitution, a further shift in power was experienced after Austria's accession to the European Union. As it is the respective Federal Minister who participates in the Council of the

---

[72] W Antoniolli, *Allgemeines Verwaltungsrecht* (Wien, Manz, 1954) 12; H Klecatsky, 'Die Köpenickiade der Privatwirtschaftsverwaltung' (1957) 79 *Juristische Blätter* 333.

European Union which passes the regulations and directives in cooperation with the European Parliament, the power of the Federal Parliament
(as well as the state parliaments) has thus been curtailed.

Aiming at counterbalancing the power shift, Arts 23e–23k, in their
2010 version,[73] were incorporated into the Austrian Federal Constitution.
These provide for the involvement of the Federal Parliament in the law-
making procedure of the European Union and are quite comprehensive
and substantial from a comparative point of view, at least on first sight.[74]

The responsible member of the federal government has to inform
the National Council and the Federal Council of all projects within the
framework of the European Union and to give them the opportunity to
air their opinions. If such an opinion concerns a project that aims at passing a legal act that would have a bearing on federal legislation, it would
be binding on the member of the cabinet acting on Austria's behalf in the
Council of the European Union. The member of cabinet may only deviate from it in case of imperative reasons relating to foreign or integration
policy. Should the European Union legislation require implementation
by a federal constitutional law or would take the rank of a constitutional
law, the National Council may even object to such a deviation. If such
a constitutional law would require the Federal Council's agreement, the
responsible cabinet member could be bound in a similar way by an opinion expressed by the Federal Council.

A 2009 survey[75] demonstrated that the National Council's initial
euphoria in issuing such binding opinions rapidly vanished. While in
1995, Austria's first year of membership, the National Council passed
no fewer than 16 binding opinions, the numbers came down to seven in
1996 and four in 1997 respectively. They further decreased in the following years and between 2004 and 2007 this instrument was not used at all.
The reasons given were multifold. Two are probably the most convincing. First, the opinion has to be passed on a majority vote in the Main
Standing Committee of the National Council (*Hauptausschuss*) or its

[73] BGBl I 57/2010.

[74] E Miklin, 'The Austrian Parliament and EU Affairs: Gradually Living Up to Its Legal
Potential' in C Hefftler et al (eds), *The Palgrave Handbook of the National Parliaments and
the European Union* (Basingstoke-New York, Palgrave Macmillan, 2015) 389, 390ff.

[75] J Pollak and P Slominski, 'Zwischen De- und Reparlamentarisierung: der öster-
reichische Nationalrat und seine Mitwirkungsrechte in EU-Angelegenheiten' (2009) 38
Österreichische Zeitung für Politikwissenschaft 193, 198. See B Blümel and C Neuhold,
'The Parliament of Austria: A "Normative" Tiger' in O Tans et al (eds), *National
Parliaments and European Democracy* (Groningen, Europa Law Publishing, 2007) 143,
160. See also J Pollak and P Slominski, 'Influencing EU Politics? The Case of the Austrian
Parliament' (2003) 41 *Journal of Common Market Studies* 707.

sub-committee respectively, where parties are represented proportionally. Therefore, it is hardly conceivable that such opinions would not reflect government's policy and would be raised against the will of a minister. Second, the first binding opinion passed by the National Council had an adverse effect. According to the binding opinion expressed by the National Council, a directive on animal transport should force a time limit on animal transport of only six hours. The Austrian Federal Minister of Agriculture had to find out in Brussels that this time limit was unacceptable to other Member States. But as the opinion was binding on him, he was not able to negotiate this time limit (the offer was to force this time limit only on transport within national boundaries). Consequently, he had to vote against the directive, thus provoking a result much more unfavourable to the genuine Austrian position.[76]

As a result of this experience, government parties informally agreed that binding opinions should be phrased more vaguely to give the respective Federal Minister enough room to negotiate. Such opinions typically start off with phrases like: 'The responsible minister is asked to try to achieve ...' This style has been kept until today; one example is a 2020 opinion in which 'the Austrian government is asked to effectively engage in ...'[77] It is obvious that with opinions phrased like that, parliament has given up any attempt to effectively influence European legislation, although the numbers of such opinions aired have risen again over time.[78] Anyhow, from a European point of view the idea of binding a minister to a strict mandate may be seriously questioned: in so far as the Council has to define a European commonwealth, it may not be helpful if ministers are bound by strict mandates. Or in other words: if all ministers representing the Member States are bound by a strict mandate of their national parliaments, European legislation may come to a standstill.

On the other hand, the administration met the demands of parliament with respect to the obligation to disclose information on EU matters, which the constitution provides for. Initially, this obligation was fulfilled by merely passing on EU documents to parliament – the more the better. But without any comments at all, it was practically impossible for delegates to filter out the relevant information. This situation slightly improved in 2003, when the Federal Cabinet decided to instruct the

---

[76] See S Griller, 'Zur demokratischen Legitimation der Rechtsetzung in der EU: Stärkung der nationalen Parlamente oder Aufwertung des Europäischen Parlaments?' (1995) 3 *Journal für Rechtspolitik* 164, 172.

[77] www.parlament.gv.at/PAKT/VHG/XXVII/SEU/SEU_00004/imfname_848319.pdf, accessed 14 June 2022.

[78] Miklin (n 74) 389, 395.

administration to provide comments on EU documents. Although not all of these comments seemed to be helpful, nevertheless Austrian members of parliament seem to be fairly well informed about European projects and about the Austrian position.[79] This gives delegates of the opposition parties at least the possibility of publicly criticising the government's position.

The 'Protocol on the Role of National Parliaments in the European Union' and the 'Protocol on the Application of the Principle of Subsidiarity and Proportionality', both attached to the Lisbon Treaty, attribute to national parliaments the power to invoke the principle of subsidiarity and in this respect also to challenge a legislative act in the CJEU.[80] In order to meet the requirements of these protocols, the constitution allocates corresponding responsibilities to both chambers, the National Council and the Federal Council.[81] It may be interesting that the Federal Council has tried to take advantage of this new power and rebranded itself into the 'Europe Chamber'. According to a more recent survey,[82] it has submitted 13 reasoned statements between 2013 and 2016 but none of them was supported by other parliaments in sufficient numbers to initiate at least a 'yellow-card' procedure.

A 2012 amendment to the constitution,[83] introducing Arts 50a–50d, provided for the participation of the National Council in matters of the European Stability Mechanism (ESM). In cases that might have a bearing on the Austrian budget, the Austrian representative may only agree or abstain from voting on approval of the National Council. These provisions, according to which the National Council has to issue a strict mandate, already reflect the change in Austrian politics. As the implementation of the ESM needed a two-thirds majority in parliament and the People's Party and the Social Democrats together had failed to achieve that in 2012, they had to negotiate with the Green Party which was basically willing to support the coalition government. However, this support came with the price of stricter scrutiny of government action.[84]

---

[79] Miklin (ibid) 392.

[80] See A Rosas and L Armati, *EU Constitutional Law. An Introduction*, 3rd edn (Oxford, Hart, 2018) 29.

[81] BGBl I 57/2010.

[82] J Grames, 'Der österreichische Bundesrat und die Subsidiaritätskontrolle – eine Entwicklung hin zur "Europakammer"?' Centre of European Integration Research, Working Paper 02/2019, eif.univie.ac.at/downloads/workingpapers/wp2019-02.pdf, accessed 10 January 2022.

[83] BGBl I 63/2012.

[84] Miklin (n 74) 389, 399ff.

V. PARLIAMENTARY FUNCTIONS II: OVERSEEING
THE EXECUTIVE BRANCH OF GOVERNMENT

Chapter E of the Federal Constitution allocates parliament the power to 'participate in the administration of the Federation' as the constitution roughly puts it. Surprisingly, this chapter contains provisions on the federal budget and on the conclusion of state treaties. Formally, parliament has to pass a law in these cases. There are historical reasons why these powers do not appear within the chapter on federal legislation. The conclusion of state treaties was the prerogative of the monarch and parliament only had to give its consent to trade agreements and other specified treaties according to a 1867 law. The Federal Finance Act, often referred to as the federal 'budget', was not regarded as a law in the late nineteenth century because it had no effect on third parties (citizens), but was viewed as an 'administrative act in the form of a law' (*Verwaltungsakt in Gesetzesform*).[85] Nevertheless, parliament's approval of the budget, thereby controlling the monarch's war chest, is seen as the historical root of parliamentarianism. It might be argued that dealing with the law on the federal budget and on the conclusion of state treaties within this very chapter of the constitution again reveals how the republican constitution is based on its monarchical antecessor. In both cases, the federal budget and the conclusion of state treaties, the executive branch of government takes a dominant role. In substance, they are therefore dealt with in Chapter 4.

A. Legal and Political Accountability of the Administration

Overseeing the administration or the executive branch of government is the other important function of parliament alongside legislation. It is a vital element of democracy because it imposes a democratic control on the administration. The head of the federal administration, the Federal Cabinet, is legally and politically responsible to parliament. Legal control implies the power of parliament to sue the Federal Cabinet (or a single minister) at the Constitutional Court for legal contraventions resulting from their official activity. Political control deals with the much broader issue whether the administration of a minister, or of the entire

---

[85] P Laband, 'Das Budgetrecht nach den Bestimmungen der preußischen Verfassungsurkunde unter Berücksichtigung der Verfassung des Norddeutschen Bundes' (1870) 4 *Zeitschrift für Gesetzgebung und Rechtspflege in Preußen* 619.

cabinet, conforms to moral or ethical standards, political conventions, or – simply – professionalism. Cabinet ministers are responsible not only for their own activities, but also for the entire sector of the executive branch they direct. To meet this responsibility, all ministers may issue instructions to influence the enforcement of laws within their realm.

As already outlined above, parliament's contribution to legislation is poorer in substance than the framers of the Federal Constitution might have envisaged. In fact, the Federal Cabinet and the administration play a decisive part in the legislative process. Overseeing the executive branch of government therefore seems to be an even more important issue. Unsurprisingly, Austrian political scientists have noted that parliament did not excel in this area either.[86]

As controlling the executive branch of government and, foremost, the Federal Cabinet and/or the Federal Ministers in a parliamentary system can effectively only be exercised by opposition parties, it has to be noted that neither the Federal Constitution nor the Standing Orders of the National Council that regulate overseeing the executive branch of government in detail attribute any power specifically to the 'opposition' or an 'opposition party' as such.[87] Instead, the Standing Orders provide for 'minority rights'. This had the consequence that at times when some of these rights could only be exercised by a relatively large minority, say for instance by 20 members of parliament, the only opposition party to a government controlling more than 90 per cent of parliamentary seats – the Freedom Party – was completely powerless. Parliamentary control was totally ineffective in those days. In the late 1980s, however, minority rights were generally given to a group of five, synchronising this number with the number it takes to form a parliamentary group. Each party that is able to establish a parliamentary group therefore has some tools at its disposal albeit their use may be restricted to a certain number of times per year to avoid hampering the legislative machinery.

There are several measures to assert the political liability of Cabinet Ministers. Traditionally, the core element is the right to interrogation, which may be exercised in many ways according to the Standing Orders of the National Council and those of the Federal Council. Every member of the National Council or the Federal Council is entitled to address

---

[86] A Pelinka, 'Eine Verwestlichung Österreichs? Zum Wandel des politischen Systems durch den EU-Beitritt' (1995) 26 *Zeitschrift für Parlamentsfragen* (Sonderband) 279.

[87] See also C Konrath, 'Parlamentarische Opposition in Österreich: Recht und Praxis in Zeiten eines fragmentierten Parteiensystems' (2017) 48 *Zeitschrift für Parlamentsfragen* 557, 561ff.

short oral questions during sessions to cabinet ministers on any subject pertaining to the enforcement of the law and to demand all related information. More complex questions have to be provided in writing and need the support of five members in total. Cabinet ministers, in principle, have to answer the questions and can refuse to do so only on the grounds that they are bound by confidentiality or data privacy. The constitution still generally pledges all functionaries entrusted with federal duties and others to confidentiality – imparting information being the exception. All efforts to introduce more transparency and to turn the system around have been unsuccessful so far. Parliament has the right to classified information as any leaks would be subject to criminal prosecution. Cases of refusing to provide information may not be reviewed by a minority which could only try to exploit them politically. The most important function of the right to interrogation is to refer issues to the public. As the right to interrogation is not restricted to members of the opposition, it can also be claimed by members of parliament supporting the government and is quite often used to give cabinet ministers a chance to raise their profile.

With regard to authorities that are independent in accordance with Art 20 para 2 of the Federal Constitution, the committees of the National Council are entitled to summon the heads of those authorities and question them on all issues of administrative business.

The National Council may also establish committees of inquiry (Art 53 of the Federal Constitution). Until a 2014 amendment[88] such committees could only be set up by obtaining a majority decision. Nevertheless, several committees of inquiry were established after World War II. In the late 1980s two such committees were mildly 'successful' in examining the political background of what was otherwise a crime story. As a result, the social democratic Minister of the Interior had to retire. As it was mainly a social-democratic background these committees were to look into, it was the People's Party that supported establishing these committees, very much to the upset of the Social Democrats. Therefore, the grand coalition government of the following decade abstained from setting up such committees, to the criticism of the opposition parties.[89]

In 2006 and 2008, the Social Democrats voted with the opposition parties to set up committees to oversee what they believed were cases of corruption that the conservative/far-right government was responsible for. The establishment of the 2006 committees raised questions as to

---

[88] BGBl I 101/2014.
[89] M Stelzer, 'Neuere Tendenzen im österreichischen Parlamentarismus: Zur Entwicklung oppositioneller Rechte' (1997) 9 *European Review of Public Law* 1079, 1101.

whether there were constitutional limits on the subjects parliament may enquire into. Further, questions of data privacy were raised, as details of a tax file concerning a private company appeared on the website of a member of the Green Party chairing the committee. Partly as a consequence, fiscal authorities submitted their files with large parts blanked out, which led to further disputes between parliament and the federal ministers involved, who were all representing the People's Party, or in other words, disputes between the People's Party and all other parties.

The ongoing arguments over these committees of inquiry were partly responsible for the dissolution of the grand coalition government in 2008. In the following elections, the Social Democrats and the People's Party lost their combined two-thirds majority. Unlike in 1994–95 it could not be restored quickly and it has not been restored so far. As the opposition parties were needed to pass amendments to the constitution, they saw a chance that their long-time request to make it a minority right to establish a committee of inquiry could be fulfilled.

Finally, the 2014 amendment to the constitution introduced the obligation to set up a committee of inquiry on the demand of at least a quarter of the members of the National Council. It restricted the subject matter to 'a certain completed process regarding matters in which the Federation is responsible for implementing the laws' (Art 53 of the Federal Constitution). Generally, all authorities and courts have to produce files and documents pertaining to the subject matter of the inquiry, although exceptions apply. Disputes between the quarter of the members who demanded the establishment of the committee and the majority and/or the government, regarding, for instance, the scope of the subject matter or the relevance of the files demanded, have to be settled by the Constitutional Court (Art 138b of the Federal Constitution).[90]

The new law has encouraged a competitive style of parliamentary discussions, sometimes turning them into belligerent disputes. Usually, the opposition accuses the government of playing 'hide and seek', while the government rues the inquisitorial style of the interrogations. A temporary peak in the struggle between government and opposition was reached when an incumbent chancellor was accused of having lied to an inquiry committee and was prosecuted.[91] (At the time of writing, the case is still pending.) Further, the incumbent Minister of Finance refused to follow an order of the Constitutional Court[92] to disclose certain

---

[90] VfGH 14.9.2018, UA 1/2018; 2.12.2020, UA 3/2020; VfSlg 20370/2020.
[91] orf.at/stories/3212744, accessed 14 January 2022.
[92] VfGH 3.3.2021, UA 1/2021.

e-mail accounts to the same inquiry committee – a disobedience which was previously unheard of. Consequently, the court decided to file an application[93] with the Federal President to execute the court's decision. Only with a possible house search of the Federal Ministry of Finance looming, did the minister eventually disclose the accounts.

The most effective instrument of control at the disposal of parliament would be a vote of no confidence (Art 74 of the Federal Constitution). Should a vote of no confidence be passed, the respective member(s) of the cabinet or even the entire cabinet would be removed from office. The Federal President is thus obliged to dismiss the minister(s) or even the entire cabinet. A vote of no confidence must be supported by the majority of the members of the National Council (the Federal Council therefore cannot pass a vote of no confidence). The main function of the vote of no confidence lies in securing parliament's political and legal influence on the formation of the Federal Cabinet which is appointed by the Federal President. This instrument is therefore particularly important in balancing the powers between the National Council and the Federal President.

In practice, votes of no confidence are regularly proposed by the opposition and rejected by the government majority. Indeed, it would need specific conditions under which a vote of no confidence may be successful. These conditions were met in May 2019 when the coalition government between the People's Party and the Freedom Party suddenly collapsed following the 'Ibiza-scandal'.[94] As the People's Party successfully demanded the dismissal of the Minister of Interior, who was a member of the Freedom Party, the Freedom Party no longer felt bound by the coalition agreement and voted with the opposition parties on a motion of no confidence. Consequently, the whole cabinet had to be dismissed by the Federal President.

As this short overview demonstrates, under grand coalition governments that were sometimes supported by up to 95 per cent of the members of the National Council, a parliamentary opposition that could have held government to account was non-existent. Opposition at those times was found more within the governing parties than in parliament and came from various groups inside the parties and party wings. This type of opposition was barely visible to the public as it operated, more or less, behind closed doors. This is probably one reason why parliamentary instruments to control the government were initially

---

[93] VfGH 5.5.2021, UA 1/2021.
[94] See ch 4 for details.

rather underdeveloped. The attitudes towards the powers of parliamentary minorities changed only (mildly) when the traditionally large parties experienced life in opposition. A probably game changing event was the already mentioned loss of the two-thirds majority that the People's Party and the Social Democrats had enjoyed together until 2008. As smaller parties are now needed to enact constitutional changes, they have some leverage over the two former large parties that they may use to strengthen minority rights. As a consequence, overseeing the executive branch of government has become more effective, or at least more visible.

B. The Audit Court and the Ombudsman Board

There are two bodies attached to the National Council designed to support it in overseeing the administration. Both bodies remarkably gained a large reputation in public, where they are not really perceived as supporting parliament but rather as authorities in their own right. Those two are the Audit Court (*Rechnungshof*) and the Ombudsman Board (*Volksanwaltschaft*). The task of the Audit Court basically is to oversee the administration of public funds; the Ombudsman Board has to investigate into all forms of possible maladministration.

The National Council has a decisive influence on the organisation of both institutions, although they are not exclusively agents of the National Council. In overseeing the management of public funds in states and municipalities, the Audit Court acts as an agent for the respective state parliament. Although these competences cannot be abrogated by the states, they are free to establish their own audit units. States may accept the competence of the Ombudsman Board in the sphere of their administration or they may establish their own boards. Vorarlberg and Tyrol have established their own Ombudsman Boards; all other states have chosen to accept the competence of the Federal Ombudsman Board in their sphere of administration so far.

i. The Audit Court

The Audit Court is directed by a president, who is elected by the National Council for a 12-year period; only one term may be served. The president may be relieved from office by a vote of the National Council. Staff members of the Audit Court are appointed by the Federal President on a proposal from the president of the Audit Court who then has to countersign the appointment.

The Audit Court's tasks include overseeing the administration of public funds (*Gebarungskontrolle*), drawing up final federal budget accounts (*Bundesrechnungsabschluss*), conducting an income inquiry in accordance with the Federal Constitutional Law on the Limitation of Emoluments of Holders of Public Offices and scrutinising the yearly statements of political parties. Overseeing the administration of public funds involves the assessment of all operations within the audited institutions that have a financial impact. Audits are performed on the whole state economy of the Federation, the states and all communities with at least 10,000 inhabitants. Several other legal entities are subject to oversight by the Audit Court, as they are substantially influenced by federal or regional bodies or because they operate on public funds. These include endorsements, funds and institutions administered by federal authorities or by individuals appointed for this purpose by authorities of the Federation, and enterprises which are owned or partly owned by public entities or controlled in a way similar to ownership. The Audit Court also examines the financial administration of corporations established under public law that use federal funds as well as the financial management of the social insurance bodies, the professional corporations (*gesetzliche berufliche Vertretungen*) and Austria's national broadcasting corporation (*ORF*).

The criteria the Audit Court has to apply in overseeing the administration of public funds are those of arithmetical correctness; compliance with existing regulations; and the employment of thrift, efficiency and expediency. These economic principles were of particular interest at the beginning of the new millennium as they served as a constitutional basis for administrative reforms that tried to strengthen the effectiveness and efficiency of the administration, implementing concepts of new public management. The fact that the Audit Court is entitled to scrutinise whether the administration acts in compliance with the law might clash with the powers of the administrative courts and the Constitutional Court respectively. It might happen (and it has already happened) that especially in the field of public funding, the Audit Court criticises the spending habits of an authority, holding it to be illegal. When the authority follows the opinion of the Audit Court, however, the Constitutional Court may find that the authority's policies were legal in the first place as the law had to be read in the light of the constitution, something the Audit Court failed to do. Disputes over the interpretation of a law between the Audit Court and the Constitutional Court may therefore prove to be costly for the holder of a substantive right who would have to file an application with the Constitutional Court because the administration denies her or him a right under pressure from the Audit Court.

The influence the Audit Court may have on the administration results mainly from the authority it derives from public opinion rather than from the legal consequences of its examinations.

The Audit Court has no legal mechanism available other than to submit the results of its reviews to the appropriate legislative body, whose task it is to decide whether there should be (legal) consequences. Before the Audit Court files its report to the appropriate legislative body, a draft version (*Rohbericht*) is sent to the audited entity, which is entitled to express its opinion. Although the draft version of the report is strictly confidential, it happens very frequently that important parts are leaked and published by the media. As the Audit Court enjoys a good reputation and a wide-ranging authority with the public, the audited institution, especially a government department or a public body, is under heavy pressure to change its fiscal management. Even if it could reject the criticism on reasonable and conclusive grounds, its counter statement will never find the same public attention as the leaked report and could easily be ignored. Reports of the Audit Court may therefore also be used by the government to get on with reforms in the field of public administration that would otherwise be successfully blocked by the civil service.

ii. The Ombudsman Board

The Ombudsman Board was established in 1977 and is based on the Swedish model of the 'ombudsman'. It consists of three members, with the chair rotating annually between them. They are elected jointly on the basis of a recommendation by the Main Standing Committee of the National Council. Each of the three political parties with the most seats in the National Council is entitled to nominate one member, who will serve a term of six years and may be re-elected only once. This provision reflects the situation of the 1970s, when only three parties were represented in the National Council. The idea was that each party should nominate one ombudsman. Until 2006, the third ombudsman was actually always nominated by the Freedom Party, as it was the party that always came at least third in the elections. In 2006, when the Ombudsman Board had to be re-elected, the Green Party and the Freedom Party jointly held the third place, controlling exactly the same number of seats. This was a situation the constitution did not provide for. Parliament's decision was that the right to nominate the third ombudsman should be exercised by the party that had gained more votes, which in this case was the Green Party. A 2012 amendment to the constitution[95] entrenched this additional criterion.

The task of the Ombudsman Board is to investigate into any form of potential maladministration within the executive branch of government. Maladministration means more than a failure to comply with legal regulations. Virtually everything that could give rise to complaint from the public may be reviewed: unfriendly behaviour of civil servants, excessively complicated application forms etc. A special focus, however, has to be given to a purported infringement of human rights.

The Ombudsman Board may take action following a complaint that may be lodged by anybody who considers her- or himself to be a victim of maladministration and who has no further recourse to legal remedy. The Ombudsman Board may also investigate its suspicions of maladministration *ex officio*. In reality, however, these two avenues are not clearly separated. That means that citizens might refer a case to the Ombudsman Board at a time when their case is still pending. Although the constitution might be read in a way that provides that the Ombudsman Board is not to intervene in pending cases, it may do so by claiming to further investigate on its own suspicions. As interventions by the Ombudsman Board are not necessarily performed on legal grounds, but also on political grounds (the ombudsmen are all politicians), their intervention may sometimes clash with due course procedures and lead to preferential treatment of a single person. The activities of the Ombudsman Board are therefore not always in line with the principle of *Rechtsstaat*.

As the Ombudsman Board has to protect and endorse human rights, it and its own commissions may visit prisons and facilities for disabled people as well as scrutinise police action.

Again, the influence the Ombudsman Board may have on the administration stems from its political authority rather than from its legal power. Administrative authorities must submit all requested information and provide access to their files. The Ombudsman Board may issue recommendations on measures to be taken in, or resulting from, particular cases. Authorities must either follow the recommendations or state in writing their reasons for not complying with them. The Ombudsman Board summarises its activities in an annual report presented to the

[95] BGBl I 1/2012.

National Council and the Federal Council.[96] It remains with these Councils to formally react to maladministration by amending laws or by calling government to account. The Ombudsman Board has a specific legal power with respect to ordinances: it may request the Constitutional Court to pronounce on their legality.

The popularity and the high esteem the Ombudsman Board enjoys in public are not a result of its reports filed to the appropriate parliaments or the contesting of an ordinance. They largely stem from weekly TV shows that were aired in the 1970s and in which cases were referred to the public. The ombudsman was given a forum to publicly exchange arguments with a representative of the authority (who was, to her or his disadvantage, neither a politician nor specifically trained to appear on TV). However, sometimes the state of affairs of the Austrian administration disclosed to the public in this way seemed to be alarming.

VI. CONCLUSION

Despite the fact that some Austrian scholars frequently claim that parliament is the 'central state body' of the republic, in reality, it is probably not the most powerful decision-making organ of the state. This claim may even be questioned from a mere normative point of view as parliament cannot enact any law without the participation of the executive branch of government which would have to authenticate and publish it. Moreover, parliament has comparatively little influence on the substance of the laws it passes. In general, bills are drafted by the ministerial bureaucracy under the direction of cabinet members. At least until the mid-1980s, social partners exercised a significant influence on many laws, further diminishing the role of parliament which was more often than not reduced to a legislative machinery passing bills on demand. The power of the executive branch of government vis-à-vis parliament mirrors the party hierarchy, which is supported and upheld by an electoral system that mostly leaves it to the political parties to select candidates. Thus, their loyalty to the political party and the party hierarchy is ensured.

In respect to its other main function, exercising control over government, parliament initially did not excel either. During the times of grand coalition governments, when the People's Party and the Social Democrats

---

[96] The annual reports are published on the Ombudsman Board's own website, www.volksanwaltschaft.gv.at.

enjoyed a majority of 90 per cent and more, the 'opposition' was barely visible. The more so, as the Standing Orders of the National Council do not attribute any rights to the opposition as such. They merely define 'minority rights', which are attributed to groups of representatives, usually, since the late 1980s, consisting of a minimum of five members.

A decisive step in expanding minority rights was taken in 2014 when the right to demand the establishment of a committee of inquiry was passed to any possible group with the support of at least a quarter of parliament's members.

Hence, minority rights were strengthened during the last decade and the style of confrontation became more competitive and sometimes belligerent. It remains unclear whether the conduct of parliamentary debates and procedures have become more animated in general. In this regard, it is probably important to distinguish between parliament's legislative business and its oversight of the executive branch of government. With regard to legislation, it may be noted that although the concept of consociational democracy was pushed back under conservative/far-right governments, political parties still have a tight grip on the composition of their slates and consequently, cabinets exercise a tight control over the legislative process. Only in the second half of 2019 under an interim government of 'experts' (civil servants and former judges), did parliament take a more prominent role in shaping policies allowing for more volatility in forming coalitions. In overseeing the executive branch, it may be argued that the new powers to establish committees of inquiry have indeed strengthened parliamentarianism.

FURTHER READING

Gottweis, H, *Die Welt der Gesetzgebung* (Wien-Graz, Böhlau, 1988).

Heinisch, R (ed), *Kritisches Handbuch der österreichischen Demokratie* (Wien, Böhlau, 2020).

Hengstschläger, J, *Rechnungshofkontrolle* (Wien, Manz, 2000).

Holzinger, G and Holzinger, K, 'Artikel 26' in Korinek, K and Holoubek, M (eds), *Österreichisches Bundesverfassungsrecht* (Wien, Verlag Österreich, 2017).

Jenny, M and Müller, WC, 'Austria: Individual Talent, Official Functions, and Party Size' in Bäck, H et al (eds), *The Politics of Legislative Debate Around the World* (Oxford, Oxford University Press, 2021).

Konrath, C, 'On Concepts of Parliament and Parliamentarism in Austrian Public Law' (2009) 3 *ICL Journal* 80.

Konrath, C, Neugebauer, C and Posnik, R, 'Das neue Untersuchungsausschuss-verfahren im Nationalrat' (2015) 23 *Journal für Rechtspolitik* 216.

Lanser, I, 'Die Volksanwaltschaft als Menschenrechtsagentur' (2017) 25 *Journal für Rechtspolitik* 34.

Lienbacher, G and Pürgy, E, *Parlamentarische Rechtsetzung in der Krise* (Wien, Jan Sramek Verlag, 2014).

Tálos, E (ed), *Die schwarz-blaue Wende in Österreich* (Wien, LIT-Verlag, 2019).

Wiederin, E, 'Die Rechtsstellung der Abgeordneten' (2020) 142 *Juristische Blätter* 609.

4

The Executive Branch of the Federal Government

Introduction – Federal President – Federal Cabinet – Civil Service – Foreign Affairs and European Membership – Federal Budget – E-Government – Nationalised Industry – Conclusion

I. INTRODUCTION

AS ALREADY DISCUSSED in Chapter 3, there is a tendency for powers to be shifted from parliament to government or the cabinet respectively. In Austria, this tendency has been intensified by the 1929 constitutional amendment introducing features of a presidential system, some Austrian peculiarities and, moreover, the accession to the European Union. According to the efficient constitution, the executive branch of government arguably holds the greatest political power.

Two bodies will be analysed in depth in this chapter. First, this chapter will deal with the role of the Federal President. Although strengthened by the 1929 constitutional amendment, the Federal President's powers may only be exercised on recommendations by the Federal Cabinet and a Federal minister respectively, with two notable exceptions. One such is the appointment of the Federal Chancellor, and the other is the authentication of laws passed by parliament. We will consider how federal presidents have used these powers and how the development of the political system, especially in the last few years, has expanded the margin of discretion presidents have to exercise their powers.

The major part of the chapter will be devoted to the Federal Cabinet, which is arguably the most powerful body under the Austrian constitution. The Federal Cabinet and Federal ministers respectively control the entire federal administration by means of instructions and, moreover, almost all armed forces. They are in charge of negotiating international treaties and participate in the law-making process of the European

Union. They appoint Austrian members to bodies of international organisations and the European Union. The cabinet, most notably the Federal Minister of Finance, has to draft the federal budget act – a decisive instrument to allocate tax revenues and, thus, implement political programmes. The Federal Chancellor plays an important part in publishing all laws passed by parliament and would, under the framework of e-government, have the (unintended) power to invalidate all laws passed after 2004. Responsible ministers operated nationalised industries and, after the privatisation of large parts, continue to manage the shares the republic has retained.

This vast field of powers attributed to the Federal Cabinet has provided governing parties with ample opportunities to fill vacancies with their affiliates and to establish systems of patronage appointments. This has encouraged corrupt behaviour on all sides. Only the federal structure, outlined in Chapter 5, and the more recent introduction of a two-tier administrative jurisdiction, discussed in Chapter 6, have curtailed the influence of the cabinet on the entire administration. The latter might have even shifted powers from the executive to the judicial branch of government.

II. THE FEDERAL PRESIDENT

A. Election and Legal Position of the Federal President

The National Council apart, the Federal President is the only state body at federal level to be directly elected by the people.[1] Direct popular election of the Federal President was introduced by the 1929 constitutional amendment, which was to some extent designed on the model of the Weimar Constitution. It aimed at establishing 'law and order' as a reaction to violent clashes between partisan militias.[2] It therefore attributed additional powers to the Federal President, entrusting the Federal President with a more prominent and powerful role within the political and constitutional system. Direct popular election was meant to strengthen the political position of the Federal President, who initially had to be elected by the Federal Assembly, with the democratic legitimation of the

---

[1] The people of Austria would also elect the Austrian members of the European Parliament directly. However, the European Parliament is a European institution and not a state body.

[2] See ch 1.

office being only derived from parliament. Popular election was seen as a means to allow the Federal President to be an effective counterpart to the National Council.

The Federal President is elected for a period of six years. Re-election for a consecutive term of office is possible only once (Art 60 para 5 of the Federal Constitution) – in other words, a person can hold the office of Federal President for two consecutive terms, that is for 12 years. After that, another person would have to be elected Federal President for at least one term of office. However, this person would not even have to complete the tenure to enable re-election of the former president for another two consecutive terms. In reality, however, no president who has served two full terms has ever been re-elected a third time – which would have been impossible in most cases anyhow, as presidents more often than not have died in office.

The type of popular election follows the same principles as elections to the National Council, except that – unsurprisingly – elections are not based on a proportional system. The Federal President is elected by an absolute majority of votes, and as no instant run-off system applies, a second ballot is needed if no candidate wins an absolute majority in the first round. All Austrians eligible for election to the National Council are entitled to vote. Citizens who are 35 years of age by the end of the election day may stand as candidates. In reality, however, candidates are chosen and supported by political parties. Members of 'ruling houses' or of 'formerly ruling families' (as the constitution phrased it) were not permitted to stand for election until 2011. As this provision clearly aimed to prevent the re-establishment of the Habsburg Monarchy, it was challenged unsuccessfully by members of the Habsburg family in the Constitutional Court. As some members again threatened to challenge it at the European Court of Human Rights, the republic chose to rescind it in 2011,[3] probably to avoid the publicity of a possible defeat on the European level.

Presidential elections may be challenged in the Constitutional Court, but this only rarely happens. In 2016, however, the court had to pronounce on the results of the run-off ballot. The 2016 election was remarkable for many reasons. Surprisingly, the candidates fielded by the two former major parties, the People's Party and the Social Democrats (traditionally, one of their candidate had always won), had no chance of even reaching the run-off stage. This stage was reached by the candidate

---

[3] BGBl I 43/2011.

of the Freedom Party and the candidate of the Green Party. This split the electorate in two camps. One camp supported or could at least tolerate a far-right candidate who had already threatened during his election campaign to be willing to exploit the competencies of a president. The other camp, opposed to the idea of a far-right president, united behind the candidate of the Green Party.

The run-off was won by the very small margin of 30,863 votes by the candidate of the Green Party and only after all postal votes were counted, which had made the difference. The Freedom Party immediately alleged that the election was rigged. They attacked the system of postal voting that purportedly allowed for voter fraud. Further, they identified many formal illegalities that had appeared during the counting procedures. Moreover, they alleged that predicted election results, based on the first results of the actual vote count, were circulated on social media. They believed that this might have influenced the behaviour of voters. Therefore, the election was challenged before the Constitutional Court on the grounds of the possible impact on the outcome.

According to Art 141 of the Federal Constitution, the court has the power to rescind an election if the illegality could have influenced the election result. The court, although upholding the postal voting system, found that formal illegalities affected 77,769 postal votes. It could not rule out the possibility that the predicted results circulated on social media were actually based on the first results of the vote counting. As the number of illegalities exceeded the margin of votes, it found that the illegalities could have had an influence on the results. This was despite the fact that no such influence was either witnessed or likely to have occurred.[4] The result of the lawsuit obviously hinged on the interpretation of the relevance clause.[5] Instead of a more substantive reading, the court basically chose a formal, almost mathematical approach.

The second run-off election was won by the candidate of the Green Party, Alexander Van der Bellen, on a clear margin of 348,211 votes. With hindsight, the decision of the court settled the matter for all parties. It is difficult to assess what would have happened had the second run-off overturned the result of the first.

---

[4] VfSlg 20071/2016; see also SL Frank, 'Austrian Constitutional Court: The Annulment of the Run-off for the Presidency' (2017) 11 *Vienna Journal on International Constitutional Law* 99.

[5] E Matti, 'Austrian Constitutional Court: Presidential Election – Counterevidence and Influence of New Media' (2017) 11 *Vienna Journal on International Constitutional Law* 123ff.

Holding the office of the Federal President is incompatible with the exercising of any other function. Therefore, Federal Presidents may not be a member of any general representative body or exercise any other occupation during their tenure. For compensation, they are entitled to the highest amount of emoluments a holder of a public office may receive according to the 'income pyramid' (*Einkommenspyramide*, see Chapter 3). This currently amounts to almost €350,000 annually.

Austrians do not elect a vice president. If the Federal President is prevented from performing her or his duties, the Federal Chancellor shall deputise. The three Presidents of the National Council collectively deputise for the Federal President if the impediment lasts longer than 20 days, if the National Council has voted on a motion to demand the Federal President's removal from office, or if the position of the Federal President is held in abeyance, as, for instance, in the case of premature death.

B. The Powers of the Federal President

Initially, the 1920 Constitution attributed a more or less ceremonial role to the Federal President, formally filling the void left by the outgoing monarch. The main function of the Federal President was (and still is) to act as a 'Head of State' and represent the republic internationally. With this respect the legal position of the Federal President is peculiar, as on one hand, it seems to be placed above all other state organs and the president's powers relate to all state functions (legislative, executive and judicial branch of government). On the other hand, however, the Federal President is only one of several 'highest executive authorities' (Art 19 of the Federal Constitution).[6] The acts of the Federal President are legally classified as executive acts; that is, as ordinances or administrative decisions. Nevertheless, most of the actions a Federal President might take are directly based on the constitution and not specified by ordinary laws.

The role of the Federal President changed in 1929 when distinctive political powers were attributed to the office holder as a reaction to armed conflicts between party militias. The main powers added by the 1929 amendment were the power to dissolve the National Council

---

[6] Constitutional theory defines the position of being 'highest' not in a political but in a strictly formal sense. According to this definition such authorities can only be author of, but never subject to, an instruction. See, for instance, W Berka, *Verfassungsrecht*, 8th edn (Wien, Verlag Österreich, 2021) 215.

(but only once for any particular reason) and to govern on the basis of emergency decrees until its re-election, as well as the power to appoint and dismiss the Federal Cabinet (until the 1929 amendment the Federal Cabinet had to be elected by the National Council). But the legal framework for the exercise of presidential power has not been eased: the Federal President still needs a recommendation, usually from the Federal Cabinet, that entitles the president to act. Although the president might refuse to act at all, the recommendation, however, ensures the influence of the governing parties.

There are two notable exceptions to this rule: first, the appointment and the dismissal of the Federal Chancellor and, second, the power of the president to sign bills into laws. In both cases no specific recommendation is required. In the former, the power of the National Council to pass a motion of no confidence ensures the influence of parliament and therefore also of the (governing) political parties.

The legal situation outlined above is a result typical of a compromise. Whereas the Social Democrats feared that a powerful president could threaten democracy, the Conservatives demanded a strong, almost monarchical presidency to constrain a fractured parliament.[7] Therefore, the position of the Federal President was strengthened, but only to a certain extent. Compared with other constitutions, it does not amount, for example, to the position of the President of the United States of America, the Russian Federation or France. Therefore, since 1929, it is fair to describe Austria as a parliamentary democracy with features of a presidential system.

The constitutional amendment was motivated by the hope that a more powerful president would be able to 'maintain' law and order, prevent a civil war and thus uphold the democratic constitution. As history demonstrates, these hopes were dashed. With hindsight, it may be said that President Wilhelm Miklas, who held the office from 1928 to 1938, mishandled the powers of the president to dissolve parliament and dismiss the cabinet respectively. One of the reasons might have been that he was not elected by the people but by the Federal Assembly (the first directly elected president actually being Theodor Körner in 1951).

However, in 1930, Wilhelm Miklas, siding with the conservatives, dissolved the National Council on recommendation of the cabinet for the first and, so far, only time in Austrian history. In doing so, he merely

---

[7] See M Welan, 'Der Bundespräsident im System der österreichischen Bundesverfassung' in G Schefbeck (ed), *75 Jahre Bundesverfassung* (Wien, Verlag Österreich, 1995) 483, 488.

prevented a Christian-social minority government from being ousted by a looming vote of no confidence.[8] In the subsequent general elections, the Social Democrats, for the first time since 1919, gained a relative majority. The (anti-parliamentarian) '*Heimwehr*' won a presence in the National Council, while the Christian-social party suffered heavy losses. The outcome of the election obviously had an adverse effect on the policy of the president and demonstrated that dissolution of parliament in particular and the use of presidential powers in general might be a risky business. Maybe also for that reason, President Wilhelm Miklas did not intervene to stop the illegal actions taken to introduce the authoritarian constitution in 1934. Rather, he acquiesced in holding the presidency even under the authoritarian constitution.

After World War II, during a period of exceptional political stability, the Federal Presidents basically restricted themselves to their ceremonial role. In times of grand coalition governments, even appointing the Federal Chancellor was not a question of choice. It became the usual practice to appoint the leader of the party which won a (relative) majority in general elections. In 1966, the Federal President swore in a conservative government as the People's Party had won the absolute majority, albeit he – a Social Democrat – might again have preferred a grand coalition government. In 1970, he appointed a minority government formed by the Social Democrats that was supported by the Freedom Party, although the conservatives were furious and accused him of not allowing enough time to negotiate on other options.[9]

During the first decades of the Second Republic, Austrians perceived their Federal President as a highly regarded elder statesman, who represented the country but otherwise lacked any essential political power. This image was mainly a result of two factors. First, the political system enjoyed a high degree of stability which did not provide the Federal President with much room to manoeuvre. Second, until the 1980s all presidents of the Second Republic were either Social Democrats or social democratic candidates, and the Social Democrats were never in favour of a politically powerful presidency.

Again, the 1980s mark a turning point. With the party system becoming more diversified, the power of the Federal President to influence the

---

[8] See B Skottsberg, *Der Österreichische Parlamentarismus* (Göteborg, Elanders, 1940) 409ff; K Berchtold, *Verfassungsgeschichte der Republik Österreich*, Vol 1 (Wien-New York, Springer, 1995) 584ff.

[9] See N Schausberger, 'Franz Jonas' in F Weissensteiner (ed), *Die österreichischen Bundespräsidenten – Leben und Werk* (Wien, Österreichischer Bundesverlag, 1992) 258, 297.

formation of a Cabinet gradually increased. In addition, the presidency was gained by conservative candidates, who promised to play a more 'active' part.

Remarkably, the first attempt of a president to deliver on such promises failed completely. The formerly highly regarded Secretary-General of the United Nations, Kurt Waldheim, became probably the weakest president the country has ever experienced. What allegedly started as a social democratic conspiracy ended up in a self-inflicted personal crisis and a crisis of the presidency and the republic as a whole. During the election campaign, Kurt Waldheim was confronted with allegations that he had lied over his wartime past and – at some point – that he had even been a war criminal. His reactions were largely held to show a remarkable lack of diplomacy and sympathy with the victims of the Nazi regime when, already elected, he insisted that he had only carried out his duties during World War II – in the same way so many other Austrians had done. His statement, aired on TV, also ridiculed the solemn 1945 proclamation of independence[10] in which Austria had declared that it was the first victim of Nazi Germany and was dragged into a war no Austrian had ever wanted. This position is obviously irreconcilable with a 'duty' to serve in the Nazi army. His statement laid bare Austria's dishonesty in grappling with the Nazi past.

It became clear fairly quickly that allegations that he had committed any crimes during the war could not be proven, but the way he dealt with the question and the allegations did a huge amount of damage. He was put on the 'watch list' by the US administration and was subsequently isolated by the rest of the world, with the remarkable exception of the Holy See and of some Arab countries. He therefore never had the chance to gain the authority to play a more powerful and active part domestically.

The role of the Federal President only started to change under his successor Thomas Klestil, who already surprised the political system when he refused to follow the routine of appointing a member of the Constitutional Court on the basis of a proposal by the National Council. Although the National Council had to submit a list of three candidates according to the constitution, it nevertheless had become a habit that the Federal President appointed the first candidate on the list. President Thomas Klestil did not follow that habit but appointed the third

---

[10] See ch 1.

candidate on the list, arguing that she was better qualified especially with regard to the federal principle of the constitution.[11]

The reaction to this decision was really remarkable: the constitution was amended[12] – the National Council (and the Federal Council) no longer had to submit a list of three candidates, but only one candidate (as the Federal Cabinet has always had to) thus curtailing the power of the Federal President and ensuring that selection of a candidate remained entirely in the hands of the political parties.

The year 2000 saw the formation of a coalition government between the People's Party and the Freedom Party following seemingly endless negotiations after the 1999 elections in which the Freedom Party gained almost 27 per cent of the votes and came second. President Thomas Klestil tried to influence the negotiations between the political parties, aiming at avoiding the right-wing Freedom Party becoming part of the government, especially as he saw repairing Austria's image as one of his main tasks. At one point, the president even reportedly considered dismissing the newly elected National Council, but as polls suggested that the Freedom Party would even get stronger in a possible re-election, the plan was dropped. (Maybe, the recollection of the adverse consequences of the dissolution of the National Council in 1930 also informed his decision to abstain from using this power.)

In the end, President Thomas Klestil had to swear in a Federal Cabinet formed by representatives of the People's Party and the Freedom Party, as they had a majority in parliament. He did it, however, only on the condition that the leaders of both parties signed a preamble to their policy statement in which they explicitly had to support respect and tolerance for all people regardless of nationality or religion and to fight discrimination, intolerance, xenophobia, anti-semitism and racism. Further, the Federal Cabinet was required to explicitly stand up for human rights, the European integration process and the social welfare state.[13] Moreover, he refused to appoint two representatives of the Freedom Party that were recommended as Federal ministers. Their appointment was deemed to be a provocation in the eyes of aliens, immigrants and probably also the Jewish and Muslim communities.

---

[11] This episode was so significant that it was even mentioned in an otherwise short obituary – see Wiener Zeitung, 8 July 2004, www.wienerzeitung.at/nachrichten/politik/oesterreich/307843_Erdberger-in-der-Hofburg.html, accessed 11 January 2022.

[12] BGBl 1013/1994.

[13] Bundesregierung, *Zukunft im Herzen Europas: Österreich neu regieren* (Wien, Bundespressedienst, 2000).

Due to the political situation, President Thomas Klestil was the first president of the Second Republic who demonstrated that he had political powers and was willing to exercise them. This came very much as a surprise to his compatriots and some representatives of the political parties, who were used to presidents signing off whatever political parties had decided. Nevertheless, he could not prevent the provocation that the participation of the Freedom Party in a coalition government meant to the fundamental principles of the European Union and the so-called 'sanctions' imposed on the country by all other EU Member States.[14] The fact that some representatives of the Freedom Party not only spread antisemitic and xenophobic ideas, but from time to time played down the cruelty of the Nazi regime, effectively undermined the post-war commitment to prevent a restoration of National Socialism or national socialist ideas. The right-wing/conservative government was neither installed in an undemocratic way nor was it *per se* a fascist government. But again, Austria was haunted by the demons of its past, which it had never dealt with properly and which therefore never went away.

In 2019, the incumbent Federal President, Alexander Van der Bellen, had to deal with an even more tumultuous situation in which he had to further exhaust the powers attributed to the president. The chairman of the Freedom Party, vice chancellor in a 2017-built coalition government between his party and the People's Party under Chancellor Sebastian Kurz, had walked into a trap set up on the island of Ibiza before the 2017 election. He had been caught on camera bragging about his ability to broker investment deals and, once in office, to hand out government contracts in return for the (financial) support of the Freedom Party. Further, he suggested avoiding the scrutiny of the Audit Court by donating money to private associations affiliated with his party rather than to the party itself.

When the video was aired in spring 2019 on Austrian TV's prime-time news, he had to resign. The People's Party further demanded that the Minister of the Interior should also retire because he had been the Freedom Party's general secretary and therefore he was under suspicion of involvement in illegal party financing. As he refused to offer his resignation, the chancellor recommended his dismissal to the Federal President who followed this recommendation. Thus, he became the first

---

[14] L Adamovich, 'Bericht zur Lage in Österreich vor der EU-Delegation des französischen Senats' (2000) 27 *Europäische Grundrechte Zeitschrift* 399; M Ahtisaari, J Frowein and M Oreja, 'Österreich-Bericht für 14 Mitgliedstaaten der Europäischen Union' (2000) 27 *Europäische Grundrechte Zeitschrift* 404.

minister of the Second Republic to be dismissed by the Federal President against his will.

Consequently, almost all ministers fielded by the Freedom Party resigned and the party no longer felt bound by the coalition agreement. In this situation the Social Democrats introduced a motion of no confidence against the whole cabinet which for the first time in the Second Republic gained enough support – the support of the Freedom Party included – and therefore was successful. Subsequently, the whole cabinet was dismissed and snap elections were promised.[15]

In the meantime, the Federal President, after consultations with all party leaders, appointed a so-called 'expert' cabinet, consisting of high-ranking civil servants and former judges. It has to be emphasised that, theoretically, the president had had a range of options to form a new government. From a democratic point of view the most obvious option would have been to ask the leader of the strongest opposition party to form a new government. This was ruled out because the Social Democrats were willing to cooperate with the Freedom Party in a motion of no confidence but not in a coalition government. Further, it is debatable, with snap elections already promised, whether he could have asked the dismissed government to conduct business on an interim basis until the formation of a successor government. Although this would somehow have undermined the motion of no confidence, the constitution, at least formally, would have tolerated it, thus leaving ample discretion to the Federal President.

All these events, although standard procedures in many other democracies, were treated as an exceptional government crisis by Austrian media. This may be understandable against the background of the stability of the political system this country enjoyed in decades after World War II, but ultimately, it may only be a small step towards a more open and competitive democracy and a new normalcy.

The interim government lasted for about half a year and was followed by a coalition government between the People's Party and the Green Party, again under the chancellorship of Sebastian Kurz. This government was on the brink of breaking up in October 2021 as corruption charges against the chancellor himself had been brought forward. In the course of investigations into the Ibiza scandal, text messages had been – coincidently – found and restored. They suggested that his seizure

---

[15] For more information on the so-called 'Ibizagate' see J-M Eberl, LM Huber and C Plescia, 'A Tale of Firsts: The 2019 Austrian Snap Election' (2020) 43 *Western European Politics* 1350.

of power over the People's Party was supported by corrupt and unfair methods. With another, probably successful, motion of no confidence looming, he retired only to become leader of the parliamentary group of the People's Party[16] for two months before relinquishing all political offices. Again, it was for the Federal President to moderate the conflict between the political parties.

As already mentioned above, the other responsibility the Federal President may exercise without further recommendations by the Federal Cabinet is the authentication of laws. According to Art 47 para 1 of the Federal Constitution, the Federal President must confirm the 'constitutional enactment' of federal laws. The phrasing of this constitutional provision has led to a discussion on the extent of the president's power of review.[17] Two points are generally accepted amongst public law scholars. First, the Federal President has the power to review the law-making process for compliance with procedural rules, for instance, the rules on voting as provided for in the Standing Orders of the National Council. And, second, the Federal President is not allowed to refuse his or her signature on political grounds. Thus, the Federal President has no right to veto a bill. All actions that a Federal President might take must be based on constitutional grounds.

Constitutional commentators do not agree over whether the Federal President may consider constitutional questions of more substantive character, such as fundamental rights, for instance. It is sometimes held that the Federal President has full power to review a bill,[18] whereas other scholars concede the president the power to refuse signature only in cases

---

[16] Details of the story were covered by The New York Times, 9 October 2021, www.nytimes.com/2021/10/09/world/europe/austrian-chancellor-sebastian-kurz-resigns.html, accessed 11 January 2022; with a follow up: The New York Times, 17 October 2021, www.nytimes.com/2021/10/17/world/europe/austria-sebastian-kurz-scandal-chancellor.html, accessed 11 January 2022; and The Guardian, 10 October 2021, www.theguardian.com/world/2021/oct/10/sebastian-kurz-departure-further-blow-europe-centre-right?, accessed 11 January 2022.

[17] See F Melichar, 'Geschichte und Funktion der Gegenzeichnung, insbesondere in der österreichischen Verfassungsentwicklung' in N Grass and W Ogris (eds), *Festschrift für Hans Lentze* (Innsbruck, Wagner, 1969) 397; F Koja, 'Die Stellung des Bundespräsidenten in der Verfassung. Seine politische Funktion' in Weissensteiner (ed) (n 9) 9; D Jahnel, 'Die Mitwirkung des Bundespräsidenten an der Bundesgesetzgebung' (1987) 109 *Juristische Blätter* 633; K Korinek, 'Die Beurkundung der Bundesgesetze durch den Bundespräsidenten' in A Mock and H Schambeck (eds), *Verantwortung in unserer Zeit* (Wien, Verlag der Österreichischen Staatsdruckerei, 1990) 121; and more recently, for instance, S Hinghofer-Szalkay, 'Die neuere Auslegung von Art 47 Abs 1 B-VG im Spannungsfeld zu den Wurzeln und Funktionen dieser Bestimmung' (2014) 136 *Juristische Blätter* 28.

[18] Koja (n 17) 13.

of serious and obvious violations of the constitution, such as threatening human dignity or endangering democracy.[19] Initially, however, Federal Presidents have not even considered claiming the power to review a law on substantive constitutional grounds. The former Federal President Rudolf Kirchschläger even explicitly denied the existence of such a power, arguing that he would otherwise block a law that had found a majority in parliament. He would deprive the majority of enacting it at all, as his refusal would effectively terminate the law-making procedures. The constitution does not provide for the National Council to be able to overturn the president's decision nor does it provide for a court to settle the case. The only way forward for parliament, other than changing the law, would be to initiate proceedings at the Constitutional Court to remove the president from office. For the sake of democracy, questions of compliance with the constitution on substantive grounds should therefore be left to the Constitutional Court to answer.[20]

This view, however, was not shared by his (initially conservative) successors. It was due to their claim to play a more active part in domestic politics that they occasionally delayed the process of signing a bill or threatened not to sign it at all. It remains speculation whether a president has influenced legislation by making such a threat in advance, so that parliament would consider his view before passing the law.

In January 2008, however, President Heinz Fischer – the irony not being missed that he was a Social Democrat – denied his signature to a bill[21] already passed by parliament on the grounds that it contained a provision that clearly and openly violated Art 7 of the European Convention on Human Rights (ECHR). The National Council submitted to the Federal President's view and redrafted the bill, omitting the offending provision. Once passed, the bill was subsequently signed by the Federal President. It is interesting that parliament had at no stage (at least officially) doubted the power of the Federal President. It may be asked whether state organs have thereby accepted the Federal President's power to deny signing a law on substantive constitutional grounds.

---

[19] For instance Jahnel (n 17) 633, 639f.

[20] President Rudolf Kirchschläger's view is reported by K Korinek who remarkably argues against this position assuming that Federal Presidents have the duty to review laws on substantive grounds; Korinek, 'Die Beurkundung der Bundesgesetze durch den Bundespräsidenten' in Mock and Schambeck (eds) (n 17) 121, 124. To understand the significance of Kirchschläger's view it is decisive to know that the Constitutional Court would only in very rare cases rescind a whole statute but rather the affected provision(s).

[21] RV 283 BlgNR 23. GP.

In fact, a precedent has been created and time will tell if it will open up a new dimension of presidential power previously not considered.

Should future presidents limit this power to cases in which the violation of the constitution is obvious and clear, the increase of presidential powers would only be marginal, as in most cases the violation of the constitution would be more or less debatable, especially with regard to fundamental rights. It remains to be seen how future presidents will cope. However, presidents did not make a habit of not signing laws that include a retroactive criminal provision. The Second Covid-19 Act (*2. COVID-19-Gesetz*, BGBl I 16/2020), with which a bundle of laws were amended in order to fight the spread of the virus, contained such a retroactive provision in Art 137 para 14 of the Telecommunications Act. Nevertheless, the law was signed by President Alexander Van der Bellen, albeit the provision was not overlooked. It was argued that not having signed the whole bundle of amendments would have been more damaging than the (mild) retroactive effect that might not even have materialised.[22]

C. Accountability of the Federal President

German and Austrian constitutional theory traditionally see the main difference between a monarchy and a republic in the liability of the head of the state.[23] While a monarch would not be liable at all, the president of a republic would be accountable for the performance of her or his function. When Austria became a republic in 1918/20, the constitution provided for the accountability of the Federal President.

The 1920 Constitution adopted an unambiguous concept: politically, the Federal President was not accountable. All of the Federal President's acts had to be countersigned by the Federal Chancellor or the respective Federal minister. By means of their signature, they accepted political responsibility. In the context of the 1920 Constitution, this was conclusive: the Federal President could only act on recommendations and the president's actions needed to be countersigned to enter into force. Legally, the Federal President was nevertheless responsible: the Federal

---

[22] M Moser, 'Gesetz zu COVID-19: Verfassungswidrig, aber notwendig?' Addendum, 25.3.2020, addendum.org/coronavirus/covid-19-gesetz-verfassungswidrig, accessed 11 January 2022.

[23] P Pernthaler, *Allgemeine Staatslehre und Verfassungslehre*, 2nd edn (Wien-New York, Springer, 1996) 164f.

Assembly could sue the Federal President in the Constitutional Court for any alleged culpable breach of the constitution. The Federal Assembly had to convene if either the National Council or the Federal Council so demanded. For such a decision a majority of two-thirds – with half of the members present – in either chamber was needed. If the president was found guilty, the Constitutional Court had only the option to decide on loss of office and – in severe cases – additionally even a temporary loss of political rights (such as the right to vote). Apart from that, the Federal President enjoyed immunity and a legal process against the Federal President was only admissible with the consent of the Federal Assembly.

In 1929, when the direct election of the Federal President was introduced, this concept was slightly altered and provisions pertaining to the political accountability of the Federal President were added.[24] Politically, the president is accountable to the people. Removal from office therefore requires a referendum that has to be initiated by the Federal Assembly following a motion of the National Council. Again, such a motion must be supported by at least two-thirds of the members with half of them present. If the referendum accepts the deposition, the Federal President is removed from office. However, rejection by the referendum counts as a new election of the Federal President (whereby the period of office must not exceed 12 years) and at the same time automatically effects the dissolution of the National Council.

Procedures to remove a Federal President from office have never been initiated. This is not only due to the fact that tensions between parliament and a Federal President never reached a point where such a motion could have duly been considered. It also lies in the way procedures are designed. Neither a decision from the Constitutional Court nor the result of a referendum would be predictable. In particular with regard to the latter, procedures would only make sense if polls suggested that the president might lose the referendum. Otherwise, initiating such procedures might prove suicidal (as the National Council would automatically be dissolved).

As long as a president enjoys public support and especially support by the most influential media, it might even be politically unwise to initiate proceedings against the president before the Constitutional Court. In 2008, for instance, it would have been completely unreasonable to take an action against the Federal President for an alleged breach of

---

[24] Remarkably, however, presidential acts still needed to be countersigned – with one exception, of course: the dismissal of the Federal Chancellor.

the constitution because he had not signed a law that included a provision that violated Art 7 ECHR. First, the violation of Art 7 ECHR was so obvious that nobody could publicly be in favour of this provision. Second, as the president acted on legal advice, he could have hardly been found culpable of breaching the constitution, even if the theory that denies the president the power to review laws on substantive grounds had prevailed in court. A lawsuit would have ended only to the embarrassment of parliament.

In general, it will be apparent that as long as a Federal President enjoys the support of a party which commands at least one-third plus one seat in the National Council, a motion to convene the Federal Assembly in order to take action against the Federal President could always be blocked. Such a president may be tempted to exhaust her or his powers, for instance, the power to refuse signing a law on purported substantive constitutional grounds as there would be no risk of any immediate consequences. The constitution thus provides for a legal framework which – under specific circumstances – offers substantial political powers to the Federal President.[25] The dispute between constitutional law scholars over the extent of presidential powers would therefore be decided on political rather than on legal grounds.

Substantial conflicts between a Federal President and parliament (at least its majority) sooner or later have to be resolved by the people – either in a referendum or in a general election. Therefore, neither the Federal President nor parliament can be certain of who would prevail in the event of a conflict (even polls may deceive). The political and legal significance of the framework described above lies in the aim of avoiding such a conflict escalating. Instead, the conflicting parties should try to find a compromise.

III. THE FEDERAL CABINET

A. The Appointment of the Federal Cabinet

As already mentioned, the Federal Chancellor has to be appointed by the Federal President. As the appointment of the Federal Chancellor does not require a recommendation, the Federal President is legally free to choose any person who is eligible to the National Council. It is merely

---

[25] See earlier in this chapter.

a matter of convention that the Federal President usually invites the leader of the largest party to form a government. The same applies in respect of the custom that the Federal Cabinet offers its resignation after general elections have been held. Its is only on the recommendation of the Federal Chancellor that other cabinet members may be appointed. As a cabinet must enjoy the National Council's confidence, the powers of the Federal President to influence the formation of a government depend on the result of general elections and the composition of parliament. The more split a parliament may be, the more influence on the composition of government the Federal President may gain. The Federal President may even be needed to moderate conflicts between parties. In such a situation, the peaceful transfer of powers from the previous government to its successor may hinge on the president's personal skills, authority and genuine interest in upholding democracy.

The Federal President might refuse the appointment of cabinet members in rare and exceptional cases, but, usually, presidents have followed the recommendations of the Federal Chancellor which, in the case of a coalition government, are based on the parties' agreement. Traditionally, each coalition party has the power to nominate its own candidates once the distribution of ministries has been settled. The other coalition party normally will not interfere. In nominating cabinet members each party will meet its own internal requirements. The Federal Chancellor will therefore not deliberately choose the members of 'her or his' cabinet but recommend candidates according to party agreements and party decisions. This convention was broken twice in recent years. In 2019, the chancellor successfully recommended the dismissal of a minister who was a member of his coalition partner. In 2021, the coalition partner of the chancellor doubted the chancellor's further capacity to perform his duties after allegations of corruption had been brought forward against him. As it would not rule out supporting a motion of no confidence, the chancellor was forced to resign. Both examples demonstrate that conventions developed under the system of consociational democracy seem to be no longer valid, or at least, they can no longer be relied on.

The Federal Cabinet is quorate when half of its members are present (Art 69 para 3 of the Federal Constitution in its 1997 version). It needed the Second Covid-19 Act to formally entrench the principle of unanimity, which previously had only been accepted for historical reasons. Following the demands of the pandemic, the possibility of circular resolutions (without meeting in person) was also enshrined into the constitution.

B. The Powers of the Federal Cabinet

According to the constitution, the Federal Cabinet and the Federal ministers are the heads of the federal administration.[26] They are subordinate to parliament – bound by its laws and accountable to it. From a political point of view, however, the Federal Cabinet and its members are arguably the most powerful organs of the Federation and, thus, the entire republic. The Federal Cabinet as such performs mainly strategic responsibilities. It effectively controls the legislative branch of government, predominantly because of the two reasons already discussed above. First, the most influential officials of the political party (or parties in the case of a coalition government) or their stakeholders usually become members of the Federal Cabinet. That ensures the ongoing support of the majority in parliament, as otherwise the party hierarchy might be overthrown. Should an influential politician lose power or support, that politician would resign from the Cabinet and give way to somebody else. Second, it is the Federal ministers who are in charge of the ministerial bureaucracy that provides the relevant information and expertise needed to draft a bill.

Further, it is the Federal Cabinet that arranges the elections both for the National Council and the Federal President. By means of recommendations, it directs the use of presidential powers and thereby also designs foreign policy. It may decide on the deployment of the Austrian Armed Forces (or delegate this responsibility to a Cabinet member). It is the Federal Minister of the Interior who is in charge of the police forces, which are almost exclusively organised at federal level. Members of the Federal Cabinet represent Austria in the Council of the European Union and thus participate in the European law-making procedures.

The implementation of federal law resides with an individual Federal minister rather than the entire Federal Cabinet. Each Federal minister who is in charge of a portfolio is also the head of a Federal ministry that supports the minister in performing her or his duties. The power of a minister extends over the territory of the whole Federation, but is limited to certain matters, thus introducing a departmental system (*Ressortsystem*). The number of Federal ministers and the powers allocated to them are determined by the Federal Ministries Act.[27]

It is quite common for the Federal Ministries Act to be amended in the aftermath of the formation of a new government, as ministries

---

[26] See Art 69 of the Federal Constitution.
[27] *Bundesministeriengesetz*, BGBl 76/1986 in the applicable version.

may not only be renamed but also re-organised. The allocation of responsibilities between ministries often changes on that occasion, especially when representatives from other parties are taking over. Such strategies will be chosen foremost to cut 'networks' within the ministries and the civil service that might jeopardise the enactment of new policies.

C. Instructing the Administration

Federal ministers may control the entire federal administration within their fields of responsibility by means of instructions or directions. Instructions may be issued as general instructions, for instance, guiding the implementation of laws in accordance with the policy of the Federal minister or they may relate to an individual case. Instructions do not count as 'administrative acts' as they lack an external impact – by definition, they cannot interfere with substantive rights and are therefore, in general, not subject to review by administrative courts. Constitutional and administrative theory has nevertheless paid special attention to illegal instructions,[28] mainly when they were politically motivated and came from Federal ministers. Politicians can influence law enforcement and may do so on political grounds. Officials have to comply even with unlawful instructions but are entitled by law to demand such an instruction in writing. This rule was clearly designed in a pre-digital era. Nowadays, as the internal communication of the administration is done electronically and largely via e-mail, instructions will generally be issued in writing. Documentations of e-mail communication or text messages between politicians and the administration or within the administration that had to be submitted to parliamentary inquiry committees or even criminal courts have occasionally been leaked to the public. They sometimes display an astonishing brazenness in disregarding the law or moral standards. However, the Federal Constitution would allow officials to refuse to comply with instructions if they were not issued by a responsible authority or if compliance would infringe the criminal code.

---

[28] G Kucsko-Stadlmayer, 'Legalitätsprinzip und Weisungsgebundenheit des Beamten' in R Walter and C Jabloner (eds), *Strukturprobleme des öffentlichen Rechts* (Wien, Manz, 1995) 77; R Novak, 'Weisungsprinzip und Verwaltungsbegriff' in H Schäffer (ed), *Im Dienst an Staat und Recht* (Wien, Manz, 1983) 359; H Walter, 'Zur Ablehnung einer strafgesetzwidrigen Weisung' (1983) *Österreichische Gemeindezeitung* 546.

The idea is that instructions rule the entire administration, create a hierarchical system and thus ensure the overall influence of a minister answerable to parliament. This forms an essential part of Austrian democracy, at least in theory. Hans Kelsen,[29] for instance, has argued that only a hierarchical administration strictly bound by instructions may ensure that the will of the democratic law-making authority is enacted. Instructions or at least the possibility to be bound by them underpins the administration with democratic legitimation. Authorities that operate outside the system of ministerial responsibility are therefore problematic with regard to democratic legitimation and accountability.

Nevertheless, quite a few such authorities have existed and still exist in Austria, although the constitutional framework has been amended over the course of time. Independent authorities may be established by a specific constitutional law or provision (for example, the Independent Political Parties Transparency Panel[30] is set up by a constitutional provision) or by an ordinary law on the basis of Art 20 para 2 of the Federal Constitution[31] that lists eight different categories of such authorities (a state constitution may even add further categories). This offers vast possibilities for setting up independent authorities. To compensate for the lack of democratic legitimation, laws establishing authorities under Art 20 para 2 of the Federal Constitution must provide for supervision by the highest federal or state authorities. As a minimum, they would have to have the right to information on all the authority's administrative business. In some cases, supervision must also comprise the right to dismiss members of independent authorities on certain serious grounds. Additionally, Art 52 para 1a of the Federal Constitution empowers the responsible committee of the National Council to summon the heads of such authorities and to question them on all their administrative business.

From the 1970s onwards, numerous independent tribunals have been established in order to meet the requirements of Art 6 ECHR, as the ECtHR had demanded that – within the scope of Art 6 ECHR – an independent tribunal had to hear the facts of a case and not just review its legal aspects, as the Austrian system of judicial review would

---

[29] H Kelsen, *The Essence and Value of Democracy*, ed by N Urbinati and CI Accetti, trans by B Graf (Lanham, Maryland, Rowman and Littlefield Publishers, 2013, Kindle Edition) 80f.

[30] See ch 2.

[31] This – renewed – system was introduced by a 2008 amendment (BGBl I 2/2008) and was further amended in 2010 (BGBl I 50/2010) and 2012 (BGBl I 51/2012).

have provided for. All these tribunals were abolished in 2014 when the two-tier system of judicial review was introduced. As administrative courts are encouraged to decide on the merit of the case rather than repeal an administrative decision, cabinet ministers can no longer influence the application of a law in (many) individual cases. The introduction of the two-tier judicial review therefore, has to some extent limited the power of the cabinet and therefore also its responsibility vis-à-vis parliament. Powers have been shifted to the judicial branch of government.[32]

Other authorities that do not operate under instructions of the state authorities are established within the framework of municipal autonomy and other concepts of self-administration which allow the formation of autonomous bodies. The lack of democratic legitimacy of these authorities has to be compensated by direct or indirect elections by the members of these autonomous bodies.[33]

Independent authorities and autonomous bodies counterbalance the power of the Federal Cabinet to a certain extent. In practice, however, this may be overshadowed by the party system and thus by party loyalty. Federal ministers who are entitled to appoint members of independent authorities may exercise their responsibilities in the interest of political parties. Elections to the organs of autonomous bodies, for instance municipalities, may be won by candidates chosen by political parties. Members of the organs of the (autonomous) social insurance bodies are delegated by social partner institutions, again guaranteeing the influence of the political parties affiliated with these institutions.

D. The Accountability of the Federal Cabinet and Federal Ministers

On the one hand, it may be argued that the Federal Cabinet is accountable to the Federal President. The Federal President has the power to dismiss the Federal Chancellor and the entire Federal Cabinet and may dismiss Cabinet members on the recommendation of the Federal Chancellor. Theoretically, the Federal President could dismiss the Federal Cabinet at any time she or he wishes to do so, for instance, when the Federal President has lost confidence in the Federal Cabinet or is not satisfied with its performance. In reality, this has never happened, although during the 2021 government crisis this possibility was at least briefly mentioned

---

[32] See for further details ch 6.
[33] See ch 5 for the principles of self-administration.

on some news programmes: the Federal President would have had the power to dismiss the chancellor Sebastian Kurz as allegations of corruption were brought forward against him and the Federal Chancellery as well as the Party's headquarters were searched. Only on the recommendation of the chancellor may the Federal President dismiss a Federal minister.

On the other hand, the Federal Cabinet mainly needs the support of parliament or, to be more precise, the majority of its members and thus the governing political parties. As already noted, the Federal Cabinet and cabinet members respectively are answerable to the National Council and the Federal Council. The right to interrogation and the power to pass a motion of no confidence have already been dealt with in Chapter 3.

Should the National Council have evidence that a Federal minister has culpably violated the law in performing the minister's official activities, it may pass a motion to prosecute the Federal minister before the Constitutional Court which, in turn, may decide upon loss of office.

In practice, the National Council has never voted to prosecute a member of the Federal Cabinet and has only once passed a motion of no confidence in the Second Republic. Normally, as a majority is required for such a motion, party discipline effectively prevents the governing parties from supporting the opposition in trying to remove a cabinet member from office. Federal ministers would not offer their resignation in cases where irregularities have been discovered within the realm of administration they are entrusted with. Although opposition parties may demand a minister to step down in such cases, it is generally held that the minister should only be liable for personal (and culpable) misdemeanours, thus jeopardising the idea of political liability. Further, no code of conduct has been established within the Austrian political system according to which a minister would have to resign. It is probably due to the catholic heritage that in the view of the public and the media, a penitent sinner has to be forgiven.

Therefore, there can be no doubt that the law on the political and legal liability of the Federal Cabinet is very ineffective. But this does not imply that there is no liability at all. What in practice works is the liability of cabinet members to their own party. Whenever the party feels that a minister who has somehow failed will affect the party's chances in the next general election, it will 'persuade' the minister to resign. The state of the public mood, gauged from opinion polls, may be the decisive spur for a party to act.

IV. THE CIVIL SERVICE

Federal ministers are supported by large bureaucracies: the federal ministries. It was a traditional feature of the Austrian constitution – as well as a heritage of the former monarchy – that the overwhelming majority of the staff members were appointed by means of an administrative ruling. These civil servants, employed under public law (*Beamte*), enjoyed a life-long tenure that could only be terminated as a result of a disciplinary hearing, which would be conducted only in exceptional cases. The legal framework, shaped under Joseph II, should ensure loyalty to the state (and – in a more modern sense – not to a political party), and to the law, without any inclination to corruption. To prevent corruption, advancements strictly followed the principle of seniority. Civil servants experienced a moderate but steady pay-rise and were rewarded for their service by a rather generous old-age pension. They filled all the core positions of the Austrian administration and they survived outgoing and incoming governments. Only a small number of mainly personal secretaries to the minister could be brought into office by a new minister, forming the so-called ministerial office (*Ministerbüro*).

The idea of an impartial civil service had already been compromised by political parties, as ministers were responsible for appointing civil servants. In fact, party membership or the affiliation to a political party – predominantly the People's Party and the Social Democrats – could be sometimes just helpful, sometimes important and sometimes even decisive. Some civil servants were no longer loyal to the state and the law but rather to the political party to which they owed their job. Filling job vacancies in the public sphere (which was, at least after World War II, not restricted to the civil service, but comprised chambers, the social insurance bodies and the nationalised banks and industry) was part of the feudal strategies of political parties.[34] Disciplinary procedures were seen as a toothless instrument to dismiss civil servants who misused their life-long tenure.

With the emergence of concepts of New Public Management, the public employment of civil servants became somehow outdated in the eyes of the public and, foremost, politicians. Moreover, with the increase in life expectancy, the old-age pension scheme proved too costly. Although initially not mentioned in the constitution, civil servants could also be employed by contract (*Vertragsbedienstete*). This seemed

[34] See ch 2.

to be admissible on the retrospective argument that civil servants had already been employed by contract in 1919 and the 1920 Constitution did not explicitly abolish this possibility.[35] Contracts may be terminated, although only on the – rather narrow – grounds listed by the relevant statutes. In reality, it may therefore not be that easy and still unusual to terminate such a contract, but the possibility does exist. In 2008, however, an amendment incorporated this category of civil service in the constitution[36] as it became the general policy, in large parts of the administration, only to employ officials by contract. This may be a more modern approach but the idea of a civil service loyal to the state and not to political parties has been more or less abandoned.

About three decades ago, a law was enacted that required the public advertising of certain (mainly higher) public functions in case of vacancies. Independent Commissions were established to assess the applications. These assessments are not binding on the minister or the responsible head of a unit but have to be duly considered.[37]

Although this law clearly provides for a more impartial procedure of appointing civil servants, it has not effectively cut the influence of the political parties as neither the procedure nor its result may be fully reviewed by law courts. Applicants therefore have no legal remedy available in cases where they feel that a less qualified person was appointed or a person was only appointed because of that person's party membership. Only if they could prove that they were discriminated against gender, religion or ethnicity would some mild compensation apply.

The law on appointing civil servants therefore effectively allows governing parties to stabilise or enhance their influence on the civil service.

V. FOREIGN AFFAIRS AND EUROPEAN MEMBERSHIP

The ongoing process of 'internationalisation' or 'globalisation' (although this may be interrupted, halted or partly revised due to the Covid-19 pandemic) and Austria's accession to the European Union have further contributed to strengthening the power of the Federal Cabinet at the

---

[35] R Thienel, *Öffentlicher Dienst und Kompetenzverteilung* (Wien, Verlag der Österreichischen Staatsdruckerei, 1990).

[36] BGBl I 2/2008.

[37] LK Adamovich, B-C Funk, G Holzinger and SL Frank, *Österreichisches Staatsrecht*, Vol 4, 2nd edn (Wien, Verlag Österreich, 2017) 119f.

expense of parliament. As already mentioned, formally it is the Federal President who represents the republic externally and therefore may issue statements that are binding on the republic under international law and conclude international treaties. But as the Federal President may only act on the recommendation of the Federal Cabinet (and/or a Cabinet Minister) in substance, it is the Federal Cabinet that basically designs Austria's external policy.

A. International Treaties

With regard to the federal system and especially the division of legislative powers between the Federation and the states, it is remarkable that in Austria, it is first and foremost the Federation which has the power to conclude international treaties. In doing so it is not bound by the allocation of powers between the Federation and the states. Consequently, the autonomous sphere of the states may be affected or states may even be bound to take measures to implement an international treaty. In any such case the Federation must give the states the opportunity to express their views before the treaty is concluded. If the treaty resolves matters that fall within the autonomous sphere of the states, the approval of the Federal Council is also required. Nevertheless, it will be the Federal Cabinet that will monitor the measures taken by the states to implement an international treaty (Art 16 para 5 of the Federal Constitution). The Federal Cabinet and the responsible Federal minister respectively may even be entitled to instruct the state governor.

Political treaties and treaties modifying or complementing existing parliamentary statutes (*gesetzesändernde* or *gesetzesergänzende Staatsverträge*) and international treaties amending the fundamental treaties of the European Union may only be concluded with parliament's approval (Art 50 of the Federal Constitution). Approval must be obtained before the conclusion (ratification) of the treaty. According to a definition initially established by the German Federal Constitutional Court and adopted by Austrian constitutional theory,[38] political treaties are treaties that substantially and directly affect the existence of a state, its territorial integrity, its independence, its position among states, its political influence on other states or the order within the community of

---

[38] H Mayer, G Kucsko-Stadlmayer and K Stöger, *Bundesverfassungsrecht*, 11th edn (Wien, Manz, 2015) 117.

states. Treaties are to be considered to modify or complement existing parliamentary statutes if their content required regulation by means of a statute. Under Austrian law, the content of a treaty would require regulation by means of a parliamentary statute if there was no legal basis that was sufficiently clear and detailed in the sense of Art 18 of the Federal Constitution.[39]

Until 2008, it was quite common to adopt an international treaty or even several provisions of an international treaty in the rank of constitutional law, thus adding to the fragmentation of constitutional law. The ECHR and its additional protocols, to name a prominent example, were adopted in the rank of constitutional law (and were made directly applicable).

This has been changed by the 2008 amendment.[40] According to this amendment, all newly concluded international treaties need ratification by an ordinary federal law only. Should the international obligation ensuing from this treaty make a constitutional provision necessary or should the National Council wish the subject matter to be constitutionally entrenched, it would have to enact a separate constitutional law covering the precise subject matter (preferably before the state treaty is concluded).

International treaties that affect the borders of the Austrian Republic (Art 3 of the Federal Constitution) are to be ratified with a two-thirds majority in the National Council with at least half of its members present, and need the consent of the states affected. International treaties amending the fundamental treaties of the European Union (primary law) need the consent of both the National and the Federal Council, which has to be given with a two-thirds majority with at least half of the members present in each chamber. Treaties amending European Union law may also be subject to a referendum.

Although parliament participates in the proceedings to conclude and adopt international treaties, it seems obvious that it has almost no influence on their substance as negotiations on the international level will be carried out by a Federal minister or ministry officials and diplomats respectively. It is, in fact, hard to imagine that the majority in parliament would not support the ratification of a treaty once the responsible minister has given consent. With regard to the European Constitutional Treaty and the Lisbon Treaty respectively, it became quite clear that

---

[39] For the reading of Art 18 of the Federal Constitution, see ch 3.
[40] BGBl I 2/2008.

parliament would not prevent ratification. Opponents to these treaties therefore tried to get them submitted to a referendum, claiming that they would constitute a further 'total revision' of the constitution[41] – a strategy that ultimately did not succeed. For the future, however, ratifications of changes to the treaties of the European Union may become more cumbersome as the People's Party and the Social Democrats no longer have a two-thirds majority together (at least not at the time of writing in Spring 2022). Therefore, it would need the consent of one or two smaller parties, which could see that as an opportunity to demand other changes of the constitution. For instance, the strict mandate foreseen in the constitution for Austria's participation in the European Stability Mechanism (ESM) had to be established to obtain the consent of the Green Party. Also with regard to the domestic situation in Austria it is quite understandable why the European Union currently shies away from changing its fundamental treaties.

Nevertheless, it has to be noted that according to the 2008 amendment, treaties reforming the fundamental treaties of the European Union enjoy a special position: Although they are not defined as 'constitutional laws', their adoption needs the same quorum as a constitutional law. Apart from that, they may be submitted to a referendum, regardless of whether this would be mandatory. All political parties in Austria have so far vowed to submit a treaty that would provide for the accession of Turkey to the European Union to a referendum. With the defensive wars against the Ottoman Empire in the sixteenth and seventeenth centuries still present in the collective memory of the Austrian population, the result of such a referendum would be highly uncertain.

B. Bodies of International Organisations

Adding further to the strengthening of the power of the executive branch of government at the expense of the legislative branch are bodies of international organisations. Many of them have increasingly been allocated the power to issue general or individual legal acts that are binding on their member states and in some cases even on their citizens.[42]

---

[41] A Schramm, 'Gesamtänderung der Bundesverfassung durch die EU-Verfassung?' (2006) 61 *Zeitschrift für Öffentliches Recht* 41.

[42] S Schmahl, 'Die Internationalen und die Supranationalen Organisationen' in W Graf Vitzthum and A Proelß (eds), *Völkerrecht*, 8th edn (Berlin, De Gruyter, 2019) 319, 328ff.

Where it applies, Austria would be represented in such a body by members of the executive branch of government and the administration respectively.

Initially, Austrian constitutional law made no reference to decisions or acts of organs of international organisations as a source of (domestic) law. It has been, therefore, necessary to incorporate constitutional provisions into all international treaties relating to Austria's accession to such an international organisation.[43] A 1981 amendment to the Federal Constitution introduced a general constitutional basis entitling the Republic of Austria to transfer specific (single) powers to intergovernmental organisations and – in its currently applicable version – also to their authorities, as well as to other states. Surprisingly, the constitution also explicitly provides for the transfer of (single) powers of foreign states or international organisations to Austrian authorities.

C. European Union

Austria's accession to the European Union has triggered another power shift from the legislative branch to the executive branch of government. With the one major exception that the Austrian representatives in the European Parliament are elected by the Austrian people, it is mainly the Federal Cabinet that is in charge of participating in the law-making bodies of the European Union on behalf of Austria and that is also in charge of nominating the (Austrian) members to various European organs.[44]

In performing the latter responsibility, the Cabinet shall reach an agreement with the Main Standing Committee of the National Council regarding the nomination of the members of the Commission, the CJEU, the Court of Auditors and the Board of Directors of the European Investment Bank. The constitution does not explicitly provide for a hearing of possible candidates at the Main Standing Committee and, therefore, various governments so far have denied such a hearing. Consequently, the committee has only little influence on the final decision as the government will always have a majority in the Main Standing Committee where parties are represented proportionally.

---

[43] R Walter, *Österreichisches Bundesverfassungsrecht* (Wien, Manz, 1972) 175f.
[44] See Art 23c para 1 of the Federal Constitution.

The influence of the social partners is guaranteed as the Federal Cabinet is bound to ask for their proposals when nominating members of the Economic and Social Committee; the nomination of members to the Committee of Regions and their deputies is effected on the basis of proposals from the states, as well as the Austrian Association of Cities and Towns and the Austrian Association of Municipalities. But, nevertheless, it is the Federal Cabinet that decides.

VI. THE FEDERAL BUDGET

Although the federal budget has to be approved by the National Council, it falls explicitly under the responsibility of the Federal Cabinet to draft the Federal Finance Act (*Bundesfinanzgesetz*) and submit it to the National Council. Traditionally, the Federal Finance Act, containing estimates of the revenue and the outlays of the Federation for an upcoming fiscal year, was drawn up on cash-flow based accounting standards, already introduced in the eighteenth century. In the 1990s these standards seemed to be outdated as they did not allow for the effective costs of the administration to be estimated, because not all non-cash expenses were represented. Further, the principle of annuity led to adverse effects: money that was not spent before the end of the fiscal year expired. It therefore used to be common administrative practice to spend all leftover money before the expiry of the fiscal year, irrespective of whether that made sense. Administrations that did not act in this way not only lost the money, but the level of expenditure allocated to them in subsequent Federal Finance Acts was reduced on the grounds that they had been proven to manage on less money. As the budget was extremely detailed and fund transfers were only admissible to a very narrow margin, on the one hand, money was often spent on goods or services no-one really needed but, on the other hand, was not available to cover necessary expenditures. This clearly undermined the constitutional principle of thriftiness, explicitly provided for by Art 126b para 5 of the Federal Constitution.

In the 1990s, federal constitutional provisions were introduced in the Federal Budget Act 1986 (*Bundeshaushaltsgesetz 1986*, BGBl 213/1986) to allow administrative units to manage their spending policy more effectively under certain circumstances. They were allocated lump sum appropriations, allowing for internal transfers of funds and forwarding leftover money into the next fiscal year(s). As these experiments seemed to be successful, a systematic reform of the law on the fiscal budget was envisaged.[45] This reform was introduced in two steps, resulting in the Federal Budget Act 2013 (*Bundeshaushaltsgesetz 2013*, BGBl I 139/2009).

In a first step, implemented in 2009, the procedural framework was altered. The Federal Cabinet not only has to draft a Federal Finance Act but also, by 30 April of each year, it must draft a Federal Finance Framework Act (FFFA – *Bundesfinanzrahmengesetz*) that covers the subsequent four financial years and submit it to the National Council. The FFFA limits the allocation of funds for the entire administration. It is binding on the Federal Cabinet when it drafts the subsequent Federal Finance Act, although exceptions apply.

The FFFA offers a comprehensive and easily accessible overview to the economic powers of the state. Thus, the relevant figures may also be seen as a part of the efficient constitution as the economic power effectively limits political power. According to the Ministry of Finance, the ordinary federal budget amounts to approximately €80 billion from which almost half is spent on the social welfare system.[46] An additional budget manages the financial debts and has risen to almost €200 billion.[47] Anyhow, a comparison with the private sector shows the rather weak economic might of a small country: the balance sheet total of the two biggest Austrian banks amount to €245 billion and €152 billion respectively,[48] notwithstanding the economic powers of 'global market players'. Even if theories on sovereignty may suggest differently, the political room to manoeuvre for a small country like Austria is effectively limited by its modest financial power.

At least 10 weeks before the expiry of the fiscal year (which happens to coincide with the calendar year), the Federal Cabinet is obliged to submit a draft version of the Federal Finance Act for the subsequent fiscal year (or the subsequent two fiscal years). If the Federal Cabinet fails to submit a draft on time, the National Council might not be able to adopt a federal budget for the upcoming year. To avoid a complete standstill of the administration, the constitution provides for revenues to

[45] G Steger, 'Austria's Budget Reform: How to Create Consensus for a Decisive Change of Fiscal Rules' (2010) 10 *OECD Journal on Budgeting* 7, 8.

[46] bmf.gv.at/themen/budget/das-budget/budgetarchiv/budget-2018-2019.html, accessed 11 January 2022.

[47] www.oebfa.at/budget-und-schulden/finanzschulden.html, accessed 11 January 2022.

[48] See the following business reports: www.erstegroup.com/de/investoren/berichte/finanzberichte, accessed 11 January 2022; www.rbinternational.com/de/investoren/berichte/geschaeftsberichte.html, accessed 11 January 2022.

be raised according to existing (tax) laws and outlays to be made on the basis of the previous Federal Finance Act. Outlays are not supposed to exceed the levels of the previous act.

Complying with the second step of the fiscal reform, implemented in 2013, the fiscal act is no longer based on eighteenth century accounting standards. In its Art 51 para 8, the constitution provides for different principles: out-put orientation, in particular also respecting the objective of gender equality, transparency, efficiency and verity in depicting the financial situation of the Federation. The International Public Accounting Standards serve as a model. Outputs have to be defined by each administrative unit. It has to give reasons for its choices, demonstrate how it will achieve them and define benchmarks against which their performance could be assessed.[49] Overachievements may be rewarded, failures may be sanctioned. This mechanism allows for a tighter grip on the administration by the Federal Cabinet and, most notably, the Federal Minister of Finance.

Further, the federal budget must aim to secure sustainable budgetary practice (Art 13 para 2 of the Federal Constitution). Federation, states and municipalities have to coordinate their budgets to implement these aims. By introducing the principle of secure sustainable budgetary practice by means of the 2008 constitutional amendment, the Austrian constitution has incorporated the requirements imposed by European law. The principle of secure sustainable budgetary practice is to be defined by the convergence criteria of the Maastricht Treaty. According to Art 126 of the Treaty on the Functioning of the European Union (TFEU), Member States should avoid excessive government deficits. Reference criteria that consider government deficit and government debts in relation to GDP are applicable (Austria's GDP would currently amount to approximately €400 billion[50]). The reference values were established in TFEU Protocol number 12 and constitute a maximum of 3 per cent of GDP for the net deficit and a maximum of 60 per cent for government debt. As the Maastricht criteria apply not to the federal budget only but to the total budget of the republic, state budgets must be included in the account. The European Commission has to monitor the development of Austria's budgetary situation. Thus, the Maastricht criteria effectively

---

[49] Steger (n 45) 17f.
[50] statistik.at/statistiken/volkswirtschaft-und-oeffentliche-finanzen/volkswirtschaftliche-gesamtrechnungen/bruttoinlandsprodukt-und-hauptaggregate, accessed 26 July 2022.

curtail domestic policies on the budget. Austria had to partly ignore these criteria to manage the economic crisis ensuing from the 2008 credit crunch and also during the Covid-19 pandemic, when these criteria were, at least temporarily, suspended.

VII. E-GOVERNMENT

The Austrian government has effectively introduced and promoted the use of digital information technologies in various fields of administration. The websites of Austrian ministries provide a lot of information and sometimes also legal advice. As part of the process, forms may be downloaded, applications may be filed electronically and, in particular, tax declarations may be submitted online. In some cases, administrative acts are distributed by electronic services. The Covid-19 pandemic has further stimulated the development of digitalisation of public administration to maintain business during several lockdowns. For instance, online-hearings before courts were made possible, video-conferences could replace meetings, etc.[51] Most of these innovations were brought in by amending ordinary laws. In one case, however, in which Austria became a forerunner, namely the publication of federal laws, an amendment to the constitution was needed.

It has always been the responsibility of the Federal Chancellor to publish federal laws. Until 31 December 2003, this was done by producing a printed version of the Federal Law Gazette (*Bundesgesetzblatt*). Nevertheless, the Federal Chancellery also started to publish the law on its website. But this was only meant as a service of the Federal Chancellery: the publication in the printed version of the Federal Law Gazette remained the only authentic one. That changed according to the 2003 amendment of the constitution and the Federal Law Gazette Act (*Bundesgesetzblattgesetz*, BGBl I 100/2003).

As of 1 January 2004, authentic publication of federal laws (and other legal provisions) is exclusively online.[52] Laws are accessible under the address www.ris.bka.gv.at and they can be accessed from any part of

---

[51] See, for instance, Art 3 of the Administrative Covid-19 Accompanying Act (*Verwaltungsrechtliches COVID-19-Begleitgesetz*, BGBl I 16/2020); Art 3 of the First Judicial Covid-19 Accompanying Act (*1. COVID-19-Justiz-Begleitgesetz*, BGBl I 16/2020); Art 69 para 3 of the Federal Constitution.

[52] M Stelzer, 'The Online Law Gazette in Austria' in S Flogaitis et al (eds), *E-Government and E-Democracy* (London, Esperia Publication, 2006) 283.

the world. It is crucial to know that only one of three versions provided is authentic. When its symbol is selected, a security check is performed. If it is successful, a safety certificate appears stating that the text has been electronically signed by a public servant to the Federal Chancellery and that the sequence of certificates can be traced back to a root certificate.

In the traditional system of publication, the law entered into force at the end of the day when the relevant issue of the Federal Law Gazette was edited and delivered (unless the law provided otherwise). As there is no such delivery within the online publication system, the law becomes legally binding at the end of the first day when access to it is granted. The electronically published documents must be accessible to the public and obtainable in the authentic version on a permanent basis. 'Permanent', by interpretation, does not mean 'at any given time': it is admissible for access to be temporarily denied due to maintenance work or software upgrades. If access is denied for a longer period, laws must be published in the traditional manner. It is not quite clear how this should be managed. The traditional system was based on subscribers to the printed copies of the Federal Law Gazette, but there are no subscribers under the current system.

Additionally, 'permanent' means that access has to be guaranteed for all the years to come. How this constitutional prerequisite can be met by the Austrian government is still hard to see. The online publication of federal law is based on the assumption that the World Wide Web as we know it will basically exist forever. But as the Austrian government has no influence on this issue, the validity of all federal laws published after 1 January 2004 depends on technical and political developments that Austria cannot control. According to the rather strict jurisprudence of the Constitutional Court regarding the publication of laws, a severe disruption to the accessibility of the authentic versions of the text would probably mean that all laws affected would have to be passed by parliament again. The chaos that would emerge from such a situation is almost impossible to imagine. However, the Constitutional Court has not addressed these problems, at least so far.

From the perspective of this chapter, which deals with the increase of power of the Federal Cabinet, another aspect may even be more important. It is in the hands of the Federal Chancellor to uphold Austria's legal system as far as laws that have been published since January 2004 are concerned. Technically speaking, it would be fairly easy to abolish all these laws or only specific laws by denying permanent access. Although there does not seem to be an imminent danger that a Federal Chancellor might misuse this power, there can be no doubt that the new system has effectively allocated to the Federal Chancellor a power previously unheard of.

VIII. NATIONALISED INDUSTRY

Although it is partly history, the responsibility to administer nationalised industries contributed decisively to the power of the Federal Cabinet and, moreover, to the power of political parties. While mail and railway services were already nationalised under the monarchy, comprehensive programmes to nationalise large parts of the industry, especially in the steel producing sector, were only implemented after World War II. This was done basically for two reasons: first, the private sector was not strong enough financially to rebuild Austria's infrastructure and industry after the war. Nationalisation was seen as a means to direct money from the European Recovery Programme to rebuild Austria's main industry. Second, and allegedly on the advice of the Americans, it was also considered to be a means to prevent the Soviets from seizing assets that were held to be 'German Property'.

In 1946, a first Nationalisation Act[53] was passed nationalising major banks as well as the steel, chemical and petrol producing industry. In 1947, a second Nationalisation Act[54] followed, pertaining to electric power producing companies. Until 1967, the Federal Chancellor and/or various Federal ministers directly represented the republic as the owner of all these companies. In 1967, this task was transferred to a trust company, established by law. Initially this was a company with licensed liability (*Österreichische Industrieverwaltungs GesmbH*), but its legal form has been subject to various changes. Regardless of its legal form, the company has always been controlled by Federal ministers. The shares of the current stock company, for instance, are all owned by the Federation. Therefore, the general meeting that elects the supervisory board (or two thirds of its members as one third will be held by the representatives of the employees) consist only of representatives of the republic, hence of Federal ministers, in that case the Minister of Finance. With the cabinet and cabinet ministers in charge, political parties, predominantly the People's Party and the Social Democrats, controlled vast fields of the

---

[53] *Verstaatlichungsgesetz*, BGBl 168/1946.
[54] *2. Verstaatlichungsgesetz*, BGBl 81/1947.

industry in addition to the administrative sector where they could hand out jobs and management careers.

Until the 1970s, the profits of nationalised industry could be used to augment the national state budget. In the 1970s, the public sector served as an instrument to tackle rates of unemployment. Although initially successful, the policy contributed to structural problems that became visible in the 1980s, when nationalised industry had to be generously subsidised from public revenue. As a consequence, a privatisation process was initiated and parts of the industry, such as the two major banks, were sold. A law enacted in 2000 provided explicitly for the Austrian Industry Holding plc to privatise the remaining parts and this process is still ongoing. Since 2015, the holding company may no longer act on its own as privatisations need to be ordered by the Federal Cabinet.[55]

Moreover, the process of privatisation was further accelerated by Austria's accession to the European Union. Within the fields governed by EU laws, such as the postal and telecommunication services, the electricity, broadcasting and railway industries, Austria has implemented the legal framework provided by the relevant EU directives.[56] This triggered the need to establish a new type of independent authority – the regulators which have to promote the transition from former government monopolies to open markets. Regulators may be supervised by the Federal Cabinet (and the responsible Federal minister respectively) and their heads may be summoned by the responsible committee of the National Council and be questioned on all the regulative administrative business.

The demise of nationalised industry and the ensuing privatisation process which was carried out against the stiff opposition of (mostly) Social Democrats and the Trade Unions effectively robbed the political system of some spheres of influence. In the remaining fields, however, nothing has changed. A survey[57] demonstrates that between 1995 and 2010 in 719 cases out of 1242 top positions in state-owned enterprises were filled with party members or party affiliates. It comes as no surprise that it were mainly the governing parties – the People's Party, the Social Democrats and between 2000 and 2006 also the Freedom Party and the

---

[55] See Art 8 of the amendment to the ÖIAG-Act 2000 (*ÖIAG-Gesetz 2000*, BGBl 24/2000 as amended by BGBl I 37/2015).

[56] See also Adamovich et al (n 37) 328ff.

[57] L Ennser-Jedenastik, 'Die parteipolitische Besetzung von Spitzenfunktionen in österreichischen Staatsunternehmen: Eine quantitative Analyse' (2013) 42 *Österreichische Zeitschrift für Politikwissenschaft* 125.

Alliance (for the) Future Austria respectively – that took advantage of 'patronage appointments'. Replacing lost spheres of influence, filling positions in regulators have offered a new field of 'patronage appointments'. It may prove significant that the 2021 government crisis somehow emerged from inquiries into corruption allegations which in turn were connected with patronage appointments by the 2017 conservative/far-right government.[58]

IX. CONCLUSION

The highest executive authorities of the Federation are the Federal President and the Federal Cabinet. The Federal Cabinet holds most of the political powers in the republic. Depending on the domestic political situation, however, the Federal President may have a more decisive role in the formation of the Federal Cabinet. With regard to using these competences, the stability of the political system until the 1980s gave little or no room at all to manoeuvre; however, things then started to change slightly. In the 2019 and 2021 government crisis the Federal President played an important part in moderating partisan disputes and used his powers to pacify the conflict rather than to escalate it. These conflicts demonstrated that the attitude with which a president holds office may make a difference.

The Federal ministers direct the whole Federal administration and decisively influence the substance of the laws enacted by parliament. The more these laws are based on or overridden by international treaties, the more the power of the executive branch of government is strengthened. This is especially true with regard to the laws of the European Union. As the Federal Cabinet is normally composed of the leaders and most influential members of the governing parties, they also may ensure the influence of the political parties in all their fields of responsibility. Only recently has the introduction of a two-tier administrative jurisdiction shifted some powers in implementing laws from the executive to the judicial branch of government.

---

[58] In 2022 the public discovered that the spheres of influence are normally agreed between the chairpersons of coalition partners and are hidden in secret side letters to the coalition agreements, see Der Standard, 28 January 2022, www.derstandard.at/story/2000132943334/sideletter-zeigt-wie-sich-oevp-und-fpoe-posten-im-staat, accessed 11 February 2022.

Within the civil service and the nationalised industry, party membership and/or party affiliation was and is more often than not decisive for
a career. Privatisation of large parts of the nationalised industry has
reduced party influence in some areas, while still giving parties ample
possibilities to patronage appointments in others.

FURTHER READING

Adamovich, LK, Funk, B-C, Holzinger, G and Frank, SL, *Österreichisches Staatsrecht*, Vol 4, 2nd edn (Wien, Verlag Österreich, 2017).

Holzinger, G and Frank, SL, 'Die Organisation der Verwaltung' in Holzinger, G et al (eds), *Österreichische Verwaltungslehre*, 3rd edn (Wien, Verlag Österreich, 2013) 81.

Lederer, G, 'Young Austrians and the Election of Kurt Waldheim' (1988) 9 *Political Psychology* 633.

Lindermuth, P, 'Das Recht der Staatsverträge nach der Verfassungsbereinigung' (2009) 64 *Zeitschrift für Öffentliches Recht* 299.

Steger, G, 'Austria's Budget Reform: How to Create Consensus for a Decisive Change of Fiscal Rules' (2010) 10 *OECD Journal on Budgeting* 7.

Stiefel, D, *Verstaatlichung und Privatisierung in Österreich* (Köln, Böhlau Verlag, 2011).

Tálos, E and Fink, M, 'The Welfare State in Austria' in Vivekanandan, B and Kurian, H (eds), *Welfare States and the Future* (Basingstoke-New York, Palgrave Macmillan, 2005) 131.

Tóth, B and Czernin, H (eds), *1986: Das Jahr, das Österreich Veränderte* (Wien, Czernin, 2006).

Welan, M, 'Der Bundespräsident im System der österreichischen Bundesverfassung' in Schefbeck, G (ed), *75 Jahre Bundesverfassung* (Wien, Verlag Österreich, 1995) 483.

——, 'Regierungsbildung und B-VG' in Hammer, S et al (eds), *Demokratie und sozialer Rechtsstaat in Europa* (Wien, WUV, 2004) 434.

Wimmer, N and Kahl, A, *Die öffentlichen Unternehmen im freien Markt* (Wien, Manz, 2001).

5

Federalism and Autonomous Public Bodies

Introduction – Concept of Austrian Federalism – Allocation of Powers (Competences) – State Legislation – Indirect Federal Administration and the Role of the State Governor – Municipal Government and Autonomous Public Bodies – Conclusion

I. INTRODUCTION

THIS CHAPTER DEALS with the vertical division of powers under the constitution. First, with reference to the historical and theoretical background we observe how Austria under its constitution was formulated as a federal state. From this analysis it will also be apparent that the Federation has been allocated the majority of the powers. In fact, the Constitution provides such a strict framework for the state constitutions that initially it was assumed that they merely had a role implementing that framework. But from 1980s onwards it will be evident that the approach changed quite significantly. Second, the core elements that deal with the allocation of powers between the Federation and the states are assessed, including the nature of the financial relationship between the Federal government and the states. The role of the Constitutional Court in interpreting the constitutional provisions pertaining to matters of power allocation will be evaluated, particularly with reference to the development of the petrification doctrine and other conceptual tools of interpretation. Finally, the Austrian concept of 'self-administration' and the role of municipal government is discussed, as this also forms an important element of the vertical division of powers.

II. THE CONCEPT OF AUSTRIAN FEDERALISM

According to Art 2 of the Federal Constitution, Austria is a federal state. Although the roots of Austrian federalism can be traced back to the monarchy, the federal system was only introduced by the 1920 Constitution.[1] Partisan disputes, between the Conservatives on one hand side and the Social Democrats and the German Nationalists on the other, resulted in a compromise that gives the impression of a rather 'weak' federal system.[2] Nevertheless, from a legal perspective, the constitution basically assumes equality between the Federation and the states. In contrast to the German constitution (Art 31 of the German Basic Law), there is no rule according to which federal law would automatically override state laws. Disputes concerning the allocation of competences have to be settled by the Constitutional Court.[3]

According to the jurisprudence of the Constitutional Court, there are four core elements of Austria's federal system: the distribution of responsibilities between the Federation and the states; the constitutional autonomy of the states; the participation of the states in the federal legislation (as discussed in Chapter 3); and the federal administration performed by state authorities.[4] In all these fields, apart from the last one mentioned, the powers of the states are rather limited. As already analysed in Chapter 3, the influence of the Federal Council on the federal legislation is rather poor and, moreover, overshadowed by party hierarchies. The allocation of legislative responsibilities is disproportionately tilted towards the Federation: the majority of the powers, and the most important powers, are vested in the Federation, and quite limited powers are in the hands of the states. Further, the Federal Constitution sets out a rather tight framework for the constitution of states. State powers seem to be so modest that some have questioned whether Austria should be considered a federal state at all.[5] However, an analysis of the efficient

---

[1] See ch 1.

[2] F Fallend, 'A Redundant Second Chamber? The Austrian *Bundesrat* in Comparative Perspective' in G Bischof and F Karlhofer (eds), *Austrian Federalism in Comparative Perspective* (Innsbruck-New Orleans, University of New Orleans Press, 2015) 34.

[3] Arts 138–140 of the Federal Constitution, see further ch 6.

[4] VfSlg 2455/1952, 11403/1987, 16201/2001; see P Bussjäger, C Schramek and MM Johler, 'Federalism and Recent Political Dynamics in Austria' (2018) 28 *Revista d'Estudis Autonòmics I Federals – Journal of Self-Government* 74, 78.

[5] It is noteworthy that Jan Erk entitles his study on Austrian Federalism 'A Federation Without Federalism': J Erk, 'Austria: A Federation Without Federalism' (2004) 34 *Publius: The Journal of Federalism* 1.

constitution may demonstrate that federalism is stronger than one might expect and the federal system, in fact, contributes to the concept of the division of powers. This is because it divides the three branches of government – legislative, executive, judicial – vertically and, as such, has the effect of limiting the exercise of their respective powers.[6]

At the same time the 'weak' concept of Austria's federalism has probably more than anywhere else begged the questions of how and why the approach adopted can be distinguished from a decentralised unitary state. Austria's constitutional scholars offer basically two different theoretical positions; one is more in line with the structure of the constitution and the other one, nowadays more popular, with the formation of the republic.

The former theory was established by Hans Kelsen, who not only distinguished between federal law and state law but also introduced a third sphere of law called the 'joint constitution'. (Accordingly, this theory, which aims to characterise federal systems, is called the 'three-sphere-theory' – '*Drei-Kreise-Theorie*'.[7]) This 'joint constitution', albeit neither specifically entrenched nor clearly designated, comprises constitutional provisions that pertain to both the Federation as well as the states. It may consist of regulations establishing 'joint institutions' such as the Constitutional Court, the Administrative High Court, the Audit Court, and, at its core, the allocation of powers between the Federation and the states. From this point of view, both – federal powers and state powers – may seem to be devolved by the 'joint constitution'. Thus, the concept of federalism is almost brought into line with the concept of a decentralised unitary state and the concept of devolution respectively. Regardless of whether Hans Kelsen's theory provides for a conclusive concept of a federal state, it perfectly reveals the structure of the Austrian federal system.

The alternative theory focuses on the main conceptual difference between devolution and Federation. While devolved powers are conceded and therefore may be revoked (at least theoretically), in a federal system both entities – the Federation and the states – exercise pristine sovereign powers of their own.[8] Although this might be difficult to square with regard to Jean Bodin's theory of sovereignty,[9] it emphasises that

---

[6] See B Ackerman, 'The New Separation of Powers' (2000) 113 *Harvard Law Review* 633.

[7] H Kelsen, *Allgemeine Staatslehre* (Berlin, Springer, 1925) 198ff.

[8] Bussjäger et al (n 4) 74, 77.

[9] See M Stelzer, 'Die (vertikale) Kompetenzverteilung' in DT Tsatsos (ed), *Die Unionsgrundordnung – Handbuch zur Europäischen Verfassung* (Berlin, Berliner Wissenschaftsverlag, 2010) 385.

in a federal system both parts are equally sovereign. Theoretical issues aside, this concept strongly reflects Austria's history: in 1918 representatives of the republic (later: the Federation) claimed sovereign powers over the whole territory, while representatives of the states claimed sovereign powers over the states' territories.

Nevertheless, whether the Austrian constitution misses exactly the decisive point of equal sovereignty may be called into question. Almost all constitutional lawyers would agree that federalism in Austria could be abolished by a 'total revision' of the constitution, thus by a nationwide referendum.[10] As there are no rules enshrined in the Austrian constitution demanding a majority of votes in each single state in such a case,[11] it might happen that a state loses its 'sovereign' powers against the will of its representative bodies and its people. Therefore, it might be questioned whether the constitution is really underpinned by a concept of dual sovereignty. However, the latter theory has informed the development of Austria's federalism during the last four decades.[12]

This may be demonstrated with regard to regulations on territory, citizenship and constitutional powers, as in all these fields the sovereignty of the Federation as well as the states would have to be equally respected, according to a doctrine of dual sovereignty.

Concerning the territory, it can be noticed that the external borders of the federal territory are established by international treaties, primarily by the State Treaty of St Germain and the State Treaty of Vienna. The borders between the states, unsurprisingly, date back to the borders of the provinces of the Habsburg Monarchy. Changing these borders nowadays would entail changes to the federal territory as well as to a state territory. External borders may only be modified with the consent

---

[10] H Mayer, G Kucsko-Stadlmayer and K Stöger, *Bundesverfassungsrecht*, 11th edn (Wien, Manz, 2015) 78; E Wiederin, *Bundesrecht und Landesrecht* (Wien-New York, Springer, 1995) 35; dissenting: P Pernthaler, *Die Identität Tirols in Europa* (Wien-New York, Springer, 2007) 29.

[11] It may be questioned whether the 2008 amendment of the constitution (BGBl I 2/2008) has altered this situation in favour of the states by providing that 'changes in the composition' of the states require an amendment of the state's constitution (see Art 2 para 3 of the Federal Constitution). But it remains unclear how this provision relates to the abolishment of the whole federal system by a 'total revision' of the constitution.

[12] Nowadays it might be argued that the theoretical underpinning of federalism has become less relevant as the Austrian states are embedded in the EU Committee of the Regions and its policies. See, for instance, A Eppler and F Staudigl, 'Europeanization of Austrian Federalism: The Case of *Länder* Rights in EU Affairs' in Bischof and Karlhofer (eds) (n 2) 86, 88.

of the respective states. Internal borders may only be changed as a result of corresponding laws of the Federation and the states concerned. In both cases the Federation and the states have to cooperate on an equal footing.

With regard to citizenship, the 1920 Constitution provided for Austrians primarily to be citizens of the states where they had their domicile. Citizenship depended on a right of domicile (*Heimatrecht*) in a municipality. After World War II, this concept was abolished and a single Austrian citizenship was introduced. Its terms of achievement and loss were provided for by a federal law, and states were thus left without a 'people'. Some states claimed that such a regulation violated the federal principle of the constitution, as a sovereign state had to have a 'people' defined by citizenship. In the 1950s, however, the states discovered that in the view of the Constitutional Court[13] this argument was only of theoretical importance, and did not raise a constitutional question. State-citizenship was not reintroduced until 1994. Nowadays, individuals are citizens of the state in which they have their principal domicile. Thus, reference can be made not only to the people of the Federal Republic of Austria but also to the people of the states. Admittedly, the introduction of state-citizenship was primarily of theoretical (and psychological), rather than legal, importance.

The legal feature of sovereignty is the allocation of constitutional powers. Therefore, under the concept of dual sovereignty, not only the Federation must be entitled to a constitution but also the states. Remarkably, the Federal Constitution contains a whole chapter (Arts 95–112) in which it provides for the legislative and executive branch of government in the states in a very detailed way. Regulations pertain to the electoral system, the legislative process, and the highest organs of the states – the state cabinet (*Landesregierung*) and the state governor (*Landeshauptmann*[14]). Further, the Federal Constitution provides for the establishment of an administrative court in each state (Art 129 of the Federal Constitution). Other constitutional laws determine the basic structure of the administration in the states or explicitly allow the introduction of a departmental system within the state government. State constitutions may only be amended or enacted in as much as the Federal

---

[13] VfSlg 2455/1952.

[14] The term '*Landeshauptmann*' dates back to the monarchy and can, for instance, be found in the 1848 draft version of the constitution that never was enacted. If a female held this position, she would be referred to as '*Landeshauptfrau*'.

Constitution is thereby not affected (Art 99 of the Federal Constitution). Should a state constitution nevertheless deviate from this framework, it would violate the Federal Constitution and, thus, might be rescinded by the Constitutional Court.[15]

In light of this legal position, it was initially assumed that states only had to implement those parts of the Federal Constitution which provided more or less precisely for state constitutions, leaving almost no leeway. This view was challenged by the concept of dual sovereignty in the 1970s,[16] underpinned by an increasing self-confidence in the states. Constitutional autonomy is accepted as a core element of Austria's federalism and states are free to legislate in areas where the Federal Constitution is silent on the matter of state constitutions ('relative constitutional autonomy of the states'). State constitutions have made use of this 'relative autonomy' in different ways and they also differ remarkably in style. Vienna and Styria have opted for a more positivistic or legalistic constitution (similar to the style of the Federal Constitution); Burgenland, Carinthia, Lower and Upper Austria have opted for a mixed system including basic rights and state objectives; while the three most western states – Salzburg, Tyrol and Vorarlberg – have opted for constitutions which are inspired by moral theories and religion, including references to values such as human dignity, freedom, independence and family life as well as state objectives. The constitution of Tyrol is promulgated in the name of God, still reflecting the deep catholic tradition of the country.[17]

III. THE ALLOCATION OF POWERS (COMPETENCES)

A. Function and Principles of the Allocation of Powers

As already mentioned, the allocation of powers between the Federation and the states is probably the most important core element of the federal principle. It is also a field of law in which highly controversial

---

[15] See, for instance, VfSlg 16241/2001.

[16] F Koja, *Das Verfassungsrecht der österreichischen Bundesländer*, 2nd edn (Wien-New York, Springer, 1988); NB: the first edition of this book, which shaped the debate in the 1970s, appeared in 1967.

[17] F Karlhofer, 'Austrian Federalism: History-Properties-Change' in Bischof and Karlhofer (eds) (n 2) xix, xxxf.

disputes occur that are far from being merely 'technical', although this is not always visible at first sight. Struggles over competences have been more often than not genuine disputes between political parties or political concepts, rather than disputes between the Federation and a state. Therefore, settling a question on competences often establishes not only which authority is responsible in a merely technical sense, but also which political concept prevails.

The Austrian constitution foremost allocates legislative and executive powers between the Federation and the states. Jurisdiction in a formal sense is to an overwhelming extent assigned to the Federation. But as of 2014, states run administrative courts (*Landesverwaltungsgerichte*) and therefore have a genuine share in judicial powers.

According to Art 17 of the Federal Constitution, the position of the Federation and the states as holders of civil rights is in no way affected by the allocation of powers. This provision contains a specific feature of the Austrian administrative and constitutional system. It constitutes the territorial corporate bodies – Federation and states – as full subjects to private law (Art 116 para 2 of the Federal Constitution provides the same for municipalities). The allocation of powers is, therefore, irrelevant when the Federation or the states act under private law.

This provision has played an important part in Austria's history. It was through this provision that it was possible for the Federation to run nationalised industries in the post World War II period. Moreover, this same provision enabled Vienna to develop its huge public residential building programmes during the First Republic, as all these activities – from a legal point of view – were performed within the field of private law.

Ultimately, competences concerning legislation or public administration (sovereignty administration – *Hoheitsverwaltung*) are allocated between the Federation and the states. By amending the constitution, the federal parliament has the power to re-distribute competences between the Federation and the states and thus has the so-called *Kompetenz-Kompetenz*. But there are also cases, especially under the Financial Constitutional Law (*Finanz-Verfassungsgesetz* – F-VG), in which the federal parliament may exercise a *Kompetenz-Kompetenz* by means of an ordinary law.

The Federal Constitution assigns specific fields of law, called 'competence matters', to the legislation or execution of either Federation or the states. It also distinguishes between a 'general allocation of powers' and the allocation of powers for special fields of law such as taxation law, the school system and public procurement law.

B. The General Allocation of Powers

Basically, the constitution distinguishes between four general types of competence allocation: (a) both legislation and implementation are the sole responsibility of the Federation (Art 10 of the Federal Constitution); (b) only the legislation is the responsibility of the Federation, while the implementation of these laws falls under the responsibility of the states (Art 11 of the Federal Constitution); (c) the Federation is only responsible for legislative principles, in which case the states have to translate these principles into laws and implement them (Art 12 of the Federal Constitution); and (d) legislation and implementation is the sole responsibility of the states (Art 15 of the Federal Constitution).

Matters which are allocated to types (a)–(c) are specified exhaustively by the constitution. Art 15 of the Federal Constitution is a basket clause providing for all competences that are not allocated to the Federation to 'remain within the autonomous sphere of competence of the states'. Seemingly, this technique of allocating competencies favours the states, but in reality, the sheer number and the importance of powers assigned to the Federation leaves very little for the states.

The most important powers, however, are specified in Art 10 of the Federal Constitution which includes areas such as external affairs; nearly all security issues; areas pertaining to trade and industry; the railway system; aviation; forestry and the use of water resources; private law and vast parts of labour legislation; social insurance and public health matters; military affairs; and many more. From the law enforcing perspective it seems to be decisive that not only is the army organised on a federal level, but also so are almost all of the police forces. With the small exception of some municipalities maintaining local forces with very little power, all armed forces in Austria are federal forces.

Notwithstanding the powers vested in the Federation right from the beginning, more powers have been assigned to the Federation throughout the course of history.[18] The only limit may be provided by the federal principle of the Constitution, should the transfer of powers be too extensive (see Chapter 1).

In areas where the Federation is responsible for legislative principles only, the states are obliged to pass detailed laws within the framework laid down by federal legislation. At first sight, this type of competence

---

[18] W Schroeder and K Weber, *Die Kompetenzrechtsreform* (Wien, Braumüller, 2006) 17; J Werndl, *Die Kompetenzverteilung zwischen Bund und Ländern* (Wien, Braumüller, 1984).

seems to be specially tailored to the federal structure of the state: it would allow setting out principles addressing the general ideas and demands of the Federation. The states, on the other hand, might respect regional peculiarities. In practice, states have rarely used this power – in many cases, they have merely copied the federal law on principles.[19] Consequently, this type of competence allocation has been eroded and its total abolition is under discussion.[20]

At a more general level, it may be observed that the federal structure of the Austrian state again meets emotional and psychological demands rather than cultural and regional peculiarities. In other words, there is very little need for different legal regulations. These emotions stem from the tension between the capital Vienna, with its roughly two million inhabitants, and the other, more rural parts of the nation. This tension was already felt during the monarchy, when Vienna was the town of residence, attracting the nobility and rich entrepreneurs (many of them of Jewish origin). This was in stark contrast to the rural surroundings. Nowadays, it might be argued that Austrian federalism satisfies an emotional need; namely, that the country should not be entirely dominated by institutions based in Vienna.

Even though Art 15 of the Federal Constitution contains a basket clause in favour of the states, the areas in which the states are fully competent are fairly small. For example, legislation relating to building, hunting and municipal law is the sole responsibility of the states. Within the fields of their exclusive responsibility, states have the power to adopt the necessary provisions also in the fields of criminal and civil law.

The allocation of the various areas of powers is understood to be exclusive. This means that an area is exclusively and unambiguously assigned to the Federation or to the states.[21] Shared competences that are exercised according to a principle of subsidiarity, for example, are alien to the Austrian constitution, with the probable exception of very few cases regarding 'legislation on demand' (*Bedarfsgesetzgebung*). Regulating administrative procedure, for instance, is assumed to be implied in any subject matter according to the so-called adhesion principle.[22] However, regulations pertaining to administrative procedure may be issued by the

---

[19] H Schäffer, 'Die Kompetenzverteilung im Bundesstaat' in H Schambeck (ed), *Bundesstaat und Bundesrat in Österreich* (Wien, Verlag Österreich, 1997) 65.
[20] Bussjäger et al (n 4) 74, 89f.
[21] LK Adamovich, B-C Funk, G Holzinger and SL Frank, *Österreichisches Staatsrecht*, Vol 1, 3rd edn (Wien, Verlag Österreich, 2020) 314; Schroeder and Weber (n 18) 9.
[22] Mayer et al (n 10) 161.

Federation, even in matters assigned to the states, to the extent that there is a demand for uniformity. Overall, the Austrian constitution assigns areas to the respective spheres of legislation and/or implementation in a rather inflexible and static manner.

Rather than challenging its static character, constitutional doctrine has defined areas of competence, which are somehow shared by the Federation and the states and are called 'cross-section areas' (*Querschnittsmaterien*).[23] Examples include environmental protection or regional planning. As the constitution does not specify these matters of competence, one might assume that they fall under the responsibility of the states, but it has been demonstrated that elements of environmental protection and regional planning are included in areas explicitly assigned to the Federation. 'Environmental protection' is thus a cross-section area because parts of it fall within the competence of the Federation whereas other parts remain with the states.[24]

Although the constitution allocates powers exclusively to the Federation or to the states, from the point of view of law enforcement several laws may apply to a specific case. These laws may be covered by different spheres of competence, as the Federal Constitution provides for abstract areas and does not settle specific cases. It may, thus, turn out that provisions of both building law and industrial law are applicable to a particular case and that one provision is incompatible with the other. The matter can only be finally settled by the Constitutional Court establishing the extent of the competence sphere of each legislative body.

The inflexibility and the static design of the allocation of powers were seen as a problem, especially when joining the European Union, as European law demands its enforcement irrespective of the internal legal structures of the Members States.[25] Therefore, a comprehensive structural reform of this part of the constitution was envisaged and – reflecting the work of the Constitutional Convention – a draft version was tabled that also included the idea of concurrent legislative powers. At one point, it seemed very likely that such a comprehensive reform could be passed by the Federal Parliament. In the end, the plans were dropped and to date have not been resumed.

---

[23] W Berka, *Verfassungsrecht*, 8th edn (Wien, Verlag Österreich, 2021) 132f.
[24] See Berka (ibid) 133 for more examples.
[25] K Weber, 'Möglichkeiten und Grenzen der Reform der bundesstaatlichen Kompetenzverteilung vor dem Hintergrund der Bemühungen um einen Vertrag über die europäische Verfassung' in M Akyürek et al (eds), *Staat und Recht in Europäischer Perspektive* (Wien, Manz, 2006) 923, 934ff.

C. 'Special' Allocation of Powers – The Finance Constitution

Apart from the general distribution of responsibilities, the constitution provides for special regulations allocating powers in particular fields of law, such as the organisation of schools, public procurement and taxation. The precise nature of fiscal provisions are fundamental for a federal system, as they establish which territorial entity is primarily responsible for levying taxes and, therefore, in charge of finance. In Austria, taxation is highly centralised. The Financial Constitution Law (*Finanz-Verfassungsgesetz*, F-VG, BGBl 45/1948 in the applicable version) defines different types of taxes, according to which the competence of legislation and implementation is allocated. The Federal Parliament has to assign each tax (for example, the income tax) to a specific type and in doing so – implicitly – decides which territorial entity is responsible for legislation and/or implementation of the tax in question. The Federation is therefore in charge of the *Kompetenz-Kompetenz*. Consequently, most taxes are levied by the Federation but as each government has to bear its own expenditures, money must be distributed fairly and equitably.[26] This is achieved by a federal law, the so-called Fiscal Equalisation Act (*Finanzausgleichsgesetz*), which is renewed periodically. Prior to passing this act, the Federation must try to reach an agreement with the states and is loosely bound to this agreement when passing the law.[27]

Under this legal regime the Federation retains most of the funds but the budgets the states administer are not negligible. According to the statistics offered by the Austrian Chamber of Commerce, in 2019 the total amounted to €51 billion, with Vienna holding the largest share of about €14 billion and the smallest states, Vorarlberg and Burgenland around €2 billion and €1.3 billion respectively.[28]

From a legal point of view, the Federation seems to be in a very strong position as it collects and distributes the tax revenue that is necessary to implement all sorts of policies. However, the system has been criticised for a lack of transparency and for a lack of clarity in setting out financial responsibilities, as well as a general lack of accountability. Reforming fiscal relations would be paramount to implementing expenditure-saving

---

[26] P Bußjäger, 'Austria's Cooperative Federalism' in Bischof and Karlhofer (eds) (n 2) 11, 30.

[27] VfSlg 12784/1991.

[28] See wko.at/statistik/bundesland/Länder.pdf, accessed 12 January 2022; and wko.at/statistik/bundesland/Gemeinden.pdf, accessed 12 January 2022.

and efficiency-enhancing policies in many fields of administration.[29] Surprisingly at first sight, these reforms are mainly blocked by the states who see no advantage in obtaining powers to levy taxes. Looking at the political effects of the system, however, this becomes fairly clear. The bargaining procedure that precedes the Fiscal Equalisation Act puts states in a much more comfortable position:[30] they spend money but do not have to raise it. The Federation may be blamed for any rise in taxation. This is obviously the main reason why a substantial reform of federal fiscal relations is still not in prospect.

D. Interpretation of Regulations Regarding Competences

As already mentioned in Chapter 1, in interpreting 'competence matters', Austrian constitutional lawyers and the Constitutional Court coined a doctrine of great importance for Austrian constitutional law that has sometimes been addressed as a general doctrine for interpreting the constitution.[31] It is based on the idea that the meaning of a constitutional term or its conceptual content may be 'petrified'. Consequently, this doctrine, euphemistically addressed as 'theory' in Austrian legal writing, is called the 'petrification doctrine'. According to it, a competence matter (or a constitutional term) must be understood in the light of the legal setting pertaining to that competence matter that was in place at the moment the constitutional law introducing the competence matter was enacted. Thus, the conceptual content of the competence matter (the constitutional term) is 'petrified' in the light of ordinary laws. As the allocation of powers between the Federation and the states was added to the Federal Constitution in 1925, most terms describing the various 'competence matters' are 'petrified' in the light of the legal situation precisely on 1 October 1925.[32]

This doctrine is best explained by means of an example. In 1994, the federal parliament wanted to extend the requirement for industrial permission for sawmills to cover those administered by farmers

---

[29] M Schratzenstaller, 'Reforming Austrian Federlism. Options, Obstacles, and Pitfalls' in Bischof and Karlhofer (eds) (n 2) 54f.

[30] Bußjäger (n 26) 11, 31.

[31] H Schäffer, *Verfassungsinterpretation in Österreich* (Wien-New York, Springer, 1971) 64f.

[32] See also the analysis of petrification by G Taylor, *Characterisation in Federations: Six Countries Compared* (Berlin-Heidelberg, Springer, 2006) 98, 110.

in addition to their agricultural or – more likely in this case – forestry business (sideline). It could only have done so if the federal competence for industrial matters covered the issue. To establish whether this was the case, the competence had to be interpreted in the light of ordinary laws that existed on 1 October 1925 relating to 'industrial matters'.

On 1 October 1925, the 1859 Industrial Code still governed the matters in question. The preamble to this code stated explicitly that the code did not apply to any sideline to an agricultural business. Thus in 1925 the 'industrial matters' area of competence did not imply the power to regulate such sidelines. As a result of the petrification doctrine, the Federal Parliament was not allowed to amend the Industrial Code in 1994 in the way it desired. The requirement of industrial permission for sawmills administered as sidelines to an agricultural business as foreseen by the 1994 amendment of the Industrial Code was, therefore, deemed to violate the constitution and was rescinded by the Constitutional Court.[33]

At first sight, it may seem to be more of a technical problem to establish which territorial corporate body – the Federation or the states – is competent to legislate on this issue. On second sight, however, a significant political issue is revealed. The exceptions made to the 1859 Industrial Code – for whatever reason they were established – nowadays privilege farmers when setting up sidelines. The decisive constitutional question would probably be whether such a privilege is (still) justified. As long as the states are responsible for regulating these issues, farmers can be confident that their privileges will remain untouched, as their influence on the legislation of the states will be strong enough. In particular, states that are governed by a conservative majority will be very reluctant to jeopardise these privileges, as the Farmers' Federation, one of the (still) strong federations within the People's Party, will prevent any such legislation (although other federations of the People's Party are not in favour of these privileges – especially those who represent entrepreneurs, who would have to cope without these privileges). At the federal level, however, the influence of the farmers' associations was obviously less significant as parliament had opted to curtail their privileges.

As a consequence of the court's ruling, the farmers' privileges remained untouched but the decisive question as to whether this could be justified was never asked. Nevertheless, Austrian constitutional lawyers would argue that this question should have been addressed at

---

[33] VfSlg 14187/1995.

constitutional level (by transferring the powers from the states to the Federation) and not resolved by the Constitutional Court.[34]

The retrospective interpretation of the allocation of powers makes it difficult to address problems of which the former legislator was not or could not have been aware. But, again, the idea behind this method of interpretation is that new problems should preferably be settled by a political compromise rather than by interpretation, thus underpinning Austria's consociational democracy after World War II. It is not surprising that the provisions concerning competences were amended frequently during the 1950s and 1960s as more and more competences were shifted to the Federation.[35] This legislation was also a consequence of the retrospective interpretation.

However, the petrification doctrine has not always been applied as strictly as in the example above. An element was soon added to broaden the scope of the constitutional provision in question, albeit undermining the basic idea of the petrification doctrine. The element in question is the so-called 'intra-systematic development' (*intrasystematische Fortentwicklung*) that allows the court to go beyond the borders of the legal setting of 1925 if the regulation to be introduced follows similar intentions as the former law.

Again, a provision from the Industrial Code may serve as an example. According to this provision, the mayor is entitled to issue ordinances prohibiting vending machines that sell sweets or similar products from being placed near schools or bus stops used mainly by children. The intention behind this law was to keep children from wasting their pocket money. The constitutional question was whether the Federation was competent to enact such a legal provision. Again, in accordance with the petrification doctrine, the legal setting on 1 October 1925 was decisive for understanding the area of competence in industrial matters. As already stated, on 1 October 1925 the 1859 Industrial Code was the law relating to industrial matters. No provision relating to vending machines was to be found in this code. The petrification doctrine would thus

---

[34] An excellent example for the traditional way of Austrian public lawyers drawing a line between interpretation and calling for the legislator is provided by R Novak, 'Die Problematik der Abgrenzung der Hoheitsverwaltung von der sogenannten Privatwirtschaftsverwaltung' in F Ermacora et al (eds), *Allgemeines Verwaltungsrecht – Festschrift Antoniolli* (Wien, Orac, 1979) 61.

[35] See, for example, P Pernthaler, 'Föderalistische Verfassungsreform: Ihre Voraussetzungen und Wirkungsbedingungen in Österreich' (1992) 21 *Österreichische Zeitschrift für Politikwissenschaft* 365.

render the provision in question unconstitutional, were it not for the doctrine of 'intra-systematic development'. The industrial law in 1925 already contained a provision prohibiting the sale of alcoholic beverages to persons under the age of 18. The Constitutional Court held that this provision was underpinned by the intention of protecting minors. Thus, the protection of minors was an intention that could be pursued within the scope of industrial matters. The provision in question, based on the intention of protecting minors, was therefore deemed to be constitutional.[36]

The doctrine of 'intra-systematic development' obviously allows for more 'flexibility' but it also introduces an element of arbitrariness, as the example above shows. At no point did the court discuss how the intentions underlying the historic laws should be determined. The chosen option, that the laws were underpinned by the intention to protecting minors *in general* was not the only one available. In a more narrow sense, the court might have argued that the former law had only intended to protect the *health* of minors. As the intention of the provision against siting vending machines near schools and other places was to prevent minors from wasting their pocket money, that obviously would have made a great difference. Were the intentions underlying the 1925 legal setting defined more narrowly, the provision under review would have been unconstitutional. Applying the doctrine of intra-systematic development therefore may contain an element of arbitrariness and it is fair to say that the Constitutional Court in some cases has overstretched the idea[37] and thus undermined the initial intention of the petrification doctrine.

The petrification doctrine apart, the Constitutional Court has developed other methods of interpreting constitutional provisions regarding competence matters. One of these is the so-called 'aspect doctrine' (*Gesichtspunktedoktrin*),[38] according to which a competence matter may cover only some aspects of a case while other aspects are covered by other competence matters, entitling different authorities to legislate. For example, regulating the construction of a railway would be indisputably the business of the Federation under Art 10 para 1 no 9 of the Federal Constitution (*Eisenbahnwesen*). The construction of a specific railway, however, may have an impact on natural resources and the environment.

---

[36] VfSlg 10050/1984.
[37] VfSlg 2721/1954, 7593/1975.
[38] Adamovich et al (n 21) 316; Mayer et al (n 10) 184.

These aspects of the case might be regulated by state laws covered by the competence 'nature conservation', which is not defined in the constitution and therefore falls under the basket clause of Art 15 of the Federal Constitution. Laws based on these competences might be in conflict with each other.[39]

Settling such a conflict has to accept that, out of mutual respect, each legislature may only exercise its power to the extent that it does not undermine the power of other legislatures. According to the jurisprudence of the Constitutional Court, one territorial corporate body therefore is not entitled to pass laws without considering the spheres of competence of the other territorial corporate body.[40] Responsibility for 'nature conservation', therefore, does not empower states to enact provisions that would make it impossible for the Federation to carry out its railway projects. On the other hand, responsibility for the railway system does not entitle the Federation to enact laws that would jeopardise state efforts for nature conservation. The idea of 'balancing' was, thus, introduced into the area of competence matters, complementing the traditional, retrospective methods of reading the constitution, although they still play a part.[41]

IV. STATE LEGISLATION

A. Institutions and Procedures

According to the Federal Constitution, state laws have to be enacted by the state parliaments. As the Federal Constitution is silent on this issue, this has triggered a discussion as to whether states are allowed to introduce referenda similar to those designed on the federal level.[42] The Constitutional Court ruled that such referenda were only constitutional as long as they could not bypass the state parliament.[43]

The members of a state parliament are elected by citizens of the state (before state-citizenship was reintroduced in 1994, the electorate was formed by Austrian citizens who had their main residence in the

---

[39] VfSlg 17212/2004.
[40] VfSlg 10292/1984; H Schäffer, 'Kompetenzverteilung und Rücksichtnahmepflicht im Bundesstaat' (1985) 10 *Zeitschrift für Verwaltung* 357.
[41] See, for instance, VfSlg 20262/2018 regarding the petrification doctrine.
[42] F Merli, 'Rechtsprobleme des Volksbegehrens in Bundes- und Landesgesetzgebung' (1988) 110 *Juristische Blätter* 85.
[43] VfSlg 16241/2001.

respective state; the reintroduction of state-citizenship, therefore, had no effect on the electorate). Further, the Federal Constitution sets out the principles applying to state elections: they have to follow the same principles as the elections to the National Council (Art 95 para 1 of the Federal Constitution). Thus, it would be impossible for a state, to introduce a majority system as the Federal Constitution requires general elections to the National Council to be based on proportional representation. Further, states may not impose more stringent conditions for suffrage and eligibility for state parliaments than does the Federal Constitution for elections to the National Council (Art 95 para 2 of the Federal Constitution). For example, a state may not introduce a higher minimum voting age than the Federal Constitution establishes for elections to the National Council, but it could introduce a lower one. This does not leave much room for states to establish their own electoral system: the states' constitutions and the respective electoral laws will have to implement preconditions set out by the Federal Constitution.

According to the Federal Constitution, the members of a state parliament enjoy the same immunity as members of the National Council. They are entitled to emoluments of up to 80 per cent of the emoluments of members of the National Council.[44] The Federal Constitution provides for a state law to require a vote by a state parliament and a publication by the state governor in the State Law Gazette (*Landesgesetzblatt*). The state constitutions may only provide for the modus of authentication and countersignature.

Until a 2012 amendment,[45] the legislation of the states was supervised by the Federation and, more precisely, by the Federal Cabinet. All state parliaments' enactments had to be notified to the Federal Chancellery before publication. Within a period of eight weeks, the Federal Cabinet had the power to submit a justified objection to a state parliament enactment, if it was deemed to threaten federal interests. Any such objection would only have had a suspensive effect: the state parliament might have repeated its vote in the presence of at least half of its members. This comprehensive supervision of state legislation was abolished by the said amendment and nowadays only applies with regard to (the rare case of)

---

[44] It is up to the State Parliaments to determine the exact amount of money their members receive. The Federal Constitutional Act on the Limitation of Emoluments of Holders of Public Offices (*Bundesverfassungsgesetz über die Begrenzung von Bezügen öffentlicher Funktionäre*, BGBl 64/1997) provides only for a limit. With regard to the limited responsibilities state parliaments have, this law still allows an enormously generous, almost disproportionate salary.

[45] BGBl I 51/2012.

state tax laws, although disputes would be resolved in a joint committee of the National and the Federal Council. Apart from that, the approval of the Federal Cabinet is nowadays only required if the implementation of the law provides for the involvement of federal authorities.[46]

B. External Powers

The Federal Constitution initially attributed the power to conclude international treaties solely to the Federation. In the 1980s, however, states demanded the power to conclude state treaties to efficiently organise regional co-operations that extended beyond the borders of the republic. If it was desirable to have a legal basis or a legal framework for implementing such a cooperation, the states only had the option to conclude treaties under private law. It is recalled that according to Art 17 of the Federal Constitution, the allocation of powers explicitly does not affect the position of both the Federation and the states as holders of civil rights.

In order to address this issue, a 1988 amendment to the Federal Constitution (BGBl 685/1988) attributed the states with the (additional) power to conclude international treaties that pertain to matters within their own spheres of competence. States may only conclude treaties with states that border on Austria or their constituent entities, provided these would have similar powers. The conclusion of such treaties (*Länderstaatsverträge*) is the responsibility of the Federal President. Before the negotiations for any such treaty may begin, the state governor must inform the Federal Cabinet and obtain its approval. The extent to which state parliaments participate in the conclusion of treaties that amend existing (state) law is a matter to be regulated by state constitutions. Treaties concluded by a state shall be revoked upon request from the Federal Cabinet.[47]

It is surprising that, following the 1988 amendment, no such treaty has ever been concluded (so far). Cooperation is still done on the basis of treaties under private law or without any legal framework at all.[48]

---

[46] This has not curtailed the power of the Federal Cabinet to contest state laws at the Constitutional Court – see ch 6.

[47] Art 16 of the Federal Constitution.

[48] Pernthaler (n 10) 309. Nowadays, cooperation on a regional basis within the framework of the European Union may even offer better options; see A Engl, 'Territorial Cooperation in a Federal Framework: Austria's Involvement in European Groupings of Territorial Cooperation' in Bischof and Karlhofer (eds) (n 2) 107ff.

It remains unclear whether the reason for this situation lies in the supervisory powers of the Federation or in the simple truth that the need was not that pressing at all. Again, it seems that the constitution mainly responded to psychological demands.

C. Cooperation in the Federal State and Participation of the States in EU Legislation

The allocation of competences between the Federation and the states sometimes triggers the need for both sides to cooperate on certain matters.[49] Cooperation can be necessary between the Federation and the states and also between different states. According to a 1974 amendment of the Federal Constitution introducing Art 15a, territorial corporate bodies are authorised to conclude agreements between each other as far as matters within their respective spheres of competence are concerned. The conclusion of such agreements (*Gliedstaatsverträge*) in the name of the Federation is, depending on the subject, the task of the Federal Cabinet or a Federal Minister. Each state constitution specifies the body responsible for concluding these agreements in the name of the state. Cooperation agreements that have a bearing on the Federation's legislation need the approval of the National Council with participation of the Federal Council. Generally, the principles of international law concerning treaties – apart from cooperation agreements between states (which can provide for different regulations in their constitutions) – are also applied to cooperation agreements.[50] Unlike international treaties, cooperation agreements cannot create directly applicable law.

The conclusion of such agreements has become common practice, both with the Federation and the states. In 1992, for instance, an agreement was reached between the Federation and all states providing for the participation of the states in matters concerning the European integration process. It was stipulated that the Federation would inform the states of any intentions or projects concerning European integration that affected the autonomous sphere of state competencies or their sphere of interest. The states were entitled to comment on these intentions or projects and the Federation was obliged to consider them. If the states

---

[49] See Bußjäger (n 26) 11ff.
[50] Mayer et al (n 10) 412.

issued a unanimous comment, the Federation would be bound by it. Such a comment could only be overridden if there were imperative reasons relating to foreign or integration policy of which the Federal Chancellor had to inform the states.[51]

Shortly before the accession to the European Union came into effect, this concept was basically adopted by a 1994 amendment to the Federal Constitution and thus transferred into constitutional law (Art 23d of the Federal Constitution) with the only modification that the states had no longer to be informed of intentions or steps to be taken in the European integration process, but of European Union projects. The original 1992 agreement left it to the states to provide for a procedure to achieve unanimous comment. In an agreement, again based on Art 15a of the Federal Constitution, the states established a so-called 'Integration Conference' composed of all the state governors and the presidents of the state parliaments. According to this agreement an opinion had to be regarded as unanimous if it had received at least five votes in favour and none against. In fact, the states have used their power to issue unanimous comments more often than the National Council has used its similar powers.[52] Between the years 2002 and 2018, 91 such comments were released.[53]

If a European Union project affects matters in which legislation falls within the responsibility of the states, the federal government may exceptionally allow a representative nominated by the states to participate in the Council's deliberations. The Federation is also obliged to initiate an action at the CJEU on the request of a state, if no other state objects to the request and if no imperative reasons of foreign or integrative policy may prevent it. With regard to this obligation, the Federation sued the European Commission on behalf of the state of Upper Austria to maintain a law that completely banned the cultivation of genetically modified (GM) crops, even though this was not the (official) policy of the Federation and it was clear from the beginning that this was a lost case anyway.[54]

---

[51] The agreement is based on Art 15a of the Federal Constitution and published in the Federal Law Gazette, see BGBl 775/1992. For more details of the participation of the states in European Policies, see Eppler and Staudigl (n 12) 86, 96ff.

[52] See ch 3.

[53] www.foederalismus.at/contentit4/uploads/foederalismus_datenbank.pdf, accessed 12 January 2022.

[54] Joined cases C-439/05 P and C-454/05 P, *Land Oberösterreich and Republic of Austria v Commission of the European Communities* (2007) ECLI:EU:C:2007:510.

V. THE INDIRECT FEDERAL ADMINISTRATION
AND THE ROLE OF THE STATE GOVERNOR

'Indirect federal administration' (*mittelbare Bundesverwaltung*) is an Austrian peculiarity that allows states to participate in the enforcement of federal laws. As this is arguably the most important task of the states in Austria's federal system, Austria may be characterised predominantly as having a unique form of 'executive' federalism. Effectively, it strengthens the position of the state governor, although it subjects this genuine state organ to instructions of the Federal Cabinet or federal ministers. According to the constitution, federal matters may be either managed 'directly' by federal organs, or 'indirectly' by organs of other entities such as the states. Art 102 para 1 of the Federal Constitution defines 'indirect federal administration' as the exercise of the Federation's executive powers by the state governors and the subordinate state authorities in the realm of the states.[55]

All matters should be administered indirectly except those explicitly defined in Art 102 para 2 of the Federal Constitution, which may be implemented by Federal authorities. The list is neither exhaustive, as with the agreement of the respective state, further matters might be administered directly, nor is it mandatory, as the Federation may transfer executive powers to the state governor even in fields where it would be entitled to direct administration. One prominent example for 'direct federal administration' is financial administration, as federal authorities which are directly subordinate to the Federal Minister of Finance exercise executive powers. However, quite a few laws are administered indirectly, including important ones such as the Industrial Code.

A key element of the Austrian system of indirect federal administration is the role of the state governor, who is bound by instructions of the respective Federal Minister[56] but has the power to issue instructions to all subordinate authorities (like district authorities). Apart from that, the state governor, being responsible for the indirect federal administration, may also issue instructions to other members of the state cabinet. This may be the case if those members are entrusted with businesses of indirect federal administration according to the respective Standing Orders of the State Cabinet. Thus, the state governor, who is otherwise an equal member of the state cabinet, may instruct other members of

---

[55] See LK Adamovich, B-C Funk, G Holzinger and SL Frank, *Österreichisches Staatsrecht*, Vol 2, 3rd edn (Wien, Verlag Österreich, 2014) 185ff.

[56] Such instructions are rarely handed down, see Adamovich et al (ibid) 191.

the cabinet on certain matters. Therefore, the state governor enjoys a privileged position within the state cabinet which further strengthens the state governor's position on top of the (local) party hierarchy.

There has been a sustained discussion as to whether indirect federal administration is already outdated. Some scholars argue in favour of abandoning this system. Instead, the matters affected should be assigned to the administration of the states thus transferring the powers of the state governor to the state cabinet, leaving only minor powers of supervision for the responsible Federal Ministers.[57] A reform of this kind would dramatically reduce the influence of the state governors and allegedly faces their resistance. Depending on their personality, of course, state governors may be prominent political figures who are able not only to represent the interests of their states, but also to strongly influence the policy of their political party on the federal level.[58] Traditionally, this has been felt by the People's Party as it held the positions of the state governor in states like Tyrol, Salzburg, Upper and Lower Austria, Styria and Vorarlberg for decades. Most notably, the State Governors of Tyrol, Styria and Lower Austria were prominent party representatives, who strongly influenced federal policies. Although the Social Democratic Party is more centralised than the People's Party, their state governors – traditionally the Mayor of Vienna, but also the current State Governors of Carinthia and Burgenland – strongly influence the party on the federal level. As already mentioned in Chapter 3, strong state governors and/or strong local groups of the relevant political party will use their powers to influence the party slates submitted to general elections, thus ensuring that their interests are represented in the Federal Parliament. In this way, it may be argued, Austrian federalism effectively contributes a counterbalance to the otherwise overwhelming central powers, even if it may seem to be 'weak' with regard to the legal framework.

VI. MUNICIPAL GOVERNMENT AND AUTONOMOUS PUBLIC BODIES

In Austria, the issues discussed in this section are covered by the rather formal constitutional concept of 'self-administration' (*Selbstverwaltung*).[59]

---

[57] G Holzinger, 'Der österreichische Bundesstaat und seine Reform' in Akyürek et al (eds) (n 25) 277, 292ff.

[58] W Pesendorfer, *Der Landeshauptmann* (Wien-New York, Springer, 1986).

[59] Arts 115–120c of the Federal Constitution.

'Self-administration' is defined as the exercise of executive powers by a public body – within a so-called 'own sphere of powers' (see below) – without being subject to instructions from external authorities, thus operating outside the concept of ministerial responsibility. These public bodies enjoy compulsory membership. The concept of 'self-administration' arguably adds to the idea of the vertical division of power, as the executive powers of the Federation and the states are curtailed.

Originally, the Federal Constitution referred explicitly only to one type of self-administration: the 'territorial' self-administration (*territoriale Selbstverwaltung*) of towns and municipalities, which had been introduced in 1848 and redesigned by an 1862 law.[60] Thus, the 1920 Federal Constitution maintained the autonomy of municipalities, which was again re-organised by a 1962 amendment of the Federal Constitution. The councils, which are the general representative organs of the municipalities, are elected according to the same principles as the National Council. The mayor may be elected directly by the electorate or – indirectly – by the council.

A municipality may perform some of its businesses without being subject to instructions in its autonomous (own) 'sphere of power' (*eigener Wirkungsbereich*). This sphere has to comprise all matters that concern exclusively or predominantly the local community and are suited to performance by the community within its local boundaries (Art 118 para 2 of the Federal Constitution). Federal and state legislation must expressly specify these matters. Should a federal or state law not assign matters that fulfil the aforementioned requirement to the municipalities' autonomous sphere of competence, it would violate the Federal Constitution. As the municipalities have a substantial 'right to self-administration', they might successfully file an application with the Constitutional Court. The federal and the states administrations have the power to supervise the municipalities when acting within their own sphere of power.

The fact that the Federal Constitution explicitly only addressed territorial self-administration triggered a debate as to whether the establishment of other autonomous public bodies by an ordinary law was constitutional, as Art 20 of the Federal Constitution provided for

---

[60] Law Establishing Principles for the Regulation of Communal Administration (*Gesetz vom 5. März 1862, womit die grundsätzlichen Bestimmungen zur Regelung des Gemeindewesens vorgezeichnet werden*, RGBl 18/1862).

all executive bodies being bound by instructions of the highest administrative authorities. The Constitutional Court nevertheless ruled[61] that autonomous public bodies were part of the design of the organisational structure of the 1920 Federal Constitution and therefore their establishment complied with the constitution, as long as it met certain requirements modelled on the prerequisites of territorial self-administration. An essential feature was the requirement for organs to be elected – directly or indirectly – by the members of the autonomous body.

The jurisprudence of the Constitutional Court added to the impression that Austria was already a nation of chambers and public bodies, a clear heritage of the monarchy and its feudal structure. The various chambers already mentioned in Chapter 2 may serve as examples. A 2008 amendment to the Federal Constitution codified the principles the Constitutional Court had set out for the establishment of 'non-territorial self-administering' bodies. There was no visible need for that; it was probably merely used to explicitly guarantee the 'social partnership' institutions.[62]

Critics of the concept of self-administration may be right that, especially in small communities (such as small municipalities), the law may not always be applied according to the principle of equality due to personal relations between citizens and law enforcing authorities. And they may also be right that as a consequence of these private relations, especially smaller communities may be prone to corruption.

VII. CONCLUSION

The Austrian Constitution is based on the idea of dividing powers not only horizontally, but also vertically. This is achieved by two concepts – the concept of federalism and the establishment of autonomous municipalities and other autonomous public bodies.

The federal system, however, based on a compromise between the Conservatives and the Social Democrats, still assigns most of the legislative powers to the Federation. The jurisprudence of the Constitutional Court has tried – to a certain extent – to limit the powers of the Federation

---

[61] VfSlg 8215/1977.

[62] W Schwartz and I Mayr, 'A New Broom Sweeps Clean? An Attempt to Gradually Change the Austrian Constitution' (2009) 15 *European Public Law* 151, 161.

by 'petrifying' them. However, the court undermined this idea by introducing the more flexible criterion of 'intra-systematic development'. Rather, it was parliament which amended the constitution in order to strengthen the federal level by increasing the legislative powers of the Federation. From the 1970s onwards, a re-interpretation of Austria's federalism focusing on the genuine sovereignty of the states has counterbalanced the centralising tendencies and, from the 1980s onwards, has led to some constitutional amendments. In the last decade, the most prominent of these resulted in the introduction of state administrative courts in 2014, thus handing a share in judicial powers to the states, and the abolishment of the overall supervision of state legislation by the Federal Cabinet in 2012. Although it still might be argued that under the written constitution Austria's federalism is underdeveloped and amounts to a type of 'executive' federalism, under the efficient constitution state governors and strong local groups of relevant political parties may influence party policies effectively even at the federal level.

FURTHER READING

Bischof, G and Karlhofer, F (eds), *Austrian Federalism in Comparative Perspective* (Innsbruck-New Orleans, University of New Orleans Press, 2015).

Bußjäger, P, 'Föderalismus als Entdeckungsverfahren – Zur Theorie und Empirie des innovativen Bundesstaates am Beispiel Österreichs' (2008) 16 *Journal für Rechtspolitik* 193.

Bussjäger, P, Schramek, C and Johler, MM, 'Federalism and Recent Political Dynamics in Austria' (2018) 28 *Revista d'Estudis Autonòmics I Federals – Journal of Self-Government* 74.

Dachs, H, 'The Politics of Regional Subdivisions' in Lauber, V (ed), *Contemporary Austrian Politics* (Oxford, Westview Press, 1996) 235.

Erk, J, 'Austria: A Federation Without Federalism' (2004) 34 *Publius: The Journal of Federalism* 1.

——, *Explaining Federalism: State, Society and Congruence in Austria, Belgium, Canada, Germany, and Switzerland* (London, Routledge, 2007).

Gamper, A, 'The Austrian Constitutional Convention: Continuing the Path To Reform the Federal State?' (2006) 2 *Revista d'Estudis Autonòmics I Federals – Journal of Self-Government* 9.

Karlhofer, F, 'Austria: Federal Politics within and beyond the Constitutional Frame' in Karlhofer, F and Palaver, G (eds), *Federal Power-Sharing in Europe* (Baden-Baden, Nomos, 2017) 11.

Koja, F, *Das Verfassungsrecht der österreichischen Bundesländer*, 2nd edn (Wien-New York, Springer, 1988).

Obinger, H et al (eds), *Federalism and the Welfare State: New World and European Experiences* (Cambridge, Cambridge University Press, 2005).

Österreichischer Gemeindebund (ed), *40 Jahre Gemeindeverfassungsnovelle 1962. Aktuelle Rechtsfragen und Entwicklungen der kommunalen Selbstverwaltung* (Wien, Manz, 2002).

Pernthaler, P, 'Die Verfassungsautonomie der österreichischen Bundesländer' (1986) 108 *Juristische Blätter* 477.

——, *Die Kompetenzverteilung in der Krise. Voraussetzungen und Grenzen der Kompetenzinterpretation in Österreich* (Wien, Braumüller, 1989).

Taylor, G, *Characterisation in Federations: Six Countries Compared* (Berlin-Heidelberg, Springer, 2006).

6

Jurisdiction

Introduction – Separation of Jurisdiction and Administration and the Road to a Two-tier System of Administrative Jurisdiction – Organisation of the Highest Courts – Powers and Policies of the Highest Courts Pertaining to the Constitution – Conclusion

I. INTRODUCTION

JURISDICTION IS THE business of independent judges (Art 87 of the Federal Constitution). This means that, other than the public administration, they may not be subject to any instructions. To protect this independent position, judges may not be deliberately removed from office or transferred against their will. Removal from office or involuntary transfer may only result from a disciplinary hearing performed by independent judges. To avoid interference from the public administration, especially politicians, the constitution explicitly provides for the separation between the executive branch of government (the public administration) and the independent (ordinary) law courts (jurisdiction). This is one of the main aspects of the horizontal separation of powers.

It will be shown that the Austrian constitution initially separated these two branches of government only according to procedural and organisational criteria without explicitly attributing certain matters to ordinary law courts. Judicial review of the administration, offered by public law courts, was far from being comprehensive. This initial approach was challenged after Austria's accession to the ECHR and we will observe how the jurisprudence of the ECtHR with regard to Art 6 ECHR forced Austria to gradually amend its design of administrative jurisdiction. This was eventually achieved by introducing a two-tier system in 2014, establishing administrative courts of first instance both at federal and at state level.

The second section will analyse the court system featuring three apex courts: the Supreme Court, the Administrative High Court and the Constitutional Court. The system was inherited from the monarchy, where it was established over a period of 30 years. It distinguishes between ordinary courts, which pronounce on private law suits and criminal charges, and public law courts. The ordinary branch of jurisdiction currently consists of the Supreme Court, and a number of district courts, provincial courts and four upper provincial courts. All these courts, despite their names, are Federal courts. Two out of 13 public law courts were already established under the monarchy: the Administrative High Court and the (former) Imperial Law Court. The 11 administrative courts of first instance were only established in 2014. While the Administrative High Court was transferred into the republic without significant changes, the same did not apply for the Imperial Law Court: it became a Constitutional Court and was additionally vested with the power to review and rescind laws (parliamentary statutes and ordinances). Although, in effect, the Austrian constitution introduced the concept of a centralised constitutional review for the first time, it will soon be apparent that the other two apex courts contribute to the interpretation and implementation of the constitution.

Finally, the discussion of the Constitutional Court and its core function, the review of laws, will reveal that the system of centralised review has changed since Austria's accession to the European Union. Despite all constitutional safeguards outlined above, it will be argued that the power to appoint judges, which rests with governments and parliaments respectively, might lead to a politicisation of courts and thus jeopardise their independency.

II. THE SEPARATION OF JURISDICTION AND ADMINISTRATION AND THE ROAD TO A TWO-TIER SYSTEM OF ADMINISTRATIVE JURISDICTION

One of the pillars of the judicial system is the separation of powers between public administration and ordinary jurisdiction. Art 94 para 1 of the Federal Constitution stipulates that (independent) judicial and (instruction bound) administrative powers shall be separate at all levels of proceedings. The concept laid down by this article has always been understood to be procedural or organisational rather than substantial.[1] The consequences are that no 'mixed' authorities (authorities that act

---

[1] H Mayer, G Kucsko-Stadlmayer and K Stöger, *Bundesverfassungsrecht*, 11th edn (Wien, Manz, 2015) 373.

as courts and administrative authorities) may exist, that no ruling of a court may be appealed at an administrative body, and that no instruction may be issued from an administrative body to a court nor vice versa.[2] In specific matters, federal or state legislation may nevertheless provide for review of an administrative decision by a court of justice rather than an administrative court. Disputes about entitlement to social insurance benefits, for instance, are initially settled by an administrative authority, but parties may subsequently bring the matter before the ordinary courts.

As a decisive consequence of the procedural or organisational reading of the principle of the separation of jurisdiction and administration, it was widely held that parliament was able to allocate powers between jurisdiction and administration almost at will. Some scholars have argued that the legislation was completely free to allocate powers, while others had assumed that courts at the least had to maintain a minimum of powers (within a sort of 'core area').[3] The latter idea was based on the observation that the Federal Constitution provided for courts; this only made sense if they had at least some business to perform. From Art 92 of the Federal Constitution, which establishes the Supreme Court as the court of final instance in civil and criminal law suits, it has been further concluded that these powers should lie in the fields of civil and criminal law. However, determining the extent of the courts' powers in these areas would still be a matter for parliament.

According to this theoretical approach, administrative authorities were entrusted with the settlement of conflicts that involved genuine questions of civil law.[4] Moreover, a rather comprehensive system of administrative penal law was maintained and under the pretext of 'decriminalisation', criminal offences were 'downgraded' to administrative offences. This did not necessarily mean that they triggered lower fines, but the stigma of being labelled a criminal was avoided. For many decades, administrative authorities worked under the review of the two public law courts only.

This Austrian concept was jeopardised by the ECHR, which in 1958 had been largely incorporated as part of constitutional law. Despite the fact that two reservations were made concerning Arts 5 and 6 ECHR,

---

[2] W Berka, *Verfassungsrecht*, 8th edn (Wien, Verlag Österreich, 2021) 122.

[3] L Adamovich, *Grundriss des österreichischen Staatsrechts* (Wien, Österreichische Staatsdruckerei, 1927) 174f; A Merkl, 'Sind die Rechtspfleger mit der Verfassung vereinbar?' (1929) 12 *Gerichts-Zeitung* 177, 178.

[4] See B Wieser, 'Zur materiellen Gewaltentrennung zwischen Justiz und Verwaltung' (2009) 131 *Juristische Blätter* 351.

the evolving case law of the ECtHR challenged the Austrian system of judicial review of the administration.[5]

Other than Art 94 of the Federal Constitution, Art 6 ECHR includes substantive requirements for the concept of the separation of judicial and executive powers. All claims regarding civil rights and obligations and all criminal charges must be heard by an independent and impartial tribunal established by law. As the ECtHR adopted a rather broad concept of 'civil rights and obligations' and 'criminal charges', it turned out that, in Austria, a large number of these procedures were in fact settled by administrative authorities. This applied, for example, to disputes concerning the approval of contracts of sale;[6] disqualification from practice as a doctor;[7] disciplinary hearings leading to disqualification from a liberal profession (like lawyers or medical doctors);[8] and the refusal to grant a permission to build on privately owned land.[9]

As the ECtHR ruled that it sufficed if the matter was heard by an independent and impartial tribunal at least in the final instance, Austrian lawyers initially felt that the requirements of Art 6 ECHR were met anyway. Administrative decisions were, however, subject to review by the two public law courts, which were both courts in the sense of the Federal Constitution and, therefore, also 'tribunals' in the sense of the ECHR.[10] This view was not entirely shared by the ECtHR, as according to Art 6 ECHR tribunals had to have the power to hear all aspects of the case and had to have full jurisdiction over questions of both fact and law. The Austrian system of administrative jurisdiction, inherited from the Habsburg Monarchy, did not satisfy this requirement on a systematic basis, as the power of the Administrative High Court to hear the facts of a case had always been severely restricted. Whether the review of an administrative authority's decision by the Administrative High Court and/or the Constitutional Court met the requirements of Art 6 ECHR depended therefore on the specific circumstances of the case. Several rulings of the ECtHR held that the Administrative High Court's review did fulfil the requirements of Art 6 ECHR in the case under consideration.[11]

[5] VfSlg 11500/1987; Mayer et al (n 1) 828.
[6] *Ringeisen v Austria* Series A no 13 (1971) 1 EHRR 455.
[7] *König v Federal Republic of Germany* Series A no 27 (1978) 2 EHRR 170.
[8] *Diennet v France* Series A no 325-A (1995) 21 EHRR 554.
[9] *Allan Jacobsson v Sweden* Series A no 163 (1989) 12 EHRR 56.
[10] VfSlg 5100/1965, 10080/1984.
[11] *Zumtobel v Austria* Series A no 234-C (1993) 17 EHRR 116; *Ortenberg v Austria* Series A no 295-B (1995) 19 EHRR 524; *Josef Fischer v Austria* Series A no 312 (1995) 20 EHRR 349.

Nevertheless, such an outcome could not be guaranteed for all future cases.

In response to this situation, numerous independent administrative authorities – tribunals – were established in various fields of administrative law. A 1988 amendment to the Federal Constitution introduced an Independent Administrative Tribunal in each state (*Unabhängige Verwaltungssenate in den Ländern*), especially to meet Austria's shortcomings with regard to its system of administrative penal law. It had turned out that the reservations to Arts 5 and 6 ECHR made to protect this system were not as far reaching as initially assumed. Politically, this amendment was partly informed by the Waldheim case: the establishment of these independent tribunals should enable Austria to withdraw the reservations pertaining to Arts 5 and 6 ECHR and, thus, help to restore its otherwise damaged reputation. But as the initial aim was to meet the requirements of the ECHR, notwithstanding foreseeable developments of the jurisprudence of the ECtHR, influential lawyers recommended upholding the reservations. Consequently, they were not withdrawn but became practically irrelevant.

Federal fiscal penal cases did not fall into the responsibility of the Independent Administrative Tribunals but were settled by Independent Appellate Tribunals (*Berufungssenate*), later by the Independent Finance Tribunal (*Unabhängiger Finanzsenat*), under the Federal Tax Penal Act (*Finanzstrafgesetz*, BGBl 1958 in the applicable version) in accordance with the requirements of Art 6 ECHR.

Additionally, amendments to the Federal Constitution introduced the Independent Federal Asylum Tribunal (*Unabhängiger Bundesasylsenat*) in 1997, followed in 2002 by the Federal Procurement Authority (*Bundesvergabeamt*). A 2008 amendment transformed the Independent Federal Asylum Tribunal (*Unabhängiger Bundesasylsenat*) into the Asylum Court (*Asylgerichtshof*).

The situation with regard to the numerous independent bodies established either by constitutional laws or ordinary laws became more and more confusing. Hence, a comprehensive reform was inevitable. First, this was because the concept of judicial review of the administration did not fulfil the requirements of the ECHR on a systematic basis and, second, because the European Union exercised further pressure as some of its laws demanded decisions of independent authorities. Nonetheless, 30 years of discussion were necessary to break down the resistance of large parts of the administration and politicians, who all feared losing their influence. The outcome was a two-tier system of administrative jurisdiction introduced by a 2012 amendment to the constitution[12] which became effective on 1 January 2014.

The reform introduces 11 administrative courts of first instance, which is understandable only against the background of the then existing independent authorities. The nine Independent Administrative Tribunals in the states were transferred into State Administrative Courts (*Landesverwaltungsgerichte*), with their organisation falling within the responsibilities of the states. For the first time, states were allocated (formal) judicial powers. The Asylum Court and the Federal Procurement Office were morphed into the Federal Administrative Court (*Bundesverwaltungsgericht*) and the Independent Finance Tribunal became the Federal Finance Court (*Bundesfinanzgericht*). Consequently, more than a hundred independent federal and state authorities in total were dissolved.

The 11 administrative courts of first instance may review administrative rulings as well as the exercise of 'direct administrative power and compulsion' (in the case of an arrest, for instance) for alleged unlawfulness. They further pronounce on complaints against an administrative authority defaulting on its (statutory) obligation to issue a ruling. These competences are rooted in the tradition of Austria's judicial review of the administration, which was far from being comprehensive.[13] This system may be cautiously expanded: it is permissible for federal and state legislation to introduce the power to review the 'conduct' of administrative authorities, clearly alluding to administrative acts that are not deemed to be 'rulings' according to the administrative doctrine. Further, state and/or federal legislation may entrust administrative courts with the review of the conduct of contract placing authorities in matters of public procurement. These courts may also be entrusted with resolving disputes in civil service matters and, according to a 2019 amendment,[14] with hearing 'complaints, disputes or applications in other matters'. Especially the latter clause opens the path to a more comprehensive judicial review.

One of the central elements of this reform, which represented a decisive power shift, was to ask administrative courts of first instance to decide on the merits of a case rather than repeal an unlawful

---

[12] BGBl I 51/2012. For a more detailed analysis see M Köhler, 'The Reform of the Administrative Jurisdiction in Austria – Theoretical Background and Main Features of the System' (2015) 14 *Public Security and Public Order* 31.

[13] See also later in this chapter.

[14] BGBl I 14/2019.

administrative ruling. Traditionally, the Administrative High Court had only the power to repeal administrative rulings which might have led to endless proceedings as the administrative authority might have issued one illegal ruling after the other, all repealed again and again by the Administrative High Court. According to Art 130 para 4 of the Federal Constitution, administrative courts nowadays have to decide on the merits of the case in administrative penal matters and in all other legal matters whether the relevant facts have been established or the establishment by the administrative court itself is 'in the interest of a speedy procedure or connected with substantial cost saving'. This clause is read in a way that deciding on the merits of a case should be the rule rather than the exception.

As a result of this reform, almost every administrative decision, not only those within the scope of Art 6 ECHR, may be contested before an administrative court without the need to exhaust administrative remedies. Formerly it was, for instance, necessary to appeal against a decision of the district administration authority at the state governor and state cabinet respectively, before a complaint could be filed with the Administrative High Court. Nowadays, the decision of the district administration authority may be immediately contested in an administrative court. Especially when the court decides on the merits of the case, the influence of the state governor and/or the state cabinet is minimised. They still could issue instructions to the district administration authority, but they would not be able to influence the decision of the administrative court. Consequently, the new system may contribute to significantly reduce political influence and, thereby, also corruption.

The allocation of responsibilities between the 11 administrative courts is rather complicated and open to interpretation. It ties in with the distinction between 'direct' and 'indirect' federal administration.[15] However, in practice, laws do not always follow this distinction, as there are mixed systems like the security management. There are also direct ministerial responsibilities, laws that combine different enforcement areas, etc. In such cases it is up to the courts, mainly the Constitutional Court, to decide which administrative court may be responsible. In the light of the principle of *Rechtsstaat*, this seems to be unsatisfactory.

---

[15] For the difference between 'direct' and 'indirect' federal administration, see ch 5.

Nevertheless, the establishment of administrative courts of first instance has filled lacunae in Austria's system of administrative jurisdiction and has shifted powers from the executive branch of government to the judicial branch of government. It is compatible with the requirements of Art 5 and 6 ECHR, and has severely relieved the Administrative High Court's burden. It became instantly popular, to the extent that a 2017 amendment to the Proceedings of Administrative Courts Act[16] had to ease some of the procedural requirements, most notably the requirement for a decision to be issued in writing, which is no longer mandatory but will only happen on demand. The reform, however, is deemed to be an overall success,[17] despite the rather unclear delineation of jurisdictions.

III. THE ORGANISATION OF THE HIGHEST COURTS

All the members of the three highest courts – the Supreme Court, the Administrative Court and the Constitutional Court – are appointed by the Federal President on the recommendation of different institutions, which can be indicative of the amount of influence political parties may take on filling vacant positions. Thus, it might be argued, the separation of power as provided for by the constitution is (again) at least partly overshadowed by the party system.

With regard to the political influence on the bench of the courts, it is necessary to distinguish between ordinary members of the Supreme Court and the Administrative High Court on the one hand and their presidents and vice-presidents as well as all members of the Constitutional Court on the other hand. The 57 ordinary members of the Supreme Court and the 66 ordinary members of the Administrative High Court are appointed by the Federal President on the recommendation of the Federal Cabinet.[18] But in these cases, the Federal Cabinet is bound by recommendations of the staff division (*Personalsenat*) of the Supreme Court and the plenary assembly (*Vollversammlung*) of the Administrative High Court respectively. This provision ensures the

---

[16] *Verwaltungsgerichtsverfahrensgesetz*, BGBl I 24/2017.

[17] See B Bierlein, 'Gedanken zu den ersten fünf Jahren der Verwaltungsgerichtsbarkeit' (2019) *Österreichische Juristen Zeitung* 448ff.

[18] The numbers are taken from the courts' own websites: www.ogh.gv.at/der-oberste-gerichtshof/richterinnen-und-richter, accessed 24 January 2022; and www.vwgh.gv.at/gerichtshof/richterinnen_und_richter/index.html, accessed 24 January 2022, respectively.

influence of the courts on the recruitment of the judges and, thus, may curtail the influence of the political parties. The president and the vice president(s) of the Supreme Court, the president and the vice president of the Administrative Court as well as the president, the vice president, six members and three alternates of the Constitutional Court[19] are appointed on the recommendation of the Federal Cabinet without the involvement of third parties. Although these vacancies have to be publicly announced, there are no public hearings of the candidates and the Federal Cabinet decides behind closed doors. The remaining members and alternates of the Constitutional Court are recommended by the National Council and the Federal Council respectively.

It has never been a secret that all these positions are more often than not filled with affiliates or members of political parties, traditionally the People's Party and the Social Democrats. Unsurprisingly, as junior partners in recent coalition governments, both the Freedom Party and the Green Party have claimed their influence on filling vacancies. In January 2022 it was revealed to the general public that spheres of influence are normally agreed in hidden side-letters to coalition agreements. The side-letters to the 2017 coalition agreement between the People's Party and the Freedom Party as well as the 2019 coalition agreement between the People's Party and the Green Party have been leaked to the media. In the former, not only had spheres of influence been settled but also the names of the president, the vice president and one member of the Constitutional Court had been agreed, long before the positions were vacant and duly announced.[20] All recruitment procedures were thus ridiculed. Maybe, in a country where corruption is fought more seriously, officials would have had to resign from positions they gained in an unfair and even somehow unlawful manner. Remarkably, this was not the case in Austria. There was not even a huge public outcry.

The issue of partisan appointments also affects the president and the vice president of the Administrative High Court, which were also mentioned in the side-letters. Moreover, in the early days of 2022, the public was informed that the vice president of the Supreme Court was partly suspended following (still unproven) allegations that she might

---

[19] Further three members and two alternates are appointed on the proposal from the National Council, the remaining three members and one alternate on the proposal of the Federal Council.

[20] See Der Standard, 28 January 2022, www.derstandard.at/story/2000132943334/sideletter-zeigt-wie-sich-oevp-und-fpoe-posten-im-staat, accessed 17 February 2022.

have been involved in a system of patronage appointments established by a conservative minister of justice.[21]

These incidents are neither surprising nor do they represent a recent development. In 1977 the president of the Constitutional Court retired because he did not concur with a decision of the court that could have only been taken after a partisan appointment had led to a social-democratic majority.[22] But step by step, the wider public is learning the extent of partisan appointments even in the judicial branch of government, because documents previously kept secret are nowadays often leaked to the media. This is obviously a consequence of the more competitive style of party politics. To be fair, the influence political parties exercise on the composition of the bench, especially of a court that is equipped with the power to review laws, is no Austrian peculiarity. Such a court is a political player, despite the efforts of Austrian scholars to argue that reading the law is a purely legal matter and can be entirely detached from political considerations. Hence, what has to be called for is more transparency in filling vacant positions, proper assessment procedures and, especially, public hearings of candidates.

IV. POWERS AND POLICIES OF THE HIGHEST
COURTS PERTAINING TO THE CONSTITUTION

A. The Constitutional Court

As it is the successor to the nineteenth century Imperial Law Court, the Constitutional Court still holds various powers it had inherited from its predecessor. Some of them may be seen as rather unusual.[23] It might be said that the court is somehow hybrid in nature. It acts as a civil law court when it decides on pecuniary claims against territorial corporate bodies, although these claims are (formally) rooted in public law. It acts as a criminal court in all impeachment trials in which it pronounces on

---

[21] See Der Standard, 25 January 2022, www.derstandard.at/story/2000132816284/ogh-vizepraesidentin-zieht-sich-nach-postenschacher-vorwuerfen-zurueck, accessed 26 January 2022.

[22] The incident is covered on the court's own website, see www.vfgh.gv.at/verfassungsgerichtshof/geschichte/zeitleiste.de.html, accessed 17 February 2022.

[23] See also A Gamper and F Palermo, 'The Constitutional Court of Austria: Modern Profiles of an Archetype of Constitutional Review' (2008) 3 *Journal of Comparative Law* 64.

lawsuits that predicate the constitutional responsibility of the highest federal and state authorities for legal contravention ensuing from their official activities. And it acts as an administrative court when it reviews ordinances and decisions of administrative courts of first instance (formerly administrative rulings) for an alleged infringement of a constitutionally guaranteed right. Pronouncing on challenges to the election of the Federal President and to elections to popular representative bodies, also hardly involves specific constitutional questions.

The core element of the powers of the court, and the most interesting here, is the responsibility to review laws. This power was conferred on the court after the demise of the Monarchy. The Imperial Law Court was re-named Constitutional Court in 1919[24] and, in a first step, vested with powers to review and rescind state laws.[25] The 1920 Federal Constitution extended the scope of reviewing laws to federal laws and attributed the power to review and rescind ordinances to the court as well. Consequently, all other courts which under the monarchy had had the power to review ordinances, were deprived of this power. Hence, Austria became the first country in which the concept of centralised review was effectively implemented.[26]

The idea of centralised constitutional review, however, was not entirely new as it had already been discussed under the monarchy, where all courts were explicitly denied the power to review parliamentary statutes.[27] Arguably, such a power undermined the sovereignty of the monarch. As it was feared that courts might adopt a US-style review of laws, the constitution explicitly prevented courts from following the example of the US Supreme Court.[28] This legal situation was intensively debated amongst scholars and Georg Jellinek suggested in 1885[29] that the Imperial Law Court should be equipped with the power to review laws. He argued that the American system would contravene the concept of monarchical sovereignty, mainly because it allowed every judge to

---

[24] StGBl 48/1919 – the court was initially named the German-Austrian Constitutional Court.

[25] StGBl 212/1919.

[26] See also R Machacek, *Austrian Contributions to the Rule of Law* (Kehl, NP Engel Verlag, 1994) 4; and more recently: H Eberhard, 'The Austrian Constitutional Court after 100 Years: Remodelling the Model?' (2021) 76 *Zeitschrift für Öffentliches Recht* 395.

[27] Art 7 Basic Law on Judicial Power (*Staatsgrundgesetz über die richterliche Gewalt*, RGBl 144/1867).

[28] J-C Bluntschli, *Allgemeines Staatsrecht*, Vol 1, 4th edn (München, JG Cotta, 1868) 457ff; R von Mohl, 'Über die rechtliche Bedeutung verfassungswidriger Gesetze' in R von Mohl, *Staatsrecht, Völkerrecht und Politik*, Vol 1 (Tübingen, H Laupp, 1860) 66ff.

[29] G Jellinek, *Ein Verfassungsgerichtshof für Österreich* (Wien, Hölder, 1885).

set aside a law. In a monarchy, it seemed inappropriate for lower court judges to scrutinise a law the monarch had enacted with parliamentary consent, but this would not be so for an apex court composed of the finest and most noble lawyers. Hence, the idea of the centralised system of constitutional review was born.

The concept of the constitutional review of laws was further backed by the doctrine of the hierarchy of laws.[30] It was robustly defended against criticism in the 1920s by Hans Kelsen,[31] who was also involved in designing the court's competence.[32] The concept of centralised review is arguably the only genuine Austrian contribution to the overall development of constitutional law. Austrian public law scholars are dutifully proud of it.[33] However, it will be observed later in this chapter[34] that the system of centralised review only initially implied that all the other courts did not have to consider constitutional questions. This is no longer the case. The clear lines drawn by the original version of the 1920 Constitution had already been blurred by the 1929 amendment, which obliged the Supreme Court and the Administrative High Court to contest the constitutionality of laws they had to apply if they doubted the constitutionality of those laws. This obligation nowadays applies to all courts. What is centralised and therefore monopolised, is the power to pronounce on laws and ordinances and rescind them on the ground that they violate domestic (constitutional) laws. The clear delineation between constitutional adjudication and the business of all other courts has been further blurred by the requirements of fundamental rights protection (see below).

Today, many constitutions have centralised constitutional review but as designs may differ, the main elements of the Austrian design choices will be briefly outlined. First, the core element of Austria's model is the organisation of constitutional review as an '*actus contrarius*' to

---

[30] See H Kelsen, *Pure Theory of Law*, trans by M Knight (Berkeley-Los Angeles, University of California Press, 1967, Kindle Edition) chapter V.35., for the hierarchical structure of the legal order.

[31] H Kelsen, 'Wesen und Entwicklung der Staatsgerichtsbarkeit' (1929) 5 *Veröffentlichungen der Vereinigung der Deutschen Staatsrechtslehrer* 30, 48ff; see also H Kelsen, 'Judicial Review of Legislation. A Comparative Study of the Austrian and the American Constitution' (1942) 4 *The Journal of Politics* 183.

[32] See E Wiederin, 'From the Federalist Papers to *Hans Kelsen's* "Dearest Child": The Genesis of the Austrian Constitutional Court', trans by M Schulze (2021) 76 *Zeitschrift für Öffentliches Recht* 313.

[33] See Wiederin (ibid) 313ff.

[34] See later in this chapter.

legislation. The court explicitly has to rescind a law that is still in force and the rescission has to be published in the respective law gazette to become effective. An entire body of law, a legal provision or even only a word or a group of words may be subject to rescission. The underlying dogma is the idea of legal certainty: probably informed by the chaotic situation after the end of World War I,[35] it seemed to be enormously important that valid laws could be clearly identified.

Second, although probably overstretching the idea of legal certainty,[36] the court may set a deadline for the rescission to become effective which may not exceed 18 months. If such a time limit is set, rescission comes into force only after expiry of the defined period. The consequences are that the already rescinded law cannot be contested within this period although it is still applicable. Unless the court pronounces otherwise, the rescission is not retroactive – the case in point (*Anlassfall*) being an exception.[37]

Third, as a consequence of this concept, the review is always 'abstract' in the sense that it only allows for a bipolar decision.[38] The law is either rescinded or not and therefore it has to be applied to future cases or not. The decision does not allow for a law to be applied in some cases and set aside in others. That may lead to problems relating to human rights issues when cases of hardship cannot be dealt with accordingly.[39] In particular, human rights issues may be at stake when a time limit for the rescission has been set and an unconstitutional law has to be applied with no redress available.

Fourth, this may lead to the observation that constitutional review was initially introduced to protect the separation of responsibilities between the Federation and the states rather than to protect fundamental rights. It may therefore be questioned whether protecting fundamental rights was ever meant to be centralised. This seems especially important for assessing the impact of the European Charter of Fundamental Rights, which will be discussed at the end of the chapter.

---

[35] See ch 1.

[36] V Ferreres Comella, 'The European Model of Constitutional Review and Legislation: Toward Decentralization?' (2004) 2 *International Journal of Constitutional Law* 461, 465, suggests that Hans Kelsen might have even been obsessed by the idea of legal certainty.

[37] For the effects of the court's decisions in time, see M Stelzer, '*Pro Futuro* and Retroactive Effects of Rescissory Judgments in Austria' in P Popelier et al (eds), *The Effects of Judicial Decisions in Time* (Cambridge, Intersentia, 2014) 63ff.

[38] See Ferreres Comella (n 36) 461, 465; Austrian constitutional doctrine distinguishes between 'abstract' and 'concrete' review on a different basis – see Stelzer (ibid) 63, and later in this chapter.

[39] See ch 7.

The power of the court to review laws in general may relate to laws that have already been enacted, which may be rescinded. It also relates to laws already invalidated, which the court cannot rescind. It may only determine that they were unconstitutional. In some cases, the power may also relate to laws that are not yet enacted and, therefore, only exist as draft bills.

This specific *a priori* review of laws may only be initiated by the Federal Cabinet and the state cabinets respectively to determine which territorial entity – the Federation or the states – is responsible for enacting a specific law on the basis of an already drafted bill.[40] No other constitutional question would be considered. The court summarises its decision in a statement (*Rechtssatz*) published in the Federal Law Gazette. The statement has the effect of a constitutional provision and may only be amended by a constitutional law.

According to the Austrian doctrine, reviews of already enacted laws may either be 'concrete' (*konkretes Normprüfungsverfahren*) or 'abstract' (*abstraktes Normprüfungsverfahren*), depending on whether the law has already been applied in a pending law suit (the former) or not (the latter). In both cases, the court would review laws against any constitutional provision including fundamental rights.

With regard to 'abstract judicial review', in the Austrian sense, the Federal Cabinet is entitled to contest any state law and every state cabinet may contest any federal law. Beyond that, federal laws can be contested by a third of the members of the National Council and state laws by a third of the members of a state parliament provided that the respective constitution of the state entitles it to do so. With regard to those bodies which might initiate an 'abstract review' of a law, such proceedings mainly result from severe disputes between political parties. In this context it is noteworthy that the 1974 law on abortion was contested by the government of Salzburg,[41] although it did not jeopardise the federal structure or the sphere of interest of the state of Salzburg in particular. Rather, the conflict was based on a deep ideological divide between the catholic-conservative camp and the Social Democrats.

'Concrete review' of a law or a legal provision may be performed on application by any law court, *ex officio* by the Constitutional Court itself, by an individual alleging direct infringement of her or his substantive

---

[40] See Art 138 para 2 of the Federal Constitution.
[41] See VfSlg 7400/1974; and, further, ch 7 for more details of this case.

rights and by a party to a lawsuit before a court of justice alleging a violation of her or his substantive rights by the court applying an unconstitutional law. Courts have the obligation to contest laws once they have 'reservations' (*Bedenken*) about the constitutionality of a certain law they have to apply or, in other words, if they seriously doubt that the provision may be constitutional.

With regard to formal or procedural requirements of an application to rescind a law, the court has developed a number of prerequisites that allow for enough flexibility to exercise sufficient docket control.[42]

Over the decades, the court has made extensive use of its power to rescind laws. The latest statistics available show that between 2011 and 2018 the court rescinded a legal provision or declared an already invalid legal provision to be unconstitutional in 611 cases. The statistics are slightly misleading as they count the cases in which applications were successful rather than revealing the number of legal provisions involved. As it is not unusual that several cases pertain to the same legal provision, the number of legal provisions found to violate the constitution was probably significantly smaller. However, between 2014 and 2019, 43 provisions were (at least partly) rescinded on the application of courts.

Although the court may review laws under any possible constitutional aspect, some provisions play an overwhelming part in the jurisprudence of the court. These are the constitutional provisions pertaining to the allocation of power between the Federation and the states, which had a dominant role especially in the 1950s and 1960s; further, Art 18 of the Federal Constitution providing for sufficiently clear and detailed laws; and, almost above all, the principle of equality. Out of the 13 legal provisions rescinded or declared unconstitutional in 2018, six were found to violate the principle of equality, two not to be sufficiently clear and detailed, two to upset the allocation of competences, and only three to violate other provisions. Although the statistics are taken from one year only,[43] nevertheless they are indicative of the jurisprudence of the court.

---

[42] See D Fontana, 'Docket Control and the Success of Constitutional Courts' in T Ginsburg and R Dixon (eds), *Comparative Constitutional Law* (Cheltenham-Northampton, Edward Elgar, 2011) 624.

[43] I am deeply indebted to Hanna Koppelent who established all the figures cited in this section by analysing the respective annual reports of the Constitutional Court, found on the court's own website: www.vfgh.gv.at/verfassungsgerichtshof/publikationen/taetigkeitsberichte.de.html.

Rescissions of laws – parliamentary statutes and ordinances alike – happen quite frequently, as the numbers quoted above show. The effects of the jurisprudence are multifold. The court is a political player and, over the decades, it has decisively helped to shape the legal order and the political life in Austria. The retrospective methods applied in the 1950s and 1960s, especially with regard to competence matters, for instance, supported the ideas of consociational democracy as many issues were left to the coalition government to be resolved rather than settled in court. The requirement for laws to be sufficiently clear and detailed had an impact on the design of laws and promoted the *Rechtsstaat* principle. Both issues have already been analysed in previous parts of this book.[44] The case law pertaining to fundamental rights, which will be analysed in depth in the following chapter, has created probably the most important benchmark against which laws nowadays are scrutinised. Especially when adopting the proportionality principle, the court has helped facilitating the Europeanisation of this country. Moreover, fundamental rights questions play an important part in almost all current topics.

To cope with the jurisprudence of the court, constitutional services at the federal and at state levels scrutinise all statutes and ordinances before they are enacted. Less surprisingly, these services are not attached to parliament but to the administration – in the case of the Federation, the Federal Chancellery.[45]

Despite its politicisation, the court is highly regarded and its judgments are, *grosso modo*, implemented. However, there still is an issue with a certain lack of transparency.[46] Neither the identity of the rapporteur nor the result of the voting is disclosed. It is not officially announced if the decision was unanimous or split. In the latter case, it is therefore not known who was in favour of the ruling and who was not, although rumours may circulate in Austria's fairly small legal community.

Moreover, no dissenting opinions are admissible. Allowing for publication of dissenting opinions has already been discussed on several occasions and demanded by many academics.[47] Recently, a new effort

---

[44] See chs 1, 3 and 5.

[45] See, for instance, the account of the tasks of the constitutional service at the Federal Chancellery, www.bundeskanzleramt.gv.at/agenda/verfassung.html, accessed 22 February 2022.

[46] G Schernthanner, 'Der Verfassungsgerichtshof und seine Unabhängigkeit' (2003) *Österreichische Juristen Zeitung* 621.

[47] F Ermacora, 'Reform der Verfassungsgerichtsbarkeit' in B-C Funk et al (eds), *Staatsrecht und Staatswissenschaften in Zeiten des Wandels – Festschrift Adamovich* (Wien-New York,

was undertaken by a draft bill providing for transparency of the administration. Immediately, the idea was again rejected by representatives of the court on the ground that it might undermine the working style of the court which aims at finding compromises.[48] It seems that the court is still acting in the spirit of the post-war consociational democracy and has failed to adapt to a more competitive environment. However, this attitude makes it impossible to assess the impact of individual judges on the case law of the court.

This attitude also shapes the almost schizophrenic style of the court's reasonings. The judges in Austria literally hide behind the institution of the court when they address themselves as 'the Constitutional Court' in the court's case law, thus pretending that the court is a completely impersonal institution enjoying almost imperial authority and dignity. This is in stark contrast, for instance, to the style of the US Supreme Court and the UK Supreme Court respectively.

B. The Administrative High Court

According to its original design, the Administrative High Court was the sole guardian of the lawfulness of the public administration. A 1946 amendment to the Federal Constitution[49] even emphatically proclaimed that the Administrative High Court ensured 'the legality of the entire administration'. Reality, however, was more prosaic. The powers of the court were restricted to reviewing specific types of administrative acts, initially to rulings (*Bescheide*) and in – negligible cases – instructions. If unlawfulness was established, the court could only repeal them. Its core function therefore was to pronounce on complaints that alleged the unlawfulness of rulings by administrative authorities (*Bescheidbeschwerde*), or, in common law terms, to exercise *certiorari*.[50]

Springer, 1992) 49, 51; R Machacek, 'Die Einrichtung der "Dissenting Opinion" im internationalen Vergleich – Einführung des Minderheitsvotums am Verfassungsgerichtshof' (1999) 7 *Journal für Rechtspolitik* 1; H Mayer, 'Die Einführung der "dissenting opinion" am Verfassungsgerichtshof aus Sicht der österreichischen Verfassungslehre' (1999) 7 *Journal für Rechtspolitik* 30.

[48] See Der Standard, 22 March 2021, www.derstandard.at/story/2000125233950/warum-der-verfassungsgerichtshof-so-stark-auf-konsens-setzt, accessed 17 February 2022.

[49] BGBl 211/1946.

[50] For the common law terminology, see, for instance, P Leyland, *The Constitution of the United Kingdom*, 4th edn (Oxford, Hart, 2021) 199.

Cases of *mandamus* – forcing an authority to act – were only admissible if an administrative authority was in breach of the statutory obligation to issue a ruling. Other remedies were not offered. The 1975 extension of the jurisdiction of the court to review the so-called 'exercise of direct power and compulsion'[51] was only due to the circumstance that the Constitutional Court had always applied a broader understanding to the term 'ruling', which also covered these type of administrative acts. The purpose of the constitutional amendment, therefore, was to deal with an unacceptable situation,[52] created by the different reading of the term 'ruling' by the two apex courts, based on a different understanding of the law – the Administrative High Court being more restrictive and formalistic than the Constitutional Court.

This example may demonstrate the structural problems created by two high courts operating on the same level, with no cross appeals allowed – one responsible for reviewing administrative rulings for a purported violation of fundamental rights and the other responsible for scrutinising such rulings for an alleged unlawfulness. It may come as no surprise that this system triggered overlaps and loopholes and was far from offering comprehensive legal protection.

Such loopholes might have stemmed from different interpretations of the applicable law. The Constitutional Court might have given the law a specific interpretation in the light of fundamental rights, while the Administrative High Court might have denied the methodological admissibility of such an interpretation and argued that, at most, the law might be unconstitutional. The 1929 amendment of the constitution conferred an obligation on the Administrative High Court to file an application with the Constitutional Court if it seriously doubts whether a law it has to apply in a pending case was consistent with the constitution. It might be said that, since then, the Administrative High Court is also obliged to consider constitutional questions (the same applies nowadays to all administrative courts). However, applications by the Administrative High Court have not necessarily been successful. The Constitutional Court might have construed the law in accordance with

---

[51] This, even with regard to the legal term's highly artificial expression, covers, for instance, arrests without a warrant, house or body searches without a warrant etc. They may be legal under specific circumstances but in many cases they are not. Without extending the power of the courts to review them, blatantly illegal and most drastic encroachments on fundamental rights would have remained without consequences.

[52] Claimants were granted standing when applying at the Constitutional Court but when the court found that no fundamental right was violated and referred the case to the Administrative High Court, their complaint was instantly rejected.

the constitution. In such a case, it would have been consequent and desirable for the Administrative High Court to follow this interpretation. But this was not always the case either, as the Administrative High Court insisted on its competence to safeguard the legality of the administration and to autonomously interpret the law. This gave the administration ample room for discretion, as it could choose which court to follow. Politicians (state governors or ministers, for example) could instruct the administration accordingly. To end the struggle between the two public law courts, which came very much at the expense of the claimant seeking legal redress, the Constitutional Court might have had no other option than to finally rescind the law.[53]

One of the most significant cases – although arguably exceptional – that revealed the structural problems of Austria's rather archaic concept, was the case of Jehovah's Witnesses requesting recognition as a religious society. Finally, the case had to be brought before the ECtHR, ending 17 years of litigation.[54] This litigation hardly ever touched the merits of the case – but revolved around the question of how *mandamus* could be effected following the inactivity of the responsible minister who did not issue what would have been an ordinance, recognising the Jehovah's Witnesses as a religious society. As the law did not explicitly provide for issuing an administrative ruling should the request be rejected (an ordinance would have been out of question in such a case anyway), the obvious lacuna gave the two courts ample leeway to consider procedural questions and reject applications the other court would have deemed to be admissible. This dispute between the two courts also revealed the almost cynical consequences of a 'positivistic' reading of laws, completely ignoring the purpose of a court to offer legal redress. The procedural question was finally solved by the Constitutional Court 'filling a lacuna' by purporting a 'negative conflict of jurisdiction' between the Administrative High Court and itself which the Constitutional Court had to pronounce upon. It is not only such exceptional cases that have led to situations which are reminiscent of the work of the great Prague-born author Franz Kafka.[55]

---

[53] See, for instance, the case of Art 3 of the Aliens Police Act (*Fremdenpolizeigesetz*, BGBl 75/1954), VfSlg 8792/1980 – interpretation in consistency with Art 8 ECHR; and VfSlg 10737/1985 – rescission of the legal provision in question.

[54] See *Religionsgemeinschaft der Zeugen Jehovas and others v Austria* (App no 40825/98) ECtHR 31 July 2008.

[55] See the great novels *Das Schloss* (*The Castle*) and *Der Prozess* (*The Trial*); readers who are more familiar with the works of Charles Dickens may be reminded of *Jarndyce and Jarndyce*, the 'interminable brief' law case before the Court of Chancery, told in the novel *Bleak House*.

However, the 2014 reform of administrative jurisdiction completely changed the role of the Administrative High Court and contributed to alleviate the structural shortcomings. The Administrative High Court nowadays forms the second tier of judicial review, and thus it has become a court of appeal. It may revise decisions of administrative courts of first instance. Such a revision, however, may only be admissible if it concerns a legal question of essential relevance, in particular if the ruling of the administrative court deviates from the case law of the Administrative High Court or if such a case law has not been established or is inconsistent. The Administrative High Court is also entitled to decide on the merits of a case although it rarely does so.

There may still be some cases of affirmative or negative conflicts of jurisdiction between these two apex courts, but the effects will be far less serious, as the Constitutional Court nowadays pronounces on decisions of administrative courts rather than administrative rulings. Situations like the ones outlined above in which an administrative court would refuse to construe a law in accordance with the constitution are less likely to occur as these courts do not have to assert themselves as being apex courts and, with regard to the state administrative courts, it is difficult to imagine that all nine courts would act alike. Apart from that, no politician would have the power to influence law enforcement by means of instructions at this stage. The case of the Jehovah's Witnesses would be resolved fairly quickly as an application arguing that the minister breached an obligation to issue a ruling would have to be filed with the Federal Administrative Court. Should it reject the application, its decision could be immediately contested in the Constitutional Court and repealed.

Although most of these cases seem to be of historic interest only, another rivalry between the three courts has been opened up by the European Charter of Fundamental Rights. This will be discussed in the last section of this chapter.

C. The Supreme Court

The Supreme Court is the apex court of the ordinary branch of jurisdiction. According to the original version of the 1920 Constitution, the ordinary branch of jurisdiction was completely separated from the public law courts. It is significant, that up to the present day, the two branches of jurisdiction also affect the training of judges: while ordinary judges have to undergo specific training after their legal studies, judges of public law courts merely have to gain some additional professional experience.

All courts of justice, the Supreme Court historically being the first, are under an obligation to contest a law whenever they doubt its constitutionality. Therefore, like the administrative courts, they also have to consider constitutional questions. The parties of the pending law suit may try to convince the court that a law violates the constitution. Should they fail to do so, remedies are limited.

Such a remedy has existed only since 2015 and it only pertains to a decision of a court of first instance. If such a decision is appealed in due course by at least one party, either party may file an application with the Constitutional Court. The party must allege that the decision of the court of justice has violated that party's rights by applying an unconstitutional law (or an unlawful ordinance). This remedy will lead to a review of the law but not of the decision of the court of justice. In situations where constitutional concerns arise at later stages of the process, it is still only in the hands of the Supreme Court as well as other appellate courts to safeguard the constitution in the fields of their jurisdiction. Unfortunately, no statistics are available that indicate how often the Supreme Court contests a law. Observers may get the impression that this very rarely arises and that the court would try to solve constitutional questions by interpretation rather than by taking the risk of challenging a law.

Further competencies pertaining to the constitution were conferred on the Supreme Court within the fields of criminal law. The court has jurisdiction to rule on complaints alleging the infringement of the right to personal freedom by someone who is detained on the order of a judge or a criminal court (*Grundrechtsbeschwerde*).[56] In such a case, the Supreme Court would basically review the reasoning given by the lower court. Should it find that the reasoning was unreasonable or inconclusive, it would quash the decision, but would not necessarily terminate the detention. The lower court, thus, would get another chance to produce better arguments.

With regard to the ECHR, the Supreme Court has been made responsible for implementing rulings of the ECtHR.[57] Should the ECtHR establish that a decision of a criminal law court has violated the ECHR,

---

[56] Fundamental Rights Complaint Act (*Grundrechtsbeschwerde-Gesetz*, BGBl 864/1992).
[57] Art 363a of the Code of Criminal Procedure (*Strafprozessordnung*, StPO, BGBl 631/1975 in the version of BGBl 762/1996).

anyone who has been affected by such a decision may apply to the Supreme Court to reopen the case. Reopening has to be granted when it cannot be denied that the infringement of a right guaranteed by the ECHR had a disadvantaging effect on the court's original decision. But the Supreme Court did not stop at this point. Empowering itself as the 'safeguard of fundamental rights' in the fields of criminal law, in a 2007 landmark decision, it held that it did not need a ruling of the ECtHR to reopen a case, but could establish on its own whether the ECHR was violated.[58] In doing so, the Supreme Court claimed that it was filling a lacuna with regard to Art 13 ECHR, which imposes a duty on the Member States to provide for efficient domestic legal remedies if a right guaranteed by the ECHR is infringed. This ruling of the Supreme Court clearly abandoned its traditional (more formal) approach of reading the Criminal Procedure Law Code (*Strafprozessordnung*). Hence, the court was heavily criticised for allegedly having blatantly crossed the fine line between judicial adjudication and policy-making.[59]

In a 2018 decision,[60] the Supreme Court denied that this power could be further extended to safeguarding the European Charter of Fundamental Rights, following a preliminary ruling of the ECJ that it had asked for.

In the field of civil law, it is the responsibility of the civil law courts and, foremost, the Supreme Court to decide whether fundamental rights may be attributed a third party effect, thus answering the question if and to what extent fundamental rights might have a bearing on the legal relationship between private actors. Initially, fundamental rights arguments played no part in civil law doctrine. Only the Data Protection Act (*Datenschutzgesetz*) explicitly endowed the fundamental right to data protection with a third party effect. It was, therefore, up to the jurisprudence of the Supreme Court to discover such an effect in other fundamental rights. In the meantime, the Supreme Court has established a considerable case law that will be discussed in Chapter 7.

Therefore it becomes clear that despite Austria's centralised system of constitutional review, there are vast fields of law in which the civil and criminal law courts under the guidance of the Supreme Court have to deal with fundamental rights and constitutional issues. In some cases, it is the sole responsibility of the Supreme Court to protect fundamental

---

[58] OGH 1.8.2007, 13Os135/06m.
[59] S Reindl-Krauskopf, 'Die neue Erneuerung des Strafverfahrens – zulässige Analogie oder Rechtsschöpfung?' (2008) 130 *Juristische Blätter* 130.
[60] OGH 30.11.2018, 13Os49/16d.

rights. Although initially reluctant, the Supreme Court has become more and more aware of this responsibility. One of the reasons for this is that, from the early 1990s onwards, specific fundamental rights courses have become integral parts of law school curricula and fundamental rights doctrine has played a decisive part in legal education.

However, substantial reforms of this system have been discussed during recent decades.[61] In particular, at one point it was envisaged that the Constitutional Court would be granted the power to decide on applications against rulings of the Administrative High Court and the Supreme Court respectively. This would have ensured that all constitutional questions ultimately could have been brought before the Constitutional Court and strengthened the concept of centralised constitutional adjudication. However, this reform has not been enacted for various reasons. Most prominently, it has faced resistance from the judges of the two other apex courts, as it would have deprived them of the status of 'highest judges'.

D. The Impact of EU Law on the Court System

Before 1995, the Constitutional Court had the power to review every law valid in Austria. After the accession to the European Union, an ever increasing part of laws applicable in Austria were removed from the court's jurisdiction. The court followed the view that it had no power to scrutinise European laws – regulations and directives – for compliance with European primary law and that it had no power to review domestic laws implementing directives for compliance with these directives. Only in the case of a directive providing for a considerable amount of discretion was the domestic law also reviewed against the Austrian constitution and, in particular, domestic fundamental rights. Thus, standards of 'double conditionality' (*doppelte Bedingtheit*)[62] were established.

This jurisprudence already undermined the concept of centralised review as each law court (and even each administrative authority) was

---

[61] This was especially discussed during the Austrian Convention (2003–05); see C Jabloner, 'Die Gesetzesbeschwerde' in A Bammer (ed), *Rechtsschutz gestern – heute – morgen* (Wien-Graz, Neuer Wissenschaftlicher Verlag, 2008) 219; M Hiesel, 'Gedanken zu einer grundlegenden Reform der Aufgabenverteilung zwischen Verfassungs- und Verwaltungsgerichtsbarkeit' (2009) 17 *Journal für Rechtspolitik* 221.

[62] K Korinek, 'Die doppelte Bedingtheit von gemeinschaftsrechtsausführenden innerstaatlichen Rechtsvorschriften' in S Hammer et al (eds), *Demokratie und sozialer Rechtsstaat in Europa – Festschrift Öhlinger* (Wien, WUV, 2004) 131.

empowered to set aside a domestic law for non-compliance with EU law, which in this case would have been a higher ranking norm. In the end, this seemed acceptable as the question of whether a domestic law was in compliance with a European directive normally did not involve genuine constitutional considerations.

This picture changed dramatically once the European Charter of Fundamental Rights was adopted and all law courts were additionally attributed the power to review domestic laws implementing European law against Charter rights. On the assumption that it was the guardian of fundamental rights, the Constitutional Court tried to claw back some of its competences. In a – probably slightly overrated – decision, nevertheless trumpeted with pomp and circumstances and even published in English on the court's own website,[63] the court stated that it would acknowledge the power to review domestic laws against Charter rights if they substantially mirrored rights guaranteed in the constitution ('be similar to rights guaranteed in the constitution with regard to their phrasing and determination').[64]

The case itself was rather unspectacular, as the court did not even find that the fundamental right was violated. A Chinese citizen had been denied asylum and had appealed the administrative decision at the (former) Asylum Court. The court had rejected the appeal but had insisted that the facts of the case had already been sufficiently established, and therefore it denied an oral hearing. The asylum seeker launched an application with the Constitutional Court invoking Art 47 of the European Charter of Fundamental Rights (as the scope of Art 6 ECHR would not have covered the case). Although the court found that Art 47 of the Charter was not violated, it nevertheless used the opportunity to basically accept Charter rights as fundamental rights in the sense of the Austrian constitution. The practical impact of this decision, however, was rather limited: it allowed for the application of principles of fair trial according to Art 47 of the Charter in fields of law that were not covered by Art 6 ECHR (mainly asylum law and tax law).

The decision, at least implicitly, suggested that each court and therefore also the Supreme Court and the Administrative High Court had to refer a case to the Constitutional Court whenever it considered a domestic

---

[63] www.vfgh.gv.at/downloads/VfGH_U_466-11__U_1836-11_Grundrechtecharta_english.pdf, accessed 18 January 2022.
[64] VfSlg 19632/2012.

law to violate Charter rights – blatantly contradicting *Simmenthal*.[65] The two apex courts applied different strategies in reacting to this decision.

The Administrative High Court basically ignored the decision, carrying on setting aside domestic laws whenever it found them in breach of Charter rights. Thus, for instance, it set aside a domestic tax provision implementing the EU's VAT directive which it found to infringe Art 20 of the Charter (principle of equality).[66] It even set aside a provision of its own procedural laws in the light of Art 47.[67] The first case is especially remarkable as it demonstrates the specific changes the legal system underwent after the adoption of the Charter. Before the adoption, the Administrative High Court would have had to contest the domestic law implementing a directive for a possible breach of the domestic principle of equality which would have been applied according to the doctrine of 'double conditionality'. After the adoption of the Charter, the court may invoke Art 20 of the Charter and set aside the law on its own. This, as already mentioned, works only if the directive allows for sufficient discretion for its implementation. Should the directive allow for no such discretion, it might itself violate Charter rights in which case the court would have to refer the question to the ECJ.

The Supreme Court chose a different strategy, opting for more publicity. It referred the case to the ECJ asking for a preliminary decision. The answer was by no means surprising: the ECJ did not explicitly deny the powers of the Constitutional Court as it would not interfere with domestic legal systems as long as any court could scrutinise and set aside domestic laws that infringed the European Charter of Fundamental Rights. Since then, it has become part of the jurisprudence of the Supreme Court to duly consider Charter rights.[68]

Consequently, this leads to a rather confusing situation. When a court considers a (domestic) law to violate a constitutional right, it has to refer the case to the Constitutional Court which will ultimately pronounce on it. Should a court hold that a domestic law implementing EU legislation

---

[65] Case 106/77, *Amminstrazione della Finanze dello Stato v Simmenthal SpA* ECLI:EU:C:1978:49.

[66] VwGH 28.6.2017, Ro 2015/15/0045; see K Spies and S Zolles, 'Harmonisierung mit Folgen: Zur Konkurrenz von VwGH und VfGH als Grundrechtsgerichte im Steuerrecht' (2018) 45 *Österreichische Zeitschrift für Wirtschaftsrecht* 134ff.

[67] VwGH 23.1.2013, 2010/15/0196.

[68] OGH 4.3.2013, 8Ob7/13g; 16.12.2014, 10ObS44/14i; 24.10.2017, 4Ob121/17y; 27.2.2019, 9ObA11/19m.

does not comply with a right enshrined in the Charter, it may simply set aside the domestic law. Therefore, it can no longer be said that judicial review – with regards to fundamental rights – is centralised. In reality, there is a mixed system in place, combining elements of centralised with elements of diffused review.

Further, this begs the question of whether a centralised review organised as a '*contrarius actus*' to legislation meets the demands of fundamental rights review. As will be shown in Chapter 7, this form of abstract review creates cases of hardship that could be eliminated under a diffused system that allows for setting aside a law in specific cases without ending the validity of the law as such. It is especially problematic that a law violating fundamental rights remains applicable when a time limit has been set for its expiry and no further avenues of redress are available. This begs the question whether the Austrian model of centralised review, which was not meant to safeguard fundamental rights in the first place, is too one-sidedly focused on legal certainty with regard to a modern system of fundamental rights protection.

V. CONCLUSION

The Austrian constitution establishes a judicial system that consists of three branches: the ordinary jurisdiction, responsible for criminal and civil lawsuits, with a Supreme Court at its apex; the administrative jurisdiction, spearheaded by the Administrative High Court and responsible for reviewing administrative acts; and a single Constitutional Court, mainly responsible for reviewing laws and ordinances. The three apex courts operate on the same level with no cross appeals allowed. This leads to overlaps and loopholes which have not been eradicated on a systemic basis but have been dealt with gradually by frequent constitutional amendments. The latest, the introduction of administrative courts of first instance as of 2014, was probably the largest reform finally meeting Austria's obligation under Arts 5 and 6 ECHR.

As the courts of the other branches were not allowed to rescind laws, judicial review was centralised in 1920 in Austria. This was the first time such a system had been effectively established anywhere in the world. This system has been challenged and severely undermined by expanding fundamental rights protection and, moreover, after Austria's accession to the European Union. Under European law and especially the European Charter of Fundamental Rights, all courts (and even administrative authorities) have the power to scrutinise domestic laws against European law and set them aside in case of non-compliance. Thus, a rather complicated mixed system has been created, comprising elements of centralised as well as elements of diffused judicial review.

FURTHER READING

Eberhard, H, 'The Austrian Constitutional Court after 100 Years: Remodelling the Model?' (2021) 76 *Zeitschrift für Öffentliches Recht* 395.

Frank, SL, *Gesetzesbeschwerde: der Parteiantrag auf Gesetzesprüfung im System der österreichischen Verfassungsgerichtsbarkeit; Entstehung, Prozessvoraussetzungen, Formerfordernisse, Verfahren vor dem VfGH, Entscheidung und Entscheidungswirkungen* (Wien, LexisNexis-Verlag, 2015).

Gamper, A and Palermo, F, 'The Constitutional Court of Austria: Modern Profiles of an Archetype of Constitutional Review' (2008) 3 *Journal of Comparative Law* 64.

Grabenwarter, C et al (eds), *Verfassungsgerichtsbarkeit in der Zukunft - Zukunft der Verfassungsgerichtsbarkeit* (Wien, Verlag Österreich, 2021).

Handstanger, M, 'Das System der Verwaltungsgerichtsbarkeit im Spiegel der Rechtsprechung' in LK Adamovich et al (eds), *Festschrift für Gerhart Holzinger* (Wien, Verlag Österreich, 2017) 275.

Kelsen, H, 'Judicial Review of Legislation. A Comparative Study of the Austrian and the American Constitution' (1942) 4 *The Journal of Politics* 183.

Klaushofer, R and Palmstorfer, R, 'Austrian Constitutional Court Uses Charter of Fundamental Rights of the European Union as Standard of Review: Effects on Union Law' (2013) 19 *European Public Law* 1.

Köhler, M, 'The Reform of the Administrative Jurisdiction in Austria – Theoretical Background and Main Features of the System' (2015) 14 *Public Security and Public Order* 31.

Müller, R (ed), *Verfahren vor dem VfGH, dem VwGH und den VwG. Leitfaden für die Praxis mit Darlegungen auch zu EMRK-Beschwerden* (Wien, Manz, 2020).

Olechowski, T, *Der österreichische Verwaltungsgerichtshof* (Wien, Verlag Österreich, 2001).

Walter, R, 'Die Gerichtsbarkeit' in Schambeck, H (ed), *Das österreichische Bundes-Verfassungsgesetz und seine Entwicklung* (Berlin, Duncker & Humblot, 1980) 443.

Wiederin, E, 'From the Federalist Papers to *Hans Kelsen*'s "Dearest Child": The Genesis of the Austrian Constitutional Court', trans by M Schulze (2021) 76 *Zeitschrift für Öffentliches Recht* 313.

7

Fundamental Rights

Introduction – General Aspects – Binding Effect on the Administration –
Binding Effect on the Legislation – Selected Case Law – Conclusion

I. INTRODUCTION

IN ITS FIRST part, this chapter will focus on the development of
fundamental rights protection in Austria. It will emphasise that
the idea of human rights was already promoted by the 1811 Civil
Law Code and that a fundamental rights charter, basically binding
on the administration, was enacted in 1867. While the 1920 Federal
Constitution did not add to the substance of the fundamental rights
charter, it nevertheless enhanced its implementation. Political negotiations on a substantive reform of the 1867 charter have remained unsuccessful so far; the only major step forward was taken by ratifying the
ECHR. When implementing European law, Austrian courts and authorities have to apply the European Charter of Fundamental Rights.

Over the years, the Constitutional Court has developed and/or
adopted several tests to review laws, administrative rulings and decisions of administrative courts respectively against fundamental rights.
These tests mirror the defensive function of fundamental rights, offering protection against encroachment by state actions. The tests vary
depending on the specific right or the specific category of rights involved.
General tests have been designed for freedom rights and the principle of
equality. In the case of other rights, especially procedural rights, singu-
lar tests apply, matching the specific demands of the right involved. The
chapter will analyse the general tests only, namely the proportionality
test and the objectivity test.

Although fundamental rights are mainly seen as 'defensive rights' and
social rights are missing on a constitutional level, it is remarkable that
this has not prevented the establishment of a comprehensive and effective social welfare system. Moreover, civil law courts, under the guidance

of the Supreme Court, have acknowledged that fundamental rights may have a third party effect.

The final section of the chapter will discuss selected cases decided by the Constitutional Court which are of more general interest. These judgments have informed the political debate in Austria and the issues involved may be relevant in many other countries. Some of these issues, like abortion, have been around for quite some time; others, like LGBTQ+ rights and digital surveillance, have become more significant recently; and measures taken to curb the Covid-19 pandemic are, at the time of writing, highly topical. The position of the court vis-à-vis the government, tilting to the political right, will be evaluated.

II. GENERAL ASPECTS

A. History and Character of Fundamental Rights in Austria

As it has already been made clear in Chapter 1, Austria was not among the first countries in the world to enact a bill of rights. Nevertheless, the philosophy of the age of enlightenment and its idea that all men (and women) were born free and equal, that inspired the various declarations of fundamental rights in the late eighteenth century, played a part in Austria's legal system at a fairly early stage. As already shown in Chapter 1, Joseph II was fascinated by these ideas, especially by the concept of equality. Hence, he commissioned a new civil law code which was drafted and tested in the province of West-Galicia before it was enacted throughout the empire in 1811. This civil law code has remained the core element of Austria's civil law system ever since. It contains a provision according to which every human being has 'inborn' or 'inherent' rights which are 'evident by reason'. Consequently, every human being has to be regarded as an equal person. Hence, every form of slavery was abolished.[1] The semantic similarity to earlier fundamental rights declarations, such as the 1776 Virginia Bill of Rights, seems to be evident.

Efforts to establish a comprehensive bill of rights were made at the Kremsier Reichstag,[2] where draft versions were debated. Although none of these became law, they are still remarkable from a linguistic and philosophical point of view as their phrasing reveals the influence of the political ideas of John Locke and/or Immanuel Kant. Two decades

---

[1] See Art 16 of the Civil Law Code.
[2] See ch 1.

later, the language would be much more sober and 'juridical', losing its philosophical tone and establishing the sober style of Austrian constitutional law.

In a first step towards curtailing state powers, two laws were enacted in 1862: the Personal Liberty Act (*Gesetz zum Schutz der persönlichen Freiheit*, RGBl 87/1862), which basically implemented the 'habeas corpus' rule, and the Rights of the Home Act (*Gesetz zum Schutz des Hausrechts*, RGBl 88/1862), which contained a universal right not to have one's home searched without a proper warrant. The latter of these two laws is still in force today.

In 1867, the Basic Law on the General Rights of Nationals (*Staatsgrundgesetz über die allgemeinen Rechte der Staatsbürger*, RGBl 142/1867) followed. It comprised a charter of classic freedom rights, such as freedom of speech, of religion, of assembly, of association, of employment and a property clause, as well as a general principle of equality and an equal right to access public functions.[3] The main task of this charter was to limit the power of the executive branch of the (monarchical) government. Nevertheless, the framers made it clear that they expected fundamental rights to serve as principles for the drafting of legislation.[4]

However, the procedural guarantees of these rights were rather poor. The Imperial Law Court was only entrusted with the responsibility of protecting the 'political' rights of this charter against infringements by the administration (other rights like those derived from the property clause were exempt from its jurisdiction).[5] Moreover, it did not have the power to repeal administrative rulings but only to assert that a fundamental right was violated. No court had the power to review laws. Therefore, it was up to the emperor and the consenting parliament to determine the influence of fundamental rights on the legislation.

When the Federal Constitution was drafted in 1920, political parties could not agree on a new charter of fundamental rights, mainly because they were split over the issue of social rights. Thus, the 1867 Basic Law on the General Rights of Nationals remained in force. Even after 1945, it was impossible to redraft the 1867 charter. In the 1960s, 1970s and 1980s,

---

[3] For a more thorough assessment of this law, see F Merli et al (eds), *150 Jahre Staatsgrundgesetz über die allgemeinen Rechte der Staatsbürger* (Wien, Manz, 2018).

[4] M Stelzer, *Das Wesensgehaltsargument und der Grundsatz der Verhältnismäßigkeit* (Wien-New York, Springer, 1991) 237; *Die neue Gesetzgebung in Österreich – Erläutert aus den Reichsrathsverhandlungen*, Vol I (Wien, GJ Manz, 1868) 310.

[5] Art 3 of the 1867 Basic Law Concerning the Establishment of an Imperial Law Court (*Staatsgrundgesetz vom 21. December 1867, über die Einsetzung eines Reichsgerichtes*) RGBl 143/1867.

further attempts were made as a Fundamental Rights Reform Commission (*Grundrechtsreformkommission*) was established. Its comprehensive proposals only led to a minor reform: in 1988, the 1862 Personal Liberty Act was redrafted (BGBl 684/1988). The Constitutional Convention took up the matter again and recommended a new charter including social rights. Although it seems that this charter was supported by both the Social Democrats and the Conservatives at one point, nothing resulted from it.

In any event, the Federal Constitution of 1920 was of major importance for the development of the protection of fundamental rights. It assigned the newly created Constitutional Court the power to repeal administrative rulings if they had infringed a 'constitutionally guaranteed right'. Although the term 'constitutionally guaranteed right' is more formal than the term 'fundamental right', it nevertheless covers fundamental rights which are generally guaranteed at the level of constitutional law.

A large and initially unforeseeable step in the development of fundamental rights was taken when Austria signed the ECHR in 1958. Convention rights were adopted at the level of constitutional law and were made directly applicable. As a consequence, any complaint filed with the Constitutional Court may invoke the rights of the ECHR. Although it was initially reluctant, the court has more or less followed the precedents of the ECtHR. This has also had a bearing on the domestic bill of rights: the 1867 Basic Law on the General Rights of Nationals.[6]

Following its accession to the European Union, Austria had to adopt the European Charter of Fundamental Rights in 2008. Those rights are directly applicable in all matters of implementing and executing European law.[7]

Apart from these three main charters, further rights are entrenched by the 1920 Constitution (most prominently, the principle of equality), the 1862 Rights of the Home Act and the 1988 Protection of Personal Liberty Act (BGBl 684/1988), both already mentioned, as well as several other constitutional laws and constitutional provisions.[8] The general

---

[6] See ch 1.

[7] See ch 6.

[8] Most notably, rights of ethnic minority groups who remained in Austria after the downfall of the monarchy, according to the 1919 State Treaty of St Germain and the 1955 State Treaty of Vienna; Art 1 of the Data Protection Act (*Datenschutzgesetz*, BGBl I 165/1999 in the applicable version), and a 1973 constitutional law transforming the International Convention on the Elimination of all Forms of Racial Discrimination (*Bundesverfassungsgesetz vom 3. Juli 1973 zur Durchführung des Internationalen Übereinkommens über die Beseitigung aller Formen rassischer Diskriminierung*, BGBl 390/1973).

impression of a highly fragmented constitution therefore also applies to the area of fundamental rights.

The Austrian constitutional system of safeguarding fundamental rights first and foremost reflects the classic understanding of these rights as defensive rights (*Abwehrrechte*). This concept means that the holder[9] of a fundamental right is entitled to challenge state actions that might encroach upon these rights. State actions, such as administrative acts, ordinances and statutes, may be rescinded by the Constitutional Court if they are held to violate those rights.

Nevertheless, it is clear that the defensive function on its own would not suffice to force states to refrain from interfering with rights: the whole concept of 'defensive rights' must be underpinned by a system of courts upheld and financed by the state. It was the German constitutional doctrine and, consequently, the German Federal Constitutional Court that first suggested that fundamental rights obliged the state not only to refrain from interfering with freedom rights, but also to protect them (*Schutzpflichten*)[10] and, moreover, to take measures to make freedom rights enjoyable for everyone (*Leistungspflichten*).[11] The reason for attaching different 'functions' to fundamental rights originates from different pre-legal concepts of fundamental rights. These concepts may be informed by more philosophical and historical considerations and revolve around the question whether fundamental rights were designed to guarantee that citizens were *legally free* to make life style choices or intended citizens to be *de facto free* to enjoy these rights.[12] If, for example, somebody owns an apartment that is contaminated by toxic gas from a nearby factory, she or he is still legally free to use it; *de facto*, however, she or he will have to abandon it in order to survive. As long as only legal freedom falls within the scope of fundamental rights, rights

---

[9] Holders of fundamental rights may not only be individuals but also legal entities if the rights are applicable to such entities. For example a public body may invoke the property clause but not the right to family life. Further, it is a specific feature of the Austrian legal system that territorial corporate bodies can also hold fundamental rights. Thus, a state may sue the Federation in case of an expropriation claiming that its property rights have been violated (and vice versa). See, for instance, VfSlg 11828/1988.

[10] See, for instance, BVerfGE 39, 1 (41) – Schwangerschaftsabbruch I; BVerfGE 46, 160 – Schleyer; P Unruh, *Zur Dogmatik der grundrechtlichen Schutzpflichten* (Berlin, Duncker & Humblot, 1996).

[11] See, for instance, M Sachs, 'Vorbemerkungen zu Abschnitt I' in M Sachs (ed), *Grundgesetz Kommentar*, 2nd edn (München, CH Beck, 1999) 93.

[12] C O'Cinneide and M Stelzer, 'Horizontal effect/state action' in M Tushnet et al (eds), *Routledge Handbook of Constitutional Law* (London-New York, Routledge, 2013) 177, 178.

are not affected in this case of contamination. The situation is different if human rights were designed to guarantee that individuals are also *de facto* free to enjoy their rights. In that case, the contamination of the apartment may be seen as an encroachment upon their rights and states may be forced to action. Usually, the answer to this question is not given in the bill of rights but lies in the theory that is supplied to interpret it.[13] In its settled case law, the ECtHR holds that the rights laid down in the ECHR may also oblige states to take protective measures, although it is not quite clear to what extent. In the case of the contaminated apartment, the ECtHR ruled that according to Art 8 ECHR it had been the duty of the state involved at least to inform the apartment owner in time.[14]

Despite the case law of the ECtHR, in Austria there are only limited possibilities to enforce the state's obligation to take (preventive) measures in order to protect fundamental rights. As laws may only be reviewed against fundamental rights after they have been enacted, there is basically no legal remedy to force the legislator to act in cases where it deliberately remains inactive.

This problem has become apparent again only recently. Several individuals, following successful examples in other countries like the Netherlands and Germany,[15] filed a 'direct' application with the Constitutional Court in order to provoke preventive measures to battle climate change. The starting point of their argument was the observation that air traffic was a main source for greenhouse gas emissions, which in general threatened their lives (Art 2 ECHR) and encroached on other fundamental rights. As they could not simply demand the court to force the legislator to act, they had to find a legal provision they could contest. Hence, they challenged laws providing tax exemptions for kerosene. But their claim was rejected for procedural reasons. As the law was only addressed to businesses and not to consumers, it did not affect the latter in their sphere of rights.[16] The case has been brought before the ECtHR and is still pending.[17]

---

[13] Exceptions may apply: Art 2 ECHR, for instance, explicitly stipulates that everybody's right to life shall be protected by law.

[14] *Lopez Ostra v Spain*, Series A no 303 C (1994) 20 EHRR 277; see further *Budayeva and others v Russia* (App nos 15339/02, 21166/02, 200058/02, 11673/02 and 15343/02) ECtHR 20 March 2008.

[15] Supreme Court of the Netherlands, 20.12.2019, ECLI:NL:HR:2019:2007 (*Urgenda*); BVerfG 24.3.2021, 1BvR 2656/18.

[16] VfGH 30.9.2020, G 144-145/2020.

[17] See www.klimaklage.fridaysforfuture.at, accessed 25 March 2022.

B. Social Rights and the Social Welfare System

The Austrian constitution guarantees freedom rights, equality rights, political rights, procedural and minority rights. Neither social rights nor a social welfare state principle is entrenched at a constitutional level. The European Social Charter, which was ratified by Austria (BGBl 460/1979 in the applicable version), was only accorded the status of simple law. The same applies to the UN Convention on Social and Cultural Rights (BGBl 590/1978), which is not even directly applicable. These observations may give the impression that Austria's constitution implements a liberal doctrine fitting a market-oriented society. Surprisingly, to the contrary, Austria is one of the most elaborate social welfare states in the world. Social spending amounts to 27.7 per cent of GNP and accounts for around 55 per cent of public expenditure.[18] To cover for this expenditure, Austria collects tax at a comparatively high rate.

Depending on the amount of their wages or salaries, people are entitled to various transfers, handed out by the Federation and states alike. This leads to a remarkable effective redistribution of wealth. Inequalities in household income are reduced by 43 per cent.[19] On the downside of this system, however, it has to be noted that it may be economically unattractive to work harder or get a better education as passing certain income thresholds may trigger the loss of transfers, which would not be adequately compensated by the pay rise.

As this system is neither underpinned by nor based on fundamental social rights or any other constitutional provision, it might be expected that it could be changed rather easily. But this does not seem to be the case. Arguably, the standards of social welfare are protected by the principle of equality which may also be invoked to fill lacunae within this highly complex social welfare system.[20]

C. Third Party Effect

Mainly influenced by German legal doctrine,[21] there has been an intensive discussion in Austria of whether fundamental rights might play a

---

[18] E Tálos and H Obinger, *Sozialstaat Österreich (1945-2020). Entwicklung – Maßnahmen – internationale Verortung* (Innsbruck, Studien-Verlag, 2020) 146.

[19] parlament.gv.at/PAKT/BUDG/ANFRAGEN/Archiv/index.shtml, accessed 18 January 2022.

[20] W Berka, *Verfassungsrecht*, 8th edn (Wien, Verlag Österreich, 2021) 426f.

[21] With regard to the earlier debate see only J Schwabe, *Die sogenannte Drittwirkung der Grundrechte* (München, Goldmann, 1971) and R Novak, 'Zur Drittwirkung der

part in legal relationships between private actors (according to the so-called 'horizontal' or 'third party effect' of fundamental rights).[22] As the 1811 Civil Law Code had already established a working system of civil law based on equality and human dignity, the 1867 Bill of Rights was clearly aimed at restricting the power of government and of the administration respectively. Earlier Bills of Rights, however, such as the 1789 French Declaration of Human Rights, were still closer connected to their philosophical origins. No clear distinction was made between a 'vertical' as opposed to a 'horizontal' effect as the Declaration centred on the protection of the free and equal human being as such. Focusing on this status guards against encroachments from all sides, private actors and the state alike.[23] With regard to this observation, it might be argued that attributing a third party effect to fundamental rights depends on pre-legal propositions. Scholars who read fundamental rights in the light of their philosophical origin may favour a third party effect, while those who tend to read them in the light of their specific historical function may oppose such an idea.

As the Constitutional Court has no power to review civil law cases, it lies entirely with the civil law courts and, at their apex, the Supreme Court to establish the third party effect of fundamental rights. Again inspired by the German discussion, the Austrian civil law doctrine initially took a rather cautious approach. Scholars suggested only a so-called 'indirect third party effect'.[24] This meant that parties of a civil law suit should not be entitled to base their claims directly on a fundamental right. Fundamental rights and freedoms should merely be used to interpret vague and ambiguous clauses of the civil law code. A good example is the 'immorality clause' in Art 879 of the Austrian Civil Law Code. According to this clause, contracts may be void if their content is immoral (*contra bonos mores*). In interpreting the term 'immoral', which is obviously rather ambiguous, fundamental rights, especially the principle of equality, may play a part. In the light of the principle of equality, for instance, a contract may be deemed immoral if the allocation of

Grundrechte – Die österreichische Lage aus rechtsvergleichender Sicht' (1984) 11 *Europäische Grundrechte Zeitschrift* 133ff.

[22] See O'Cinneide and Stelzer (n 12) 177, 181ff.

[23] M Troper, 'Who Needs a Third Party Effect Doctrine? – The Case of France' in A Sajó and R Uitz (eds), *The Constitution in Privat Relations: Expanding Constitutionalism* (Utrecht, Eleven International Publishing, 2005) 115ff.

[24] See F Bydlinski, 'Thesen zur Drittwirkung von Grundrechten im Privatrecht' in R Rack (ed), *Grundrechtsreform* (Wien, Böhlau, 1985) 173ff; H Mayer, 'Nochmals zur sogenannten "Drittwirkung" der Grundrechte' (1992) 114 *Juristische Blätter* 768ff.

rights and obligations between the contracting parties would be severely unbalanced, thus attributing most of the benefits to one party and most of the responsibilities to the other.

More recent studies have convincingly shown that there is no categorical distinction between a 'direct' and an 'indirect' third party effect.[25] As a result, it should come as no surprise that the Austrian Supreme Court has never addressed this doctrinal question. Rather, it has, for instance, based its case law on the principle of equality, according to which monopolistic suppliers of essential goods and/or services may be obliged to enter into contracts with private individuals who are in need of these goods or services. Contracts may only be denied on reasonable grounds.[26] This case law had another important effect, as public bodies acting under private law were also seen as 'monopolistic' providers of essential goods and services and could therefore face similar obligations to contract, thus reducing the inherent and otherwise unreviewed arbitrariness of the administration acting under private law.

In its case law, the Supreme Court has not only referred to the principle of equality but also to freedom rights. The following examples may briefly illustrate its jurisprudence: the freedom of expression may trump copyright, restricting it beyond statutory requirements;[27] freedom of expression may also trump personality rights should the publication of the full address of a person be justified for political reasons;[28] the freedom to religion does not entitle a father to neglect his duty to pay maintenance by joining a religious order;[29] protesters that have blocked the access to a building site can only be successfully sued for damages if the right to assembly is balanced against property rights;[30] an employer enforcing a dress code on an employee infringes the personality rights of the latter and therefore this would demand convincing and overriding reasons.[31]

These examples demonstrate that the Supreme Court attributes a third party effect to fundamental rights but also that the court has not followed a path of reconstructing every single dispute as a conflict over

---

[25] M Krumm and V Ferreres Comella, 'What is so Special About Constitutional Rights in Private Litigation? A Comparative Analysis of the Function of State Action Requirements and Indirect Horizontal Effect' in Sajó and Uitz (eds) (n 23) 241ff.

[26] See, for instance, OGH 26.11.2019, 4Ob207/19y.

[27] OGH 12.6.2001, 4Ob127/01g.

[28] OGH 23.5.2019, 6Ob83/19b.

[29] OGH 27.9.2017, 1Ob155/17a.

[30] OGH 25.3.1999, 6Ob201/98x.

[31] OGH 24.9.2015, 9ObA82/15x.

fundamental rights positions that have to be balanced. Although theoretically possible, such undertaking would oversimplify the legal approach
and would tend to undermine legal certainty.[32] Civil law doctrine has
been distinctively elaborated over hundreds of years based on a civil law
code that was already inspired by the enlightenment ideas of free and
equal human beings, which also underpins the concept of fundamental
rights. The Supreme Court appears to mould the civil law in the light of
fundamental rights in cases where the influence of fundamental rights
would otherwise almost entirely be ignored.[33] Such intervention begs
the question of the consequences of leaving the application of fundamental rights in legal relationships between private actors in the hands
of the civil courts rather than a constitutional court. The answer would
seem to be that this favours property rights as a constitutional court in
balancing property rights against political rights (such as the freedom to
assembly) might attach more value to political rights. Consequently, a
different balance might be struck and a case could therefore be decided
differently.

III. BINDING EFFECT ON THE ADMINISTRATION

A. Freedom Rights

To assess whether the decision of an administrative court (and, maybe,
already an act of the administration) has violated a freedom right, first,
the question whether the decision effectively interferes with such a right
must be resolved. Following the German fundamental rights doctrine,
technically, this involves two questions.[34] First, the scope of a freedom
right must be established to determine whether the right may be invoked
at all. Second, it must be assessed whether the decision of an administrative court can be recognised as an encroachment. It is only if these two
questions are answered in the affirmative that an interference has been
established and a constitutional justification is needed.

---

[32] See the harsh criticism of the jurisprudence of the German Federal Constitutional
Court by G Roellecke, 'Das Mietrecht des BVerfG' (1992) 45 *Neue Juristische Wochenschrift*
1649.

[33] See already M Stelzer, 'Stand und Perspektiven des Grundrechtsschutzes' in
Österreichische Parlamentarische Gesellschaft (ed), *75 Jahre Bundesverfassung* (Wien,
Verlag Österreich, 1995) 583, 610f.

[34] See W Heun, *The Constitution of Germany* (Oxford-Portland, Hart Publishing, 2011)
192ff.

The court is rather generous in answering these two questions, thereby strengthening the protection of fundamental rights. Generally, it can be observed that the court has a tendency to assume a wide scope of freedom rights, although minor exceptions may apply. With regard to encroachments, the court has adopted different positions. In some cases,[35] it has insisted that only a state action intentionally restricting a fundamental right would legally interfere with it; in other cases, however, it has been more prepared to intervene. For example, the chilling effect of criminal punishment has been recognised as an encroachment on fundamental rights.[36]

To justify an encroachment upon a freedom right by an administrative court, the Constitutional Court has established several criteria against which the interference is assessed. These criteria were already developed under its former power to scrutinise administrative actions.[37]

The starting point is the observation that all freedom rights with the exception of the freedom of science (Art 17 of the 1867 Basic Law on the General Rights of Nationals) and the freedom of the arts (Art 17a of the 1867 Basic Law) are qualified.[38] This means that they generally may be infringed by a parliamentary statute or on the basis of a parliamentary statute.

Consequently, any interference with a freedom right that is not based and/or cannot be based on a parliamentary statute, violates the constitution. This is called a 'lawless interference' (*gesetzloser Eingriff*). Apart from the relatively rare cases in which a statute is entirely missing, the court also accepts cases in which a statute has been applied only '*pro forma*'. This is assumed when the law has been applied in an unreasonable[39]

---

[35] See, for instance, VfSlg 12017/1989.

[36] VfSlg 14233/1995.

[37] They are summarised in 'set phrases' (*Grundrechtsformeln*) which appear throughout the case law of the court as a leitmotif and starting point of all legal considerations. See the landmark article by K Spielbüchler, 'Grundrecht und Grundrechtsformel' in O Martinek et al (eds), *Arbeitsrecht und soziale Grundrechte* (Wien, Manz, 1983) 289; for a more recent take on these set phrases, see M Hiesel, 'Grundrechtsformeln' in R Müller (ed), *Verfahren vor dem VfGH, dem VwGH und den VwG*, 7th edn (Wien, Manz, 2020) 101ff.

[38] H Mayer, G Kucsko-Stadlmayer and K Stöger, *Bundesverfassungsrecht*, 11th edn (Wien, Manz, 2015) 674ff.

[39] It might be tempting to compare this criterion with the Wednesbury unreasonableness test as it was developed by the UK courts. Depending on the reading of Wednesbury unreasonableness, there are many similarities but also some substantial differences. Both criteria, for instance, would cover the case in which the administrative decision defies logic but the Constitutional Court would never (explicitly) take into account moral standards (as the Austrian Constitution is not underpinned by a moral concept). On the other hand, the criterion may trigger a full proportionality test (see later in the text). For Wednesbury

manner (*denkunmögliche Gesetzesanwendung*). 'Unreasonableness' may stem from defying logic, failing to take the necessary procedural steps, or completely misunderstanding the meaning of a parliamentary statute. That the court restricts its interventions to 'unreasonableness' rather than 'unlawfulness' originates from the need to delineate its jurisdiction from the jurisdiction of the Administrative High Court, which is responsible for reviewing the legality of decisions of administrative courts.

The most important cases of unreasonableness nowadays are those in which the law is applied in an unconstitutional manner. Consequently, all administrative courts (and administrative authorities as well) are obliged to interpret all laws in conformity with the constitution and, above all, in conformity with fundamental rights. Whenever a parliamentary statute is enforced, constitutional considerations must be taken account of by a public authority. Unless explicitly prohibited by the statute, the authority has to interpret it in accordance with the constitution and in particular with fundamental rights guarantees. This would basically require a balancing exercise in making a decision.

Thus, it was possible that the Constitutional Court demanded that deciding on the expulsion of foreigners had to respect the foreigners' private and family life (Art 8 ECHR). Expulsion was deemed to be unconstitutional and thus in violation of Art 8 ECHR when the private interests of the foreigner were not properly balanced against the public interest expressed by the relevant parliamentary statute, regardless of the fact that the statute did not provide for such a balancing decision.[40] In a similar fashion, the court ruled that laws restricting businesses had to be interpreted in accordance with Art 6 of the 1867 Basic Law (right to free employment) whenever that was possible.[41] Disciplinary measures taken against lawyers, civil servants or medical doctors have to be in accordance with Art 10 ECHR where it applies and Art 6 of the 1867 Basic Law respectively.[42] Dissolution of an association or an assembly is only lawful when the grounds given meet the requirements of Art 11 para 2 ECHR, even if the phrasing of the legal provisions that apply might allow a much broader approach.[43]

Unqualified rights, such as the freedom of science and the freedom of the arts demand a similar balancing exercise. This became apparent

---

unreasonableness and the adoption of the proportionality test see P Leyland, *The Constitution of the United Kingdom*, 4th edn (Oxford, Hart, 2021) 202ff.

[40] VfSlg 14121/1995.

[41] VfSlg 11991/1989.

[42] VfSlg 11404/1987, 13612/1993, 16483/2002.

[43] See, for instance, VfSlg 8090/1977 (association); VfSlg 10443/1985, 12155/1989 (assembly).

in the case of a professional piano player, who regularly used her apartment for rehearsing piano recitals, thereby annoying her neighbours. She was reported and ultimately fined for disturbance. As the performance as well as the rehearsal of piano recitals are covered by the scope of the freedom of the arts, fining her was found to be unconstitutional, because the law enforcement authority had not even attempted to strike a balance between the legitimate interests of the neighbours and the constitutional right of the piano player. However, the statute involved did not explicitly provide for such a balancing exercise. Instead, it authorised law enforcement authorities to take action whenever people were disturbed by undue noise. It was held that the term 'undue' was broad or vague enough to allow or even demand a balancing exercise.[44]

Forcing administrative authorities (and administrative courts, for that matter) to take account of fundamental rights has not only significantly influenced the implementation of administrative law, but also changed the methods of interpreting it. Until the 1980s, administrative authorities could have easily avoided an infringement of fundamental rights mainly by closely sticking to the phrasing of the parliamentary statutes, not overstretching them and relying on the explanatory remarks, respectively. But as soon as the court required authorities to consider fundamental rights guarantees and to balance their measures against them, authorities had to follow different methods of interpreting the law and had to adopt their policies accordingly.

As the Administrative High Court did not instantly and systematically follow the standards of the Constitutional Court, a struggle between a more formal, traditional and a more substantive reading of administrative law ensued. This has ended with the requirements of European law, especially the Charter of Fundamental Rights.[45] According to the 2019 annual report of the court, 1680 out of 2174 complaints were dismissed *a limine*, 10 were rejected on procedural grounds and 102 on substantive grounds and only 307 were successful (in the remaining cases the files were closed for undocumented reasons).[46] Although the report does not specify how many of the successful cases were just 'follow-ups' to the rescission of a law, the mere fact that less than 2 per cent of complaints were successfully launched may indicate that, especially with administrative courts of first instance in place, fundamental rights have penetrated administrative law.

---

[44] VfSlg 11567/1987.

[45] This was discussed at the end of ch 6.

[46] See the annual reports (*Tätigkeitsberichte*) of the Constitutional Court, published on the court's own website: www.vfgh.gv.at/verfassungsgerichtshof/publikationen/taetigkeitsberichte.de.html, accessed 25 January 2022.

B. Principle of Equality

The general equal protection clause (*Allgemeiner Gleichheitsgrundsatz*; Art 7 para 1 of the Federal Constitution) states that all nationals (Austrian citizens[47]) are equal before the law. Privileges based upon birth, gender, estate, class or religion are excluded.

According to the jurisprudence of the Constitutional Court, the principle of equality is violated by the decision of an administrative court mainly in a case of arbitrariness, irrespective of whether it has so acted on purpose or not. This means that if a decision appears to be taken arbitrarily from an objective point of view, it is unconstitutional.[48] This may, for instance, apply to cases in which the facts are not (properly) established,[49] or to decisions which openly and seriously deviate from the applicable law.[50] Further, the equal protection clause may be violated if a legal provision is not applied in accordance with the principle of equality.[51]

However, it has to be stressed that the court will only repeal arbitrary decisions if they are unlawful, thus failing to address the problem of preferential treatment. When a civil servant, for instance, challenged disciplinary measures arguing that the authority had refrained from taking actions in comparable cases, the court instantly rejected the complaint.[52] A similar experience was made by a proprietor of a Tyrolean camping site who gave access to certain mobile homes that were arguably banned from camping sites by law. After receiving a fine from a Tyrolean authority, he challenged the ruling arguing that the authority had tolerated such mobile homes on other camping sites. The court did not even consider the facts as it found that the law was applied reasonably in the applicant's case. It insisted that there was no 'equality in injustice'.[53] Therefore, the equal protection clause cannot be invoked as long as the law has been applied correctly, notwithstanding other cases in which it might have been applied incorrectly or not at all.

---

[47] The scope has to be extended to all European Citizens according to Art 18 TFEU, which overrides Art 7 of the Federal Constitution. (Other) foreigners may enjoy a similar right with regard to the implementation of the International Convention on the Elimination of all Forms of Racial Discrimination, see n 8.

[48] VfSlg 4480/1963, 9206/1981.

[49] VfSlg 15385/1998.

[50] VfSlg 13430/1993.

[51] See, for instance, VfSlg 11284/1987.

[52] VfSlg 5372/1966.

[53] VfSlg 9169/1981.

As a consequence of this case law, in Austria there is no remedy against preferential treatment as long as the legal position of a third party remains unaffected. Administrative authorities may grant subsidies or issue permissions in favour of an applicant illegally almost without facing any consequences (except possible corruption charges which may be much harder to prove). Considering the influence of political parties on the administration,[54] the jurisprudence of the court almost endorses corrupt behaviour by political parties, which was especially common in the post-war period.[55] The court systematically fails to tackle the idea that there is one rule for party members and another rule for all others. However, with a less formal approach to the law, this problem could be solved.

One example has been set by the ECtHR, which had to deal with preferential treatment handed out by the Austrian parliament in the already discussed case of Jehovah's Witnesses.[56] This religious group had requested recognition as a religious society. The – finally – applicable law had provided for a 10-year waiting period for religious communities before they were entitled to the vast privileges of religious societies. During that period they were monitored. In contrast to the Jehovah's Witnesses who had to undergo the waiting procedure, the Coptic Orthodox Church, which had existed for a considerably shorter period than the Jehovah's Witnesses, was handed the status of a religious society by a parliamentary statute. This statute clearly constituted an act of preferential treatment. The ECtHR took that into consideration and found that the Austrian parliament had demonstrated that it 'did not consider such a waiting period to be an essential instrument for pursuing its policy in that field'.[57] Thus, Austria had violated its obligations under Art 14 in conjunction with Art 9 ECHR.

In a similar fashion, the Constitutional Court might consider rescinding laws or legal provisions that are not applied equally, arguing that the administration has shown that these provisions did not pursue a common good. It could, further, re-assess the significance of conventions in applying a law, or at least, report authorities for what would be criminal offences. The failure to react to authorities which give preferential treatment deepens Austria's problems with corruption.

---

[54] See ch 4.
[55] See ch 2.
[56] See ch 6.
[57] *Religionsgemeinschaft der Zeugen Jehovas and others v Austria* (App no 40825/98) ECtHR 31 July 2008.

IV. BINDING EFFECT ON THE LEGISLATION

Apart from Arts 5 and 6 of the ECHR, which have both greatly influenced the development of Austrian legislation and led to the establishment of a two-tier system of administrative jurisdiction, it has been, first and foremost, the equality clause that has played a decisive part in the jurisprudence of the Constitutional Court when reviewing laws against fundamental rights. Since the mid-1980s, freedom rights have been strengthened in order to curtail the legislator effectively.

A. The Equality Clause

As already pointed out, the equality clause is primarily binding on the administration, at least according to its phrasing. Nevertheless, the second limb of the clause excludes privileges based upon birth, gender, estate, class or religion. Under the monarchy, such privileges were often granted by law. As the main historical purpose of the equality clause was to abolish privileges, the clause obviously was meant to have an impact on legislation. However, the grounds listed in the second limb of the equality clause were seen as non-exhaustive. Instead, a more general view was applied, according to which the legislator was prevented from discriminating against *any* unjust reason. Discrimination was, therefore, only admissible if it was based on reasonable or objective grounds (*Sachlichkeitsgebot*). Consequently, a specific 'objectivity test' (*Sachlichkeitsprüfung*) is applied when laws are assessed against the equality clause.

The starting point of this test is the proposition that the equality clause essentially forces the legislator to treat equivalent issues alike. Exceptions are only admissible if they are supported by valid reasons. The 'objectivity test' initially required two different legal regulations to be compared with each other and to assess whether they effectively attached different legal consequences to equivalent issues. The crucial question therefore was under what aspects could issues be recognised as equivalent. The following example may demonstrate the difficulties involved. When the court had to assess a provision of criminal law that made a male homosexual relationship between an adult and a minor liable to prosecution, it had to deal with the allegation that this provision violated the equal protection clause because similar lesbian relationships were not unlawful. The court insisted that there were significant differences between homosexual male and female relationships and denied the comparability.[58] In a subsequent case, the court had to assess the same criminal law provision in the light of the allegation that the provision in question violated the equal protection clause on different grounds. A relationship, it was argued, that started between a 16 year old and a 17 year old was legal for one year and became liable to prosecution during the second year only to be perfectly legal from the third year onwards. The applicant suggested that this was unreasonable. In this case, the court followed the argument of the applicant and rescinded the contested provision.[59]

On the other hand, parliament is forced to treat issues which are not equivalent not alike unless there are valid reasons to do so. In this respect, the court held that limiting the opening hours of night clubs to the opening hours of restaurants would entail treating non-equivalent issues alike and would, therefore, violate the equal protection clause.[60] The jurisprudence of the court has gone a step further: in many cases, the court abstains from comparing different regulations with each other but simply examines whether a regulation is 'reasonable' or 'objective'. However, it accepts that parliament has a wide margin of appreciation in defining valid reasons.

With regard to this wide margin, laws meet the 'objectivity test' as long as they are reasonable '*grosso modo*' (which means that the court does not look into details). In single cases, the application of the law, therefore, may lead to citizens being treated unfairly, as long as these cases can be defined as 'cases of hardship' (and are not caused by a systematic failure of the law).[61] In other words, these citizens have bad luck as there is no avenue for redress. This jurisprudence reveals the already discussed[62] structural problems of Austria's centralised constitutional review, which was not primarily designed to safeguard fundamental rights. As the law may only be rescinded or not, there is no way of treating these cases more fairly by setting the law aside in cases of hardship without questioning its validity in general.

The court applied the objectivity test as shown above literally in hundreds of cases and it has rescinded dozens of laws or related provisions on the ground that discrimination was not supported by a good cause. Nevertheless, it can be said that according to the high sophistication of

---

[58] VfSlg 12182/1989.
[59] VfSlg 16565/2002.
[60] VfSlg 12923/1991.
[61] VfSlg 16744/2002, 19530/2011.
[62] See ch 6.

the test the jurisprudence of the court had the effect of fine-tuning the legislation rather than striking down broad policy concepts.[63]

In this respect, the court has always accepted legislation that provided for different legal systems in similar fields of administration. The court rejected comparing these legal systems with each other, thus guaranteeing equality only within the system. The most prominent example is probably the field of social security. The mandatory social insurance schemes are operated by various autonomous bodies. Individuals are members of these bodies according to the profession(s) they exercise. Different legal systems apply, triggering different amounts of mandatory contributions and different sets of benefits. As these systems should not be compared with each other according to the jurisprudence of the court, it may, therefore, be perfectly legal if a civil servant receives less payment during maternity leave than an employee (of a private business) would be entitled to. The objectivity test is not even applied.[64] It is also perfectly legal that individuals who exercise two or more professions might be forced to contribute to two or more insurance schemes, although they would not receive medical treatment twice or three times in case of illness.

However, this attitude of only fine-tuning the legislation has been overcome in some cases. For instance, when the court found that the equality clause was violated by several laws entitling women to retire five years earlier than men, it challenged the political system.[65] Although the court basically accepted that allowing women to retire earlier might be perfectly reasonable because of the extra burden they normally assumed in raising children and organising family life, it held that the scheme under scrutiny typically benefitted women who did not bear that extra burden. Nevertheless, pressure groups were strong enough to persuade parliament to enact a constitutional provision overriding the court's ruling and entrenching different legal retirement ages for females and males.[66]

It is rather surprising to observe that in most cases in which the court dealt with gender equality, it found that men were disadvantaged. In 1998, Art 7 of the Federal Constitution was amended to the effect that it requires the Federation, states and municipalities to subscribe to the *de facto* equality of men and women. Measures to promote gender equality (affirmative actions), in particular by eliminating existing

---

[63] M Pöschl, *Gleichheit vor dem Gesetz* (Wien-New York, Springer, 2008) 204ff.
[64] See VfSlg 13829/1994.
[65] VfSlg 12568/1990.
[66] *Bundesverfassungsgesetz über unterschiedliche Altersgrenzen von männlichen und weiblichen Sozialversicherten*, BGBl 1992/832.

inequalities, are, therefore, admissible. Similarly, a 1997 amendment to the constitution provides for the confirmation of the Federation, the states and the communities that equal treatment of disabled persons in all aspects of everyday life is promoted. Although not stated explicitly, affirmative action may sometimes be a requirement.

B. Freedom Rights: From Deference to Proportionality

The review of laws in the light of freedom rights was, again, informed by the fact that almost all rights enshrined in the 1867 Basic Law were qualified. Different phrasings apart, it meant that all rights could be restricted by a law or on the basis of a law without any further qualification. According to Hans Kelsen's understanding, such a qualified fundamental right was completely meaningless under the 1920 Constitution as it provided for the obvious: that any interference had to be based on a parliamentary statute.[67] But as all administrative action had to be based on parliamentary statutes according to Art 18 of the Federal Constitution, such a fundamental right did not offer any additional benefit; in particular, it could exercise no binding effect on parliament. In a 1928 ruling[68] the Constitutional Court shared this view although it conceded that an encroachment on property rights (Art 5 of the 1867 Bill of Rights) had to pursue the common good. But at the same time it determined that assessing the common good was entirely the business of parliament and not for the court to review.

After 1945, the court changed its attitude, but only gradually. Inspired by a provision of the German Basic Law (Art 19 para 2), it stated that restrictions on fundamental rights must not affect the essence (*Wesensgehalt*) of the fundamental right in question.[69]

Unsurprisingly, this statement initially had no effect but merely imposed a rhetorical threshold. Nevertheless, it hinted at the prospect that freedom rights might possibly also exercise a binding effect on the legislator. This gave ample room for discussions and speculations about the possible meaning of the court's jurisprudence as well as allowing legal scholars to elaborate various concepts establishing the 'essence' of freedom rights, borrowed from the German legal doctrine.[70]

---

[67] H Kelsen, *Allgemeine Staatslehre* (Berlin, Springer, 1925) 155.
[68] VfSlg 1123/1928.
[69] The first ruling in which the court referred to this term was probably VfSlg 3505/1959.
[70] J Aicher, *Grundfragen der Staatshaftung bei rechtmäßigen hoheitlichen Eigentumsbeeinträchtigungen* (Berlin, Duncker & Humblot, 1978); K Korinek, 'Das

In another 1959 ruling,[71] the court found that an act of expropriation was unconstitutional if the law did not provide for any specific purpose or need for the expropriation. Moreover, it held that an expropriation was only lawful if meeting a specific need or demand was in the common interest, if the object envisaged for expropriation was suitable to meet the demand and if it was impossible to meet the demand other than through expropriation. It seems that in 1959 the court had already defined some of the core elements of the proportionality test, namely that encroachments upon freedom rights had to be in the common interest, suitable and necessary.[72]

However, it took another 25 years for the proportionality test to be fully incorporated in the court's jurisprudence.[73] In the mid-1980s a couple of laws imposing limits on the right to free employment (Art 6 of the Basic Law on the General Rights of Nationals) came under the scrutiny of the court. These laws provided for licences to establish certain businesses, which were only to be issued if the level of consumer demand justified the introduction of an additional business (*Bedarfsprüfung*). Such provisions, which were fairly common in Austria, protected the existing businesses by erecting 'objective' barriers to the introduction of a new business.

In one of the leading cases, the court quashed the related provisions of a law that regulated the market for taxi drivers.[74] The need for an additional contractor mainly had to be assessed on the expert opinion of a Chamber of Commerce, which therefore could protect the contractors on the market who – by law – were all members of the Chamber. The number of licences could therefore be limited in the interest of the existing businesses. It does not need a lot of imagination to assume that the implementation of such a law was open to corruption.

The Federal Government submitted a couple of arguments supporting the idea that by limiting the number of taxicabs the common good was served. First, it argued that the law was aimed at ensuring the availability

---

Grundrecht der Freiheit der Erwerbsbetätigung als Schranke für die Wirtschaftslenkung' in K Korinek (ed), *Beiträge zum Wirtschaftsrecht* (Wien, Orac, 1983) 243; P Oberndorfer and B Binder, 'Der verfassungsrechtliche Schutz freier beruflicher, insbesondere gewerblicher Betätigung' in L Adamovich and P Pernthaler (eds), *Auf dem Weg zur Menschenwürde und Gerechtigkeit – Festschrift Klecatsky* (Wien, Braumüller, 1980) 677ff.

[71] VfSlg 3666/1959.

[72] See Heun (n 34) 43.

[73] See, for instance, M Holoubek, 'Die Interpretation der Grundrechte in der jüngeren Judikatur des VfGH' in R Machacek et al (eds), *70 Jahre Republik – Grund- und Menschenrechte in Österreich*, Vol I (Kehl am Rhein-Straßburg-Arlington, NP Engel Verlag, 1991) 43ff.

[74] VfSlg 10932/1986.

of taxicabs. The court held that limiting the number of taxicabs would obviously have the opposite effect. The measure was therefore deemed unsuitable with regard to the specific public interest pursued.

Second, the Federal Government argued that limiting the number of taxicabs would help to restrict the volume of the traffic and avoid traffic congestion. Although the court accepted that avoiding traffic congestion was a legitimate aim, it doubted that in the absence of this measure the number of taxicabs would significantly increase. Should problems occur nevertheless, they could be met with measures regulating traffic which would be less restrictive. Denying additional businesses access to the market was therefore 'not necessary'.

Finally, the Federal Government insisted that the existing law was supported by safety considerations. Again, the court assumed that these aims could be pursued by other measures more suitable and less restrictive such as technical standards for cabs and specific training for drivers respectively.

As a consequence, the court held that the law under scrutiny provided for a partly unsuitable and partly unnecessary measure to promote the public interest. It was only aimed at protecting the contractors on the market, limiting competition. But limiting competition did not serve the common good. Thus, the related provisions were rescinded. In a similar way, provisions pertaining to the establishing of skiing schools,[75] driving schools,[76] cinemas[77] and other businesses were quashed by the court.

In the case of chimney sweeps, undertakers and pharmacies, the court upheld laws that restricted the access to the market if the need for an additional contractor could be denied. In the case of pharmacies, however, Austria had to later modify its laws according to the demands of the ECJ.[78]

However, since the mid-1980s, the proportionality test has become the standard test for reviewing laws against freedom rights. Performing this test replaced the traditional reading of freedom rights – a proportionality test was not what Hans Kelsen had in mind when he defended the idea of constitutional review.[79] Rather, the jurisprudence of the court was inspired by the German Basic Law and the German constitutional

---

[75] VfSlg 11652/1988.

[76] VfSlg 11276/1987.

[77] VfSlg 11749/1988.

[78] Case C-367/12, *Sokoll-Seebacher I* ECLI:EU:C:2014:68; and Case C-634/15, *Sokoll-Seebacher II* ECLI:EU:C:2016:510.

[79] H Kelsen, 'Wesen und Entwicklung der Staatsgerichtsbarkeit' (1929) 5 *Veröffentlichungen der Vereinigung der Deutschen Staatsrechtslehrer* 30.

doctrine which was partly adopted by some Austrian constitutional scholars challenging the more traditional methods of reading the constitution.[80] In fact, the shift in the jurisprudence of the court marked a turning point in Austria's post-war constitutional history as it started the Europeanisation of the constitutional and public law doctrine. Without this pioneering case law, the accession to the European Union a decade later would have been almost impossible for the administration to cope with.

Although there was a domestic line along which the proportionality test was developed, the influence of the jurisprudence of the ECtHR, which applied a similar test when reviewing state action against Convention rights, cannot be ignored.[81] At some point, the Constitutional Court suggested that these different lines were interlinked when it hinted that the 'essence' of the right to freedom of expression (Art 13 of the Basic Law on the General Rights of Nationals) might be defined in Art 10 para 2 ECHR.[82] This clause justifies the encroachment upon the right to free expression if the encroachment would serve specific common interests and would be necessary in a democratic society. According to the view of the ECtHR, in a democratic society only a proportionate encroachment would deemed to be necessary.[83]

To a certain extent, the performance of the proportionality test has overridden design differences of qualified freedom rights. The test is applied, regardless of whether the qualification is formal or substantial. Consequently, what could have been a categorical difference is reduced to the observation that in the latter case public interests, which might justify an interference with the related freedom right, are specified. As the ECHR defines these public interests in a rather broad manner, this has basically no effect in practice.

Moreover, in the case of unqualified freedom rights – the freedom of science and the freedom of the arts – again, a proportionality test applies. Apparently, the court upholds the idea that these rights must be different in some way, when it argues that an 'intentional interference' with such a right is unconstitutional *per se*.[84] For the time being, it can only be speculated in which cases the court may assume an 'intentional interference' as

---

[80] See ch 1.

[81] F Matscher, 'Methods of Interpretation of the Convention' in R Macdonald et al (eds), *The European System for the Protection of Human Rights* (Dordrecht, Martinus Nijhoff Publishers, 1993) 63.

[82] VfSlg 11651/1988.

[83] *Informationsverein Lentia and Others v Austria*, Series A no 276 (1994) 17 EHRR 93.

[84] VfSlg 8136/1977, 10401/1985.

no definition has ever been given. Still, it is widely held that the court's doctrine might prohibit the legislator from enacting laws banning certain fields of science or arts solely because these fields are held to be detrimental or unfavourable to society.[85] Thus, a Nazi-style law banning certain fields of art as 'degenerate' would be unconstitutional *per se*. Fortunately, there is currently no real threat that the Austrian parliament might enact such a law. Consequently, it can be observed that the different types of qualifications do not play a part in the modern fundamental rights doctrine which focuses on proportionality.[86]

V. SELECTED CASE LAW

This section aims to analyse selected cases that raised questions that may be of more general interest as they are discussed more or less worldwide and are highly controversial. They define cleavages between liberal and conservative/far-right policies. Some of these issues have been around for quite a while, like abortion, others, such as migration, LGBTQ+ rights, data retention or the response to the Covid-19 pandemic are of more recent origin and sometimes highly topical. Regardless of the strategy chosen – a formal or a substantial reading of fundamental rights – the court retained a more liberal attitude, especially with a government tilting to the right. With regard to this type of intervention, it also becomes clear that the court has always been a political player.

A. Abortion

In Austria, disputes about abortion laws peaked in the 1970s. The social-democratic government enacted a revised penal code introducing a provision according to which abortion was not prosecuted when carried out by a medical doctor in the first trimester of pregnancy after comprehensive medical consultations. The government introduced this provision despite massive protests by the Catholic Church, catholic associations and groups within and outside the People's Party. On behalf of these interest groups, the Salzburg Government challenged the law

---

[85] M Pöschl and A Kahl, 'Die Intentionalität – ihre Bedeutung und Berechtigung in der Grundrechtsjudikatur' (2001) *Österreichische Juristenzeitung* 41.

[86] See C Grabenwarter, 'Verhältnismäßig einheitlich: Die Gesetzesvorbehalte des StGG 1867 im Wandel' (2018) 140 *Juristische Blätter* 417ff.

in the Constitutional Court, which primarily had to assess this provision against the right to life, guaranteed by Art 2 ECHR. According to the court's findings, the scope of Art 2 ECHR did not extend to unborn lives. This result was obtained on a rather formal, albeit perfectly reasonable legal argument. As the exceptions stipulated by Art 2 ECHR only provided for the deprivation of life of the already born, the court followed the line of argument that, should Art 2 ECHR also protect the unborn life, unborn children would enjoy unlimited protection at all costs, even if the mother's life was in danger. The court insisted that such a consequence was unacceptable. Therefore, the court concluded, protection of the unborn did not fall under the scope of Art 2 ECHR at all.[87]

The court was heavily criticised especially by catholic and conservative lawyers for its 'formal' way of treating the case.[88] Hopes that the ECtHR could take a different view were dashed decades later as the court held that it was the Member States' responsibility to decide how far they were willing to protect the unborn child as no common European standard could be established.[89] Although the law on abortion may still be opposed in catholic quarters, the issue seems to have been settled for once and for all, as even conservative/far-right governments have not even tried to touch upon that matter. As a political player, the court has contributed by upholding the law with a rather formal reading of the constitution.

B. Assisted Suicide

In 2020, the court was tasked with reviewing parts of Austria's penal code that prohibited offering assistance to people desiring to end their lives. Such desires may grow in people who suffer from a severe, painful and untreatable illness. The court held that Art 8 ECHR and the equality clause of the Federal Constitution comprised everyone's right not only to shape her or his own life but also to determine freely her or his death, especially if this meant dying with dignity. Individuals having taken such a decision may also count on assistance as otherwise they might be tempted to premature suicide (at an earlier stage of their illness, when they could still act on their own). It therefore rescinded the provision of

---

[87] VfSlg 7400/1974.
[88] W Waldstein, 'Rechtserkenntnis und Rechtsprechung. Bemerkungen zum Erkenntnis des VfGH über die Fristenlösung' (1976) 90 *Juristische Blätter* 505, 574.
[89] *Vo v France* (App no 53924/00) ECtHR 8 July 2004.

the penal code according to which assistance in suicide would expose persons to prosecution without providing for any exceptions.[90]

The court did not deny that additional measures could be needed to ensure that this right was not abused and the decision to commit suicide was always taken freely and not forced upon a person. Although it explicitly stated that it would have to stay out of political discussions in assessing the law, the applicants had made it clear that changing the law in parliament would have met fierce resistance from the Catholic Church and conservative lawmakers in general. To overcome this resistance, it needed a potent political ally – in this case, the Constitutional Court.

C. LGBTQ+ Rights

Likewise, the court was responsible for promoting the rights of LGBTQ+ people, partly by introducing standards the ECtHR had already recognised.

The 1992 Act on Medically Assisted Reproduction (BGBl 275/1992), heavily influenced by Catholic groups, was restrictive in many ways. In particular, medically assisted reproduction was only available for heterosexual couples. In a 2013 ruling,[91] the court found that lesbian couples being denied the benefit of artificial insemination violated their rights according to Art 14 and Art 8 ECHR. No proper reason could be given for this restriction. The main justification provided by the government – preventing surrogate motherhood – was found to be of no relevance. Thus, the contested provisions of the Act were rescinded as the encroachment on these rights was held to be disproportionate.

Another area of discrimination against homosexuals and lesbians was opened up by adoption laws, as same-sex couples were prohibited from adopting children. The Austrian legal situation, which allowed unmarried heterosexual partners to adopt children of the other partner but denied a similar right to lesbian and homosexual partners, had already been under scrutiny of the ECtHR which, in a 2013 decision, had found that this prohibition violated Art 14 and Art 8 ECHR.[92]

In a 2014 ruling, the Austrian court went a step further, paving the way for lesbian and homosexual couples living in a so-called registered

---

[90] VfGH 11.12.2020, G 139/2019; see *Pretty v UK* (App no 2346/02) ECtHR 29 July 2002.
[91] VfSlg 19824/2013.
[92] *X and others v Austria* (App no 19010/07) ECtHR 19 February 2013.

partnership (see below) to adopt children from other people.[93] Again, in the light of Art 14 and Art 8 ECHR, the prohibition had seemed to be disproportionate as the court did not accept that the ban could be justified on the basis of the child's welfare.

Until 2010, same-sex couples had no opportunity to legalise their relationship as marriage was restricted to heterosexual couples, in line with the Augustinian understanding, strongly upheld by the Catholic Church, according to which marriage is devoted to procreation. A 2009 Act[94] introduced the so-called 'registered partnership' which was only open to same-sex couples and provided for a legal framework similar (but not entirely equal) to matrimony.

In 2017, the court scrutinised the provisions which denied same-sex couples access to marriage. It held that same-sex relationships had, over the years, become more similar to marriage. Parenthood was no longer restricted to heterosexual couples: all same-sex couples could adopt children and lesbian couples could use methods of medical assisted procreation to give birth to children. (The court did not disclose that this assimilation was of its own doing – in both cases the court had rescinded the restrictive provisions and forced parliament to change the law.) As a consequence, the court held that distinguishing between marriage, that was reserved for heterosexual couples, and a registered partnership, that was open only to same-sex couples, had a discriminatory effect. It still expressed 'otherness' and somehow suggested that 'registered partnership' was probably inferior to matrimony. It therefore rescinded the provisions that denied marriage to same-sex couples as well as those that denied registered partnership to heterosexual couples.[95] As the conservative/far-right government, seemingly out of defiance, did not introduce legislation to abolish registered partnership, Austrian couples can nowadays freely choose between matrimony and registered partnership should they desire to legalise their relationship.

It seems obvious in all these cases that the court, again, acted as a powerful opponent to the Catholic Church[96] which had enough influence on conservative lawmakers to block all of the described developments. While the People's Party formed the government or participated in a coalition government, no similar bills would even have been considered.

---

[93] VfSlg 19942/2014.
[94] BGBl I 135/2009.
[95] VfSlg 20225/2017.
[96] See C Knill, C Preidel and K Nebel, 'Die katholische Kirche und Moralpolitik in Österreich: Reformdynamiken in der Regelung von Schwangerschaftsabbrüchen und der Anerkennung gleichgeschlechtlicher Partnerschaften' (2014) 43 *Österreichische Zeitschrift für Politikwissenschaft* 275ff.

It is significant that the fairly liberal laws on abortion were passed in the 1970s when the People's Party was out of government and strong feminist movements forced the social-democratic government to act. In all other of the referred cases, it needed the Constitutional Court and constitutional considerations to overcome the influence of the Catholic Church. It may be surprising that the court opposed catholic policies although it was dominated by judges affiliated to the People's Party. It is therefore up to speculation whether all conservatives may be unhappy about the court promoting reforms, or if they, or at least some of them, are grateful to the court. It is obvious that the party in government could not have undertaken or openly supported such reforms out of fear that it might have unsettled its (core) clientele. In other words: the court being a political player makes it sometimes difficult to determine whether it really pursues policies against the wishes of government or whether it already plays a part in government strategies.

In 2018, the court heard a case raising a legal question pertaining to a law which requires registration of all newborn children whose data are recorded and kept on file. Amongst these data, authorities would also record the gender of the child – traditionally female or male. As the application of an adult person to change the old records from 'male' to 'intersexual' or 'diverse' was finally rejected, a complaint was filed with the Constitutional Court. Following the case law of the ECtHR,[97] the court held that determining one's gender fell under the scope of Art 8 ECHR and no legitimate reason could be found to justify the encroachment in this case. Moreover, the republic even had an obligation to allow individuals to determine their own gender. But the court upheld the law as the term 'gender', referred to by the relevant legal provision, was in its view broad enough to accept recording a person's gender as 'diverse', 'intersexual' or whatever appropriate expression would apply.[98] In this way, Austria was the first country in Europe which officially accepted a human right to a third gender.[99]

D. Islamic Head Scarf

Over generations, the relationship between Austria and Islam has been problematic. The sieges of Vienna by the Ottoman Empire in the sixteenth

---

[97] A.P., *Garçon and Nicot v France* (App nos 79885/12, 52471/13 and 52596/13) ECtHR 6 April 2017.

[98] VfSlg 20258/2018.

[99] www.rklambda.at/index.php/de/groesste-erfolge, accessed 19 January 2022.

and seventeenth centuries left deep scars in the collective memory of the Austrian population. At the beginning of the twentieth century, however, the 1909 annexation of Bosnia-Herzegovina changed the narrative, as for the first time Muslims were part of the multi-ethnic polity. Their denomination was recognised by a 1912 law, partly owed to the pluralistic approach of the monarchy, and partly to colonial policies.[100] After the demise of the monarchy, Bosnia-Herzegovina was no longer part of Austria and, therefore, Islam was no longer a major issue.

In 1979, however, the Islamic Council was recognised as a corporate body, representing churches and religious communities. At that time, the social-democratic government pursued more liberal policies, opening the country to the world and establishing Vienna as a host to United Nations organisations, next to New York and Geneva. Moreover, Austria became a vanguard in opening talks with Arab countries.[101]

This liberal attitude toward Islam started to change in the early 2000s (after the 9/11 attacks in the US), initially seen with the xenophobic and islamophobic policies of the Freedom Party. Due to immigration, the Muslim part of the population grew from 4 per cent in 2001, to around 8 per cent in 2016 (14 per cent in Vienna).[102] This development, together with further terror attacks in Europe, have changed the perception of Islam in large parts of the population and political attitudes have also shifted.

Part of the discussion was directed at Islamic female dress codes which were heavily disputed. In 2017, parliament passed a law (BGBl I 68/2017) that prohibited people from covering their faces in public places. This law not only but mainly targeted face coverings like the burkha and similar pieces of clothing. Apart from the fact that this law was rather undermined by the obligation to wear masks imposed in response to the Covid-19 pandemic a couple of years later, it had almost no practical significance and was of rather symbolic nature as burkhas and similar garments were only rarely seen in Austria.

In 2019, parliament changed the laws on schools to prevent girls attending primary schools (until the age of 10 years) from wearing head scarfs. The court rescinded the relevant provisions arguing that the law violated the principle of equality as it only singled out Muslim girls and

---

[100] See F Hafez, 'Ostarrichislam. Gründe der korporativistischen Hereinnahme des Islams in der Zweiten Republik' (2016) 45 *Österreichische Zeitschrift für Politikwissenschaft* 1ff.
[101] Hafez (ibid) 7.
[102] Die Presse 5 August 2017, www.diepresse.com/5264108/religion-in-oesterreich-mehr-konfessionslose-mehr-muslime; accessed 24 January 2022: the numbers are estimated as official numbers do not exist.

thus discriminated against them. The court did not accept the reason given by the government – that the prohibition was necessary for the inclusion of Muslim girls – as it saw the danger that Muslim girls might be taken away from public schools and educated at specific private schools or at home, with adverse effects on their integration.

Although the decision of the court may be seen as fairly liberal, it nevertheless dodged one crucial question: the legal relationship between the state objective to establish gender equality and freedom of religion.

E. Immigration and Asylum

Austria was grappling with a rising number of immigrants and asylum seekers long before the 2015 refugee crisis. However, there is only space to briefly evaluate the most important case law in this field. The Constitutional Court has targeted both levels: the implementation of laws and the laws themselves. With regard to implementation, it arguably filled a lacuna, as the principle of equality, enshrined in Art 7 of the Federal Constitution, protected citizens but not aliens against arbitrary administrative action. In the 1990s, the court argued on the basis of the 1973 constitutional law transforming the International Convention on the Elimination of All Forms of Racial Discrimination into the Austrian legal system, that aliens enjoyed a substantive right not to be discriminated against on the basis of race, colour, descent, national or ethnic origin and therefore all had to be treated equally in comparison to each other. This specific principle of equality forbade any form of arbitrary administrative action.[103]

In refoulement cases, the court insisted that Art 3 ECHR had to be duly considered and aliens were not to be extradited to countries where they might experience torture, inhuman treatment or even be sentenced to death.[104] In this regard, Art 3 ECHR also trumped the EU–Dublin system.[105] Further, as already mentioned earlier, measures terminating the residence of foreigners had to be proportionate in the light of Art 8 ECHR, which was only the case if the public interest for terminating the residence of a foreigner was duly balanced against the interests protected

---

[103] K Korinek, 'Der gleichheitsrechtliche Gehalt des BVG gegen rassische Diskriminierung' in S Griller et al (eds), *Grundfragen und aktuelle Probleme des öffentlichen Rechts. Festschrift für Heinz Peter Rill* (Wien, Orac, 1995) 183; see, for instance, VfSlg 14191/1995, 17026/2003.

[104] VfSlg 14998/1997; VfGH 30.9.2021, E 3445/2021.

[105] VfSlg 19205/2010.

by Art 8 ECHR.[106] In all these cases, the court upheld human rights that were sometimes too easily brushed aside by an administration partly responding to xenophobic trends in public opinion but partly being over-stretched by the sheer number of cases.

Turning to the legislation itself, statutes on immigration and asylum have tended to become more restrictive over recent decades. The court has mainly struck down laws for lack of compliance with the *Rechtsstaat* principle. On several occasions, parliament has tried to block or close avenues of redress and to significantly reduce procedural rights for immigrants or asylum seekers respectively.

For instance, the court in general upheld the quota system introduced to regulate immigration, but nevertheless held that in cases in which family unification was mandatory according to Art 8 ECHR, quotas should not apply. Although the law providing otherwise would have clearly violated Art 8 ECHR, the court rescinded it for a very different reason.[107] As authorities were only obliged to notify the applicant that the quota was already met without being obliged to issue an administrative ruling, the applicant was deprived of all avenues of redress. Consequently, administrative action could never have been subject to scrutiny. Thus, the law violated Art 18 of the Federal Constitution and the *Rechtsstaat* principle.[108]

In 2008,[109] the court reviewed and rescinded a provision according to which a residence permit could be granted for humanitarian reasons but only '*ex officio*', as an act of grace. Once again, the court found that this violated the *Rechtsstaat* principle as the foreigner had no corresponding (procedural) right to apply for such a residence permit, no avenue of redress was offered and the administration could not be scrutinised.

According to Art 136 para 2 of the Federal Constitution, standards for procedures before administrative courts of first instance have to be set by a Federal law. Federal and state laws may deviate from these standards only if it is necessary to enforce a specific law. Under these standards, complaints may be filed with administrative courts within a period of four weeks. A law relating to asylum procedures reduced that period for asylum seekers to two weeks. It was reviewed and rescinded by the court.[110] The government failed to convince the court that the

---

[106] See, for instance, VfSlg 18233/2007; VfGH 8.6.2021, E 4076/2020.
[107] VfSlg 17013/2003.
[108] For details on this principle see ch 1.
[109] VfSlg 18517/2008.
[110] VfSlg 20193/2017.

reduction was necessary to speed up procedures, because at the same time the (standard) period for taking the decision was being extended from six to 15 months.

While the court effectively intervened to grant fair procedures in immigration and asylum cases, it has refrained from interfering with the design of immigration and asylum policies. It, for instance, upheld rather restrictive laws for those who only benefitted from subsidiary protection.[111]

F. Data Retention

In 2011, parliament implemented the EU data detention directive (2006/24/EG) by amending various laws and/or legal provisions. These laws were challenged at the Constitutional Court as they allegedly violated fundamental rights, especially Art 8 ECHR and a domestic constitutional right to data protection. Remarkably, the court requested a preliminary ruling from the ECJ, arguing that the directive did not comply with fundamental rights stipulated in the Charter. Upon that request and a similar request from the Irish High Court, the ECJ declared the data retention directive invalid.[112] Consequently, the domestic laws implementing the directive were rescinded as they were disproportionate in the light of Art 8 ECHR and the domestic constitutional right to data protection.[113] The Austrian court adopted a liberal approach in a highly controversial debate, helping to clarify the legal situation at the European level.

G. Covid-19 Response

As almost everywhere else in the world, fighting the Covid-19 pandemic led to various encroachments upon fundamental rights in Austria. Measures such as full and partial lockdowns, curfews, restrictions on meeting friends and relatives, denying access to public places and even requirements to wear face masks, to name the most prominent ones, all interfered more or less severely with fundamental human rights, such as Art 8 ECHR, Art 9 ECHR, the freedom of movement, the freedom

---

[111] VfSlg 20177/2017, VfSlg 20286/2018.
[112] Cases C-293/12 and C-594/12, *Digital Rights Ireland and Seitinger et al* ECLI:EU:C: 2014:238.
[113] VfSlg 19892/2014.

to employment, property rights and others. These measures were implemented by ordinances, initially based on a law to curb epidemics and finally, on a specific law passed in March 2020 to prevent the spread of the Covid-19 pandemic.[114]

Less surprisingly, ordinances implementing these measures, even if only temporarily, were challenged in the Constitutional Court. In general, the court upheld the law despite the fact that it granted the administration, mainly the responsible minister, a high degree of discretion to choose appropriate measures,[115] but rescinded ordinances for failure to comply with the law.[116]

It was only in a few cases that the court underpinned its decision with specific human or fundamental rights considerations. In a 2020 case, which took place after the first lockdown, a company challenged the relevant ordinance, arguing that it was treated unfairly as hardware stores and garden centres had been allowed to reopen regardless of their size, while its (shoe)store had to remain closed for the only reason that it comprised a customer area larger than 400 square meters. In this case, the court did not only find that the minister had failed to comply with the law but underpinned its decision to rescind the ordinance by arguing that the distinction between hardware stores and garden centres on one hand, and other shops comprising larger customer areas on the other hand, was unreasonable and therefore violated the principle of equality.

In 2021, a provision that restricted attendance at a funeral to 50 mourners was contested. The court found that this provision was disproportionate in the light of Arts 8 and 9 ECHR, as attendance at a funeral was a most private act and not repeatable.[117] Moreover, participation in assemblies, protected by Art 11 ECHR, was not restricted to a certain number of people. It found that the relevant provision of the ordinance that had already seen its sunset was unlawful.

The biggest challenge, however, would have posed the law the government saw fit to propose in the early stages of 2022. With approximately a quarter of the population refusing to get inoculated (for various reasons), the government decided to introduce vaccination mandates, arguing that this was necessary in order to contain the pandemic and to avoid further curfews and lockdowns. In January 2022, the National Council passed the relevant law.[118] It was not only supported by the government

---

[114] BGBl I 12/2020.
[115] VfSlg 20399/2020.
[116] See ch 3.
[117] VfGH 24.6.2021, V 2/2021.
[118] Covid-19 Mandatory Vaccination Act (*Covid-19-Impfpflichtgesetz*, BGBl I 4/2022).

but also by members of two opposition parties, the Social Democrats and the *NEOS*. It met fierce criticism from the Freedom Party, which had already positioned itself as the advocate of anti-vaccination movements. The law provided for fining unvaccinated residents of 18 years and older (exceptions regarding their health status might have applied) rather than actually administering jabs. Further, it introduced a transitional period in which unvaccinated residents were to be persuaded to get inoculated without being fined. By means of an ordinance the implementation could have been suspended at any time, thus reacting to the development of the pandemic. Possible scenarios included vaccinations becoming useless because they were not effective against a specific variant; impossible, because of supply shortages; or superfluous, because at some point, the virus might no longer have been a threat to society. Nevertheless, the law encroached upon human rights, most notably Art 8 ECHR, and has been contested. Although government has visibly tried to comply with the proportionality principle by designing the law in a rather flexible and lenient way, there might nevertheless have been issues with the ample discretion attributed to the responsible minister and with the nationwide data reconciliation upon which the enforcement of the law was based – a means reminiscent of a total surveillance state. At the beginning of March 2022, the implementation of the law was effectively suspended but might have been reactivated at any time if necessary. With regard to this suspension, the Constitutional Court held that the law was not disproportionate.[119] In July, however, the law was rescinded by parliament as the view had prevailed that it had only (further) divided society.

Notwithstanding the law being short-lived, the most remarkable aspect of the initial parliamentary debate, which was aired on TV, was the explicit and legally correct reference to the proportionality principle by many lawmakers no matter whether they argued in favour or against the law. Thus, after more than 30 years of struggle, it may be observed that the proportionality principle has, at last, arrived in parliament.

VI. CONCLUSION

The principle of equality has played the major part in Austria's fundamental rights guarantees with the Constitutional Court reviewing laws against this principle throughout the Second Republic. The court has

---

[119] VfGH 23.6.2022, G 37/2022, V 173/2022.

developed an 'objectivity test' which demands that laws have to be reasonable. In applying this test, it has rescinded many laws and/or legal provisions. This intervention has rarely if ever struck down fundamental government policies and is hardly noticed by the wider public as the decisions were unspectacular and mostly of mere 'technical' importance. From the mid-1980s onward, the court strengthened freedom rights by applying a proportionality test when scrutinising laws against these rights – initially starting with the right to freedom of employment. By intervening, it cut into a system in which political parties claimed to be in charge of handing out jobs and professional careers. To a certain extent, it introduced competition where previously there had been a closed shop.

The court's more interventionist approach to reading the constitution has been strongly criticised not only by academic traditionalists but also by representatives of the political system calling for constitutional provisions to override the court's decisions. However, it has been argued that applying and developing the proportionality test in the human rights field has helped the Austrian legal system to adjust to the demands of the ECHR and the jurisprudence of the ECtHR. This trend also assisted in the preparation of the country for its accession to the European Union a decade later. Obviously, the freedoms of the single market and the principle of proportionality are enshrined in the entire EU legal system and its laws are interpreted in a more purposeful manner.

By requiring the interpretation of parliamentary statutes in accordance with the constitution, the court also forced the administration to implicitly perform a balancing exercise for which the administration in general was neither prepared nor trained. It took quite some time to settle that matter but, finally, with the introduction of administrative courts of first instance, it seems as if, in general, the constitutional demands have been largely met. Finally, as the debates over measures responding to the Covid-19 pandemic may demonstrate, the proportionality principle has also impacted on parliament as legislator.

FURTHER READING

Baumgartner, G, 'The Relationship between European and National Protection of Fundamental Rights' in Weber, A (ed), *Fundamental Rights in Europe and North America*, Part A (Leiden-Boston, Martinus Nijhoff Publishers, 2001) 119ff.

Berka, W, 'Concretization of and Limitations on Fundamental Rights' in Weber, A (ed), *Fundamental Rights in Europe and North America*, Part A (Leiden-Boston, Martinus Nijhoff Publishers, 2001) 47ff.

——, Binder, C and Kneihs, B, *Die Grundrechte: Grund– und Menschenrechte in Österreich*, 2nd edn (Wien, Verlag Österreich, 2019).

Brauneder, W, *Die historische Entwicklung der modernen Grundrechte in Österreich* (Wien, Verlag für Geschichte und Politik, 1987).

Eberhard, H, 'Soziale Grundrechtsgehalte im Lichte der grundrechtlichen Eingriffsdogmatik' (2012) 67 *Zeitschrift für Öffentliches Recht* 513ff.

Hengstschläger, J and Leeb, D, *Grundrechte*, 3rd edn (Wien, Manz, 2019).

Holoubek, M, 'Function and Interpretation of Fundamental Rights' in Weber, A (ed), *Fundamental Rights in Europe and North America*, Part A (Leiden-Boston, Martinus Nijhoff Publishers, 2001) 99ff.

——, 'Grundrechte' in H Eberhard et al (eds), *100 Jahre Republik Österreich – Kontinuität – Brüche – Kompromisse* (Wien, Verlag Österreich, 2021).

——, 'Grundrechte im Mehrebenensystem' in P Bußjäger et al (eds), *100 Jahre Bundes-Verfassungsgesetz* (Wien, Verlag Österreich, 2020).

Merten, D et al (eds), *Handbuch der Grundrechte in Deutschland und Europa*, Vol VII/1: *Grundrechte in Österreich*, 2nd edn (Wien, Manz and CF Müller, Heidelberg, 2014).

Pöschl, M, *Gleichheit vor dem Gesetz* (Wien-New York, Springer, 2008).

Schäffer, H and Jahnel, D, 'The Protection of Fundamental Rights' in Weber, A (ed), *Fundamental Rights in Europe and North America*, Part A (Leiden-Boston, Martinus Nijhoff Publishers, 2001) 75ff.

Stelzer, M, *Das Wesensgehaltsargument und der Grundsatz der Verhältnismäßigkeit* (Wien-New York, Springer, 1991).

——, 'The Evolution of Fundamental Rights and its Influence on the Drafting of Fundamental Rights Instruments' in Weber, A (ed), *Fundamental Rights in Europe and North America*, Part A (Leiden-Boston, Martinus Nijhoff Publishers, 2001) 18ff.

——, 'Sources of Fundamental Rights' in Weber, A (ed), *Fundamental Rights in Europe and North America*, Part A (Leiden-Boston, Martinus Nijhoff Publishers, 2001) 13ff.

Epilogue

G LANCING BACK, WITH hindsight the mid-1980s marked a turning
point in the history of post-war Austria and its constitution. It
was a time which coincided with the demise of the nationalised
industry and the Waldheim affair, exposing Austria's dishonesty in grappling with its Nazi and fascist past. The first cracks were appearing in
the party system, bringing to an end a political era of remarkable stability characterised by two parties – the conservative People's Party and the
Social Democrats – which shared all political power and dominated the
running of the country. These two parties were supported by a social
partnership comprising a neo-corporatist conflict resolution model
which operated outside the constitution but relied on compromises.
Arguably, Austria's model of consociational democracy was responsible
for the nation's economic growth and its social harmony. These were
Austrian qualities much admired internationally.

Two decades into the twenty-first century, Austria has lost many of its
decisive post-war characteristics. The Austrian model of consociational
democracy no longer exists as such. With an increasingly volatile electorate, Austria's democracy has become more competitive and a multi-party
system has evolved. It seems that the People's Party and the Social
Democrats have irretrievably lost their combined supermajority. This
has significantly changed the engineering of constitutional amendments,
as these two parties can no longer facilitate them on their own. Other
parties, which are needed to achieve a two-thirds majority in parliament,
have obtained significant bargaining power.

This may lead to a more open, transparent, Western-style democracy
that overcomes the heritage of a feudal party system and battles corruption more effectively. This seems to be one of the most important tasks
necessary to keep or even increase the trust in the democratic system.
Currently, a further amendment to the law on political parties to curb
private party donations is being discussed. Moreover, with regard to
the discovery of the side letters to coalition agreements, which detailed
partisan appointments within the judiciary branch of government, the
process of appointing judges is under review and might be altered. In
both cases, amendments to the constitution may be needed.

While selective changes to the constitution still may easily be facilitated, more general and structural amendments are not in sight. A substantial reform of Austria's federal system, as desirable as it might be, seems to be rather elusive. However, Austria may be forced to reconsider its neutral status. As a small country, its security hinges on a rules-based world order. The more such an order is in jeopardy, the more the need to join a military alliance may grow. Should the plans of the European Union to implement its own military task force materialise, Austria would have to decide whether it would want to participate. In any case, it would have to further clarify its current status.

The emergence of a more competitive party system has first and foremost strengthened right-wing populism. Some of its representatives have an ambiguous relationship with Austria's fascist and Nazi past. Those daemons are still lingering. It has been demonstrated that a Federal President who is supported by slightly more than a third of National Council members might have a very influential political position. Right-wing populism has already come close to winning the presidency and gained up to 30 per cent of the votes in a general election. A further shift to the right and/or to authoritarianism may not be that far away.

All over the world, nations have arrived at a crossroads: the next decade will be decisive for fighting climate change. This might entail measures that encroach upon fundamental rights and freedoms. The analysis of the jurisprudence of the Austrian Constitutional Court, especially with regard to instruments designed to curb the Covid-19 pandemic, has demonstrated that the court is willing to tolerate even drastic infringements of fundamental rights should the commonwealth demand them.

Simultaneously, the transfer of a post-industrial society into a digital age will have to be facilitated. As the Covid-19 legislation has demonstrated, the digital means to establish a total surveillance state are already in place. As parliament seems to be willing to use them, it will mainly be the responsibilities of the courts to safeguard the private sphere.

However, all these challenges have the potential of unsettling society and jeopardising democracy. In this respect, Austrians of all people should have learnt from their past that a democratic constitution will only survive as long as it is lived in a democratic spirit.

Index

www.ingramcontent.com/pod-product-compliance
Lightning Source LLC
Chambersburg PA
CBHW061148220326
41599CB00025B/4403